THE
APOCALYPTIC VISION
IN THE
POETRY OF SHELLEY

UNIVERSITY OF TORONTO
DEPARTMENT OF ENGLISH

Studies and Texts, No. 12

THE
APOCALYPTIC
VISION
IN THE
POETRY
OF SHELLEY

Emilia: What did thy song bode, lady?
Hark, canst thou hear me? I will play the
swan,
And die in music.
Othello, V, ii, 246–8

ROSS GREIG WOODMAN

UNIVERSITY OF TORONTO PRESS

© University of Toronto Press, 1964
Printed in Canada
Reprinted, 1966

To Marion

PREFACE

This study is an attempt to examine the nature of Shelley's poetic vision and to trace its unfolding from *Queen Mab* to *The Triumph of Life*. It is not concerned with the "genesis of a radical,"[1] which Professor Cameron has brilliantly elucidated, but with the way in which Shelley's imagination transmuted his radical ideas concerning man and society into a series of visionary works. It is this imaginative act of transmutation which characterizes the apocalyptic nature of Shelley's vision. As an apocalyptic poet, Shelley sought to reveal the archetypal form of a certain set of radical beliefs by releasing them from the limitations of time and space with which, he felt, moral reformers as "promoters of utility"[2] were largely concerned. Greater attention is therefore paid to those occult writers who were primarily concerned with the mythological mode of thought than to those eighteenth-century reformers who influenced his moral, social and political outlook. For the purposes of this study the writings of John Frank Newton and Thomas Taylor are of greater significance than the writings of William Godwin and Baron d'Holbach.

. The emphasis in this study, then, is less upon Shelley as a moral and political philosopher with "'a passion for reforming the world'"[3]

[1]*The Young Shelley: Genesis of a Radical* (London: The Macmillan Co., 1951).
[2]*A Defence of Poetry*, VII, 132.
[3]*P.U.*, Preface, p. 207.

and more upon Shelley as a mythopoeic poet. In his Preface to *Prometheus Unbound*, Shelley is careful to draw a distinction between them. "But it is a mistake," he writes (p. 207),

> to suppose that I dedicate my poetical compositions solely to the direct enforcement of reform, or that I consider them in any degree as containing a reasoned system on the theory of human life. Didactic poetry is my abhorrence; nothing can be equally well expressed in prose that is not tedious and supererogatory in verse. My purpose has hitherto been simply to familiarise the highly refined imagination of the more select classes of poetical readers with beautiful idealisms of moral excellence; aware that until the mind can love, and admire, and trust, and hope, and endure, reasoned principles of moral conduct are seeds cast upon the highway of life which the unconscious passenger tramples into dust, although they would bear the harvest of his happiness.

Shelley, it will be noted, is not opposing the imaginative vision of the poet to the reasoned principles of the philosopher. On the contrary, he suggests that the poet's vision (which he rather clumsily describes as "beautiful idealisms") brings humanity to an awareness of the validity of those principles which humanity might otherwise ignore. Shelley's prose works, therefore, should not be separated from his visionary poems; the latter, at least until the composition of *Adonais* in 1821, were intended to inspire men to put into practice those reasoned principles laboriously worked out in his rather fragmentary prose. For this reason, this study of Shelley's myth-making will follow a different method from that applied by Professor Bloom in his valuable study of Shelley as a mythopoeic poet.[4] Professor Bloom,

---

[4]*Shelley's Mythmaking* (New Haven: Yale University Press, 1959). On page 206, Professor Bloom writes: "Of all Shelley's prose only the *Defence* lives, and that is because it is more a visionary poem about poetry than it is a reasoned argument. I affirm the 'unscholarly' heresy that a student of Shelley's *poetry* is best off not having read any of the prose but the *Defence*. The letters sometimes help; more usually they do not, and two years of steady reading in them have not sufficed for me to find too much of permanent literary or human value therein. . . . The poet Shelley was infinitely wiser and better than the philosopher Shelley or the man Shelley, from the beginning to the end of his career. Shelley himself wrote in a letter to the Gisbornes that 'the poet and the man are two distinct natures; though they exist together, they may be unconscious of each other, and incapable of deciding on each other's powers and efforts by any reflex act.' "
Professor Bloom is perhaps placing too great an emphasis upon Shelley's doctrine of inspiration, his Platonic notion of the poet as divinely inspired and therefore subject to influences "beyond and above consciousness." He tends to ignore the amount of attention that Shelley gave to understanding these influences, especially in his life-long interest in occult studies. Shelley was both a poet and a student of poetry who not only was inspired by what he read but sought also to understand

rejecting the value of Shelley's prose works (including his letters though excluding his *Defence*) for an understanding of Shelley as a poet, turns to Martin Buber's religious philosophy to interpret the process governing the formation of Shelley's myth. This study, on the other hand, turns to Shelley's philosophy as presented in his prose works to interpret that process. More than that, it seeks further to understand that process by examining the growth of Shelley's mind as it wrestled with the somewhat conflicting approaches to truth offered by the rationalist and occult traditions, both of which absorbed his life-long attention.

Largely under the influence of John Frank Newton and the occult group which surrounded him, Shelley at the end of 1812 recognized that there need be no opposition between the "votary of romance"[5] and the rational philosopher. Under Godwin's influence, he believed that there was an opposition and that, if he was to fulfil his duty in advancing the cause of human freedom, he must forgo his earlier interest in the occult. At the same time, however, he accepted, especially after the rather dismal failure of the Irish adventure in the early spring of 1812, Godwin's conviction that the mass of humanity is not ready for radical political change. The evidence for this conviction lay in the failure of the French Revolution, which was and remained for Shelley a central preoccupation. Change, Godwin argued, must arise out of a growth in consciousness; it cannot be imposed from without. And it was precisely here that Newton's mythical vision of the universe with its notions concerning the four ages of man served a necessary and constructive purpose. By making its appeal to the imagination it allowed the consciousness of man to expand and thus prepared him inwardly for outward change.

it in a philosophical and rational way. His view of Milton's *Paradise Lost*, for example, was no mere instinctive or temperamental response to the poem; it was rooted in a carefully worked out view of man's nature to be found not only in Greek poetry but also in Greek philosophy. While it is true that he subordinated the philosopher to the poet because he subordinated the analytical reason to the creative imagination, he did not ignore the value of the analytical reason in its efforts to raise to consciousness the revelations of the creative faculty by copying the poet's vision "into the book of common life." So long as Shelley was concerned to reform the world, he respected the philosopher's "appointed office in society." What he did not respect was the failure of many rational reformers to acknowledge their dependence upon imaginative vision. Shelley, in other words, was concerned, at least until he composed *Adonais*, to assert a hierarchy of faculties with the imagination at the top.

[5]Letter to Godwin (Jan. 10, 1812), VIII, 19.

Shelley's acceptance of imaginative vision as the chief instrument of man's psychic growth marks his passover from a moral reformer in the limited, rational sense to a visionary poet in the full, imaginative sense. The struggle to make this passover is revealed in *Alastor* (1815) and its resolution is revealed, or partially revealed, in the *Hymn to Intellectual Beauty* and *Mont Blanc* (1816). Thus, by 1817, in the composition of *The Revolt of Islam*, Shelley is ready to present his vision of an ideal revolution dedicated in part to exposing the errors of the French one. And in his Preface he addresses himself to his audience as a poet who desires to be judged by the tribunal that is worthy to judge Milton. He has, in other words, moved from the moral reformer's "appointed office in society"[6] to the poet's "abode where the Eternal are" (*Adonais*, 495). He has within himself set the stage for the composition of *Prometheus Unbound*.

On the basis of his experiential knowledge of the creative act and of Plato's doctrine of divine inspiration which provided a "probable account" of it, Shelley in his *Defence of Poetry* further clarifies the distinction between the poet and the moral reformer. As a man, reflecting on his mental growth in its temporal sequence, Shelley obviously saw his apocalyptic vision emerging from his education in the radical philosophy of the Enlightenment, as that philosophy was imaginatively transformed by his interest in the occult. As a poet, however, he saw, or with the help of Plato thought he saw, that the influences that shape a man are not the influences that govern a poet. The poet and the man, in fact, are two distinct natures. The poet, as he argues in his *Defence*, is subject to influences "beyond and above consciousness" (VII, 116); his inspiration arises from the "interpenetration of a diviner nature through [his] own" (VII, 136). The poet, therefore, is not a man subject to "the influences under which others habitually live" (VII, 139), but the "divinity in Man" (VII, 137) which finds release through his ascent to those "eternal regions" (VII, 135) where divinity dwells. The poet is the divinely possessed being whom Plato describes in the *Ion* with an irony that Shelley in his *Defence* chose to ignore. The poet, in other words, stands in the presence of the archetypes (which Shelley says forever exist in the mind[7]) in that condition of pure being which the soul

---

[6]*A Defence of Poetry*, VII, 132.
[7]*A Discourse on the Manners of the Ancients*, VII, 228.

enjoys prior to its descent into body and which Shelley describes as the soul's "proper paradise"[8] existing within man.

Viewed in this anagogical perspective, which is the perspective governing the movement of *Adonais*, the poet's vision belongs not to time but to eternity. It arises not out of man's earthly existence but out of the poet's divine existence. Thus, from this anagogical point of view, Shelley's Promethean vision is not the imaginative recreation of Godwin's philosophy; on the contrary, Godwin's reasoned principles of political justice are the result of that vision. Shelley's archetypal vision is prior to Godwin's philosophy as eternity is prior to time, or spirit is prior to body, or archetype is prior to its constructed likeness. Shelley makes this crucial point clear in his *Defence of Poetry*. "Poetry," he writes,

is indeed something divine. It is at once the centre and circumference of knowledge; it is that which comprehends all science, and that to which all science must be referred. It is at the same time the root and blossom of all other systems of thought; it is that from which all spring, and that which adorns all; and that which, if blighted, denies the fruit and the seed, and withholds from the barren world the nourishment and the succession of the scions of the tree of life. [VII, 135]

Shelley's experience as a visionary poet served more and more to shift his attention from time to eternity, from a concern for man as an earthly being to a concern for the "divinity in Man" eager to escape the dungeon of flesh. Following the path of ascent marked out by Plato's Eros in the *Symposium*, he moved from existence to preexistence. And having made this final passover, he found it increasingly difficult to address himself to men. Thus in *Adonais* he asks himself (469–74):

> Why linger, why turn back, why shrink, my Heart?
> Thy hopes have gone before: from all things here
> They have departed; thou shouldst now depart!
> A light is passed from the revolving year,
> And man, and woman; and what still is dear
> Attracts to crush, repels to make thee wither.

The poems upon which Shelley worked after the completion of *Adonais* reveal, with the exception of the exquisite lyrics to Jane Williams, a repulsion for that which attracts him. On June 18, 1822,

[8]*On Love*, VI, 202.

he writes to John Gisborne, echoing the sentiments expressed in the final stanzas of *Adonais*: "I stand, as it were, upon a precipice, which I have ascended with great, and cannot descend without *greater*, peril, and I am content if the heaven above me is calm for the passing moment" (X, 404). The contentment in a calm heaven for a passing moment is the subject of his lyrics to Jane Williams. *Hellas*, when viewed in terms of the speeches of Ahasuerus, is a belated effort to celebrate the monotonous round of Nature's cycle out of which will emerge a reborn Greece. *Charles the First* is a drama that might have applied that same cyclic round, though somewhat more ironically, to an earlier period of history had Shelley been able to bring his waning energies to bear upon it. *The Triumph of Life* is a vision of that "mad trance" (*Adonais*, 345) in which the poet's vision turns to nightmare because of his lingering, his turning back. All three works reveal to different degrees and in different ways Shelley repelled and crushed by his efforts to revive his hopes for man.

This repulsion was accentuated by the serious doubts which assailed him towards the end of his life about the constructive character of his earlier Promethean vision. When, in *Adonais*, Urania calls upon him to reveal his identity, he is not sure whether he should be associated in his suffering with Christ or Cain. This doubt was partly influenced by Byron's conviction that there was something daemonic (in the Christian sense) about Shelley's Promethean vision. There can be little doubt, for example, that in Shelley's rejection of the Christian God in favour of the "divinity in Man" Byron found an inspiration for his conception of Cain in *Cain, A Mystery*. "How happy should I *not* be," Shelley writes to Horace Smith (April 11, 1822), "to attribute to myself, however indirectly, any participation in that immortal work" (X, 378, italics added).

Perhaps more important than Byron's daemonic treatment of Shelley's Promethean vision was the knowledge that Plato, whom Shelley admired more than any other philosopher, exiled from his republic the type of visionary poet that Shelley had sought both to defend and to become. So long as Shelley chose to ignore the real significance of the Socratic irony which governs Plato's account of the poet's divine madness in the *Ion*, he could view Plato's treatment of the poet in the *Republic* in much the same way as he had viewed Milton's assertion in *Paradise Lost* that he is justifying the ways of the Christian God to men. Milton, in declaring that he is justifying the Christian God, Shelley suggests in his *Defence*, is speaking as a man subject to the conditions of the age in which he lived. As a poet, however, he is subject to influences "beyond and above consciousness" which completely reverse his conscious endeavour so that the poem itself contains a direct refutation of the very system which it appears to defend. In precisely the same way, Shelley could argue that Plato's treatment of the poet in the *Republic* is refuted by a very different treatment in the *Ion*. Once, however, he had recognized both the presence and the significance of the irony in that dialogue he was forced to reconsider Plato's reasons for exiling the poet. That Shelley did recognize that irony is evident both in *Adonais* and the poems which followed it.

In the final phase of his mercurial career (the phase that begins with *Adonais*) Shelley struggled to impose an ironic perspective upon his apocalyptic vision. It is this struggle which is evident in his presentation of Archy in *Charles the First*, Ahasuerus in *Hellas*, and Rousseau in *The Triumph of Life*. The irony itself is contained in the words of Demogorgon in *Prometheus Unbound*: "the deep truth is imageless" (II, iv, 116). There is the danger of the poet's mistaking the visionary world constructed by his imagination for the reality which it can only adumbrate. The poet can merge with that reality ("the white radiance of Eternity," *Adonais*, 463) not through his submission to the muse, but through his abandonment of her. All that men create, whether it be institutions or visionary works, is but "a dome of many-coloured glass" (462) which must be trampled into fragments if the truth which it darkly reflects is to be disclosed. Once the poet realizes this truth (the apocalypse itself as distinct from the vision of it) he sees his imaginative frenzy as a "mad trance" in which he strikes with his "spirit's knife / Invulnerable nothings" (*Adonais*, 347–8). It is precisely this ironic view of the poet's creative acts that Ahasuerus offers in *Hellas* and that Shelley in *The Triumph of Life* brings into brilliant focus.

Once Shelley had substituted the real apocalypse for the vision of it, he was forced by the dialectic that is propelled by the Platonic Eros to conclude that only death can join together what life divides. Thus his *Adonais* emerges as a metaphysical defence of suicide. And since the metaphysic governing *Adonais* is but an anagogic extension of the metaphysic governing *Prometheus Unbound*, Shelley was forced to recognize that the vision of that earlier work might have more to do with death than it had to do with life. Depending on the angle from which that vision was seen, the Promethean poet could be viewed either in the likeness of Christ or in the likeness of Cain. *Faust*, he tells John Gisborne in a letter (April 10, 1822) is "an unfit study for any person who is prey to the reproaches of memory, and the delusions of an imagination not to be restrained" (X, 371).

It is this final phase of Shelley's career in which he moves beyond vision to its primal source that cannot be explained either in terms of his radical ideas derived from the eighteenth-century philosophers or in terms of his myth-making powers quickened by his conception of the poet's role in the reformation of society. This final phase, towards which his whole career as a visionary poet moves with an inevitability similar to the dialectic of those Platonic dialogues which influenced him profoundly, can perhaps only be understood in the light of an occult Platonism. It is for this reason that a major emphasis in the study which follows is devoted to an examination of that final phase. Through an examination of some of Shelley's major visionary works within the framework of his growing insight into the meaning of Plato's philosophy, it is hoped that there may be gained some new appreciation of Shelley as a profoundly metaphysical poet concerned to discover and to reveal what he considered to be man's true nature.

R.G.W.

ACKNOWLEDGMENTS

I am deeply indebted to Professor A. S. P. Woodhouse who, as a supervisor of my doctoral dissertation, first suggested revising the dissertation for publication. Without his initial interest, assistance and encouragement this book would not have been written.

Both Principal Northrop Frye and Professor Milton Wilson read the manuscript at an early stage. Their many suggestions and criticisms greatly assisted me in preparing a final draft of the text.

To most of my colleagues in the Departments of English at the University of Western Ontario I am indebted for their patience in hearing and discussing a series of papers which I delivered every fortnight throughout one academic year primarily on the subject of this book. I am especially indebted to Hugh MacCallum (now at the University of Toronto), Ronald Bates, and Earle Sanborn who, during that lecture series, read valuable papers on the relation of Shelley's poetry to the works of Milton, Joyce, and Yeats.

I am indebted to Miss Tina Vandermeer for typing and partly re-typing my manuscript and to Miss Jean C. Jamieson, Associate Editor at the University of Toronto Press, for her expert guidance in seeing it through to publication.

I am grateful to the Canada Council for two short-term grants which assisted me to complete in England my research for the present volume. To the Nuffield Foundation I am grateful for permission to make the final preparations for the publication of this book while at work on another project for which the Foundation granted me a fellowship.

Finally, I would like to point out that this work has been published with the help of a grant from the Humanities Research Council, using funds provided by the Canada Council, and of a grant from the Publications Fund of the University of Toronto Press.

R.G.W.

CONTENTS

A NOTE ON SOURCES

All quotations from Shelley's prose, except for the prefaces and notes to the poems, are taken from *The Complete Works of Percy Bysshe Shelley*, ed. Roger Ingpen and Walter E. Peck, 10 vols. London: Ernest Benn Limited; New York: Charles Scribner's Sons, 1930, for the Julian Editions.

All quotations from Shelley's poetry and from his prefaces and Mary Shelley's notes to the poems are taken from *The Complete Poetical Works of Percy Bysshe Shelley*, ed. Thomas Hutchinson. London, New York, Toronto: Oxford University Press, 1956.

All quotations from Blake's poetry are taken from *The Poetry and Prose of William Blake*, ed. Geoffrey Keynes. London: Nonesuch Press, 1948.

All quotations from Coleridge's poetry are taken from *The Poems of Samuel Taylor Coleridge*, ed. Ernest H. Coleridge. London, New York, Toronto: Oxford University Press, 1960.

All quotations from Keats's poetry are taken from *The Complete Poetical Works of John Keats*, ed. H. W. Garrod. Oxford: The Clarendon Press, 1958.

All quotations from Wordsworth's poetry are taken from *The Complete Poetical Works of William Wordsworth*, ed. A. J. George. Boston, New York: Houghton, Mifflin and Company; Cambridge: The Riverside Press, 1904.

All quotations from Pope's poetry are taken from *An Essay on Man*, ed. Maynard Mack, vol. III, i. London: Methuen and Company, 1947, for the Twickenham Editions (6 vols.).

All quotations from the *Timaeus* are taken from the second volume of *The Works of Plato*, trans. Floyer Sydenham and Thomas Taylor. 5 vols., London: R. Wilks, 1804.

All quotations from Nonnos are taken from the *Dionysiaca*, trans. W. H. D. Rouse, with notes by H. J. Rose and L. R. Lind. 3 vols., London: William Heinemann Limited; Cambridge: Harvard University Press, 1940, for the Loeb Classical Library.

All quotations from Euripides are taken from *The Bacchae*, trans. Gilbert Murray. London: George Allen and Unwin Limited, 1948.

The abbreviation Godwin has been used throughout the footnotes for William Godwin, *Enquiry Concerning Political Justice and Its Influence on Morals and Happiness*, ed., with Introduction and notes, by F. E. L. Priestley, 3 vols. Toronto: University of Toronto Press, 1946.

Part One

THE NATURE OF THE
VISION

"This object, or its archetype, forever exists in the mind, which selects among those who resemble it, that which most resembles it; and instinctively fills up the interstices of the imperfect image, in the same manner as the imagination moulds and completes the shapes in clouds, or in the fire, into the resemblances of whatever form, animal, building, &c., happens to be present to it."

A Discourse on the Manners
of the Ancients

1

CREATIVE

IMAGINATION

Shelley's life was governed by two powerful passions: a desire to reform the world and a desire to transcend it. Once only—in *Adonais* —was he able to bring them together in a perfectly sustained, perfectly coherent work of art. The whole of Shelley is present in *Adonais* as in no other poem that he wrote. It both recapitulates his brief career and gives it an anagogical focus that he never found in life. The elegy is at once a defence of poetry that incorporates his reforming zeal and a statement of his desire to find a reality beyond the reach of art. This chapter will focus on that first passion, his desire to transform the familiar world to which man is bound by custom and habit. Other chapters will examine that other passion which led inevitably to his death both as reformer and poet.

The interdependence of the desire to create and the desire to transcend is clearly described in *A Defence of Poetry*. There Shelley writes that "the interpenetration of a diviner nature through our own" quickens the imagination to create "anew the universe, after it has been annihilated in our minds by the recurrence of impressions blunted by reiteration."[1] But *A Defence of Poetry* was written in 1821; in 1812 Shelley did not believe in a "diviner nature." He believed, or

[1]VII, 136, 137.

thought he believed, that matter in a state of motion was the only reality, that the physical universe was the only universe. Fortunately William Godwin, among others, persuaded him otherwise. And once he was persuaded, his career as a poet was safely launched. It grew in stature under Plato's influence, and ended, again under Plato's influence, in some final acceptance of the "deep truth" that is "imageless" (*P.U.* II, iv, 116). The journey begins with Godwin and the materialists, whose impact on Shelley the first part of this chapter will explore. It will move on to the first phase of Plato's influence, and conclude with some general remarks about Shelley's view of the creative imagination which took shape during these two stages of his mental and spiritual development.

While at Oxford, Shelley wrote to Stockdale on November 19, 1810, requesting him to send a copy of Godwin's *Enquiry Concerning Political Justice.* The immediate effect of his first reading (he reread the work in 1811, 1812, 1814, 1816, 1817 and 1820) was to turn Shelley's interests away from Gothic literature and magic in favour of "philanthropy and truth," as he wrote in a letter to Godwin (Jan. 3, 1812) shortly after discovering that Godwin was still alive. "I was no longer the votary of romance," he wrote a week later; "till then [i.e. until reading Godwin] I had existed in an ideal world—now I found that in this universe of ours was enough to excite the interest of the heart, enough to employ the discussions of reason; I beheld, in short, that I had duties to perform."[2]

As conceived by Shelley in the first months of 1812, those duties were multiple: they included, among other things, writing "'An inquiry into the causes of the failure of the French Revolution to benefit mankind'" and going to Ireland to promulgate Godwin's ideas. Godwin was not convinced that Shelley was equipped to do either, and within a week of receiving Shelley's second letter, wrote to him admitting his "'deep and earnest interest'" in Shelley's welfare, but suggesting at the same time that he ought "'to have no intolerable itch to become a teacher.'"[3]

Shelley's rather naïve understanding of Godwin's philosophy had not prepared him for this. "But could I not," he writes in reply, "at the same time, improve my own powers and diffuse true and virtuous principles?" If others are "scattering the seeds of prejudice and selfish-

²VIII, 19, 233, 240.   ³VIII, 241, 242, 243.

ness" might not the truth, exhibited "with equal elegance and depth, suffice to counteract the deleterious tendency of their principles?"[4] Apparently Godwin thought not. Shelley now refused to listen and, against Godwin's wishes, went to Ireland in February of 1812 to perform his missionary work.

The Irish campaign was the first serious crisis in the relations between Godwin and Shelley. It came within the first month of their initial correspondence. The cause of the crisis was, at bottom, Shelley's refusal in 1812 fully to accept the fundamental nature of Godwin's philosophy, especially with reference to the doctrine of progress. "It appears to me," he wrote to Godwin on March 18, "that on the publication of 'Political Justice' you looked to a more rapid improvement than has taken place." Just what Shelley here meant by "rapid improvement" is clear from his letter to Godwin written ten days earlier. "But 'Political Justice' was first published in 1793; nearly twenty years have elapsed since the general diffusion of its doctrines. What has followed? Have men ceased to fight? Have vice and misery vanished from the earth?"[5]

To this earlier letter, Godwin replied: "Oh, that I could place you upon the pinnacle of ages, from which these twenty years would shrink to an invisible point! It is not after this fashion that moral causes work in the eye of him who looks profoundly through the vast and —allow me to add—venerable machine of human society."[6] The "pinnacle of ages" suggested a rather dismal prospect to Shelley at the age of nineteen; however, confronted by the evident failure of the Irish campaign, he told Godwin in his letter of the 18th that he was willing to withdraw. "I shall address myself no more to the illiterate," he states (VIII, 301). "I will look to events in which it will be impossible that I can share, and make myself the cause of an effect which will take place ages after I have mouldered in the dust; I need not observe that this resolve requires stoicism. . . . There is not a completer abstraction than labouring for distant ages." By March of 1812, therefore, Shelley had come to realize that his passion for reforming the

---

[4]VIII, 244.

[5]VIII, 301, 287–8. In *An Address to the Irish People*, written in England in January, 1812, Shelley is much more moderate. He makes it clear in his *Address* that he does not expect that the egalitarian state will be achieved in his time.

[6]Quoted in C. Kegan Paul, *William Godwin: His Friends and Contemporaries* (London: H. S. King and Co., 1876), II, 207.

world would have to find some other outlet. That outlet was destined to be poetry. His new resolution required, in the first instance, a deeper understanding of Godwin's position, and to that task he addressed himself upon his return from Ireland.

The Godwin whom Shelley met in 1812 was, as Professor Priestley points out, "an 'immaterialist' and an admirer of Berkeley" who, in his conversations with Shelley, would be bound "to emphasize immaterialism, the belief in a governing spirit (not personal, however) of the universe, and a rational benevolence capable of developing, with some further Platonic modification, into Shelley's principle of Intellectual Beauty."[7] Shelley, on the other hand, considered himself a materialist, and, without giving it much thought, tended to identify Godwin's philosophy with that of the *philosophes*. Godwin's first task was to show Shelley that his system, while it had certain superficial similarities to that of the *philosophes*, was fundamentally opposed to it.

In *Political Justice*, Godwin rejects David Hartley's materialistic basis for his theory of association because it reduces the mind to the mere physical organ of sensation, enslaved by what Godwin calls "material automatism." Opposing the materialists, he asserts that the mind in its mode of functioning is independent of matter because it has the power of reflection, the ability to stand aside from the mechanism of perception and observe it. This power of observation is what constitutes consciousness, which Godwin is careful to distinguish from what he calls "unconscious thought." "By the consciousness which accompanies any thought," he writes, "there seems to be something implied distinct from the thought itself. Consciousness is a sort of supplementary reflection, by which the mind not only has the thought, but adverts to its own situation, and observes that it has it. Consciousness therefore, however nice the distinction, seems to be a second thought."[8]

To the extent that man asserts his independence of matter by taking "second thought," he becomes a disinterested spectator, able to distinguish between his own personal and temporary good and the good of mankind. He is able to forgo any purely selfish desire in the interests of humanity. And here again Godwin disagrees with the materialists, including Baron d'Holbach and Helvetius, who assert that man is selfish by nature and governed in all his acts by the pleasure-pain motive. Godwin agrees that the pleasure-pain principle is present in every human act, but, unlike the materialists, he introduces a qualitative scale of pleasures in which the direct pleasures of the senses are subordinated to the higher pleasures of the mind, the pleasures found in the disinterested pursuit of virtue. He writes that the man who seeks the benefit of others and finds his happiness in the consciousness of their good ascends "to the highest of human pleasures, the pleasures of disinterestedness."[9] If the mind is chained to and determined by physical impulses, Godwin argues, there is no way in which man can rise above his own immediate desires and perform disinterested acts of benevolence. A materialist is incapable of disinterestedness.

In the summer of 1812, Shelley found it difficult fully to grasp this point. He refers, in his letter of July 29th, to Godwin's charges against Baron d'Holbach's *Système de la nature* (although he confuses the author with Helvetius) and admits that, while it is a book of "uncommon powers," it is "too obnoxious to accusations of sensuality and selfishness." However, he then goes on:

Although, like you an irreconcilable enemy to the system of self love, both from a feeling of its deformity and a conviction of its falsehood, I can by no means conceive how the loftiest disinterestedness is incompatible with the strictest materialism. In fact, the doctrine which affirms that there is no such thing as matter, and that which affirms that all is matter, appear to me, perfectly indifferent in the question between benevolence and self love. [IX, 11]

Had Godwin been unable to dislodge him from his materialistic bias, Shelley could never have arrived at his mature view of the creative imagination. For Godwin, the shift from the self to a perception of the universal system involved the imagination. "We are able in imagination," he writes,

to go out of ourselves, and become impartial spectators of the system of which we are a part. We can then make an estimate of our intrinsic and absolute value; and detect the imposition of that self-regard, which would represent our own interest as of as much value as that of all the world beside. The delusion being thus sapped, we can, from time to time at least, fall back in idea into our proper post, and cultivate those views and affections which must be most familiar to the most perfect intelligence.[10]

[9]Godwin, I, 447.   [10]Godwin, I, 427–8.

From the context in which Godwin here uses the term imagination it is evident that he means reason in the intuitive, as distinct from the discursive, sense. The intuitive grasp of the universal order makes possible an examination of man's proper place within it.

When he wrote to Shelley concerning his desire to place him on the "pinnacle of ages," it was this intuitive grasp of the universal system that Godwin had in mind. Until he had achieved it, Godwin believed, Shelley could never really understand his "proper post" or "cultivate those views and affections which must be most familiar to the most perfect intelligence." That Shelley in 1812 was moving towards this understanding is evident in *Queen Mab*, which he began after his return to England in April, 1812. In the poem, Ianthe is visited by the Fairy Queen (Godwin's perfect intelligence), her soul is separated from her body, and "on fancy's boldest wing" (IV, 155) she is granted a vision of the universe. The universe which she perceives in vision, however, is the materialistic one of the *philosophes*. Shelley was still trying to reconcile the two systems. Not until 1815 could he, looking back to this period, fully recognize that he "was discontented with such a view of things as [materialism] afforded." And the reason for his discontent was Godwin's:"man is a being of high aspirations, 'looking both before and after,' whose 'thoughts wander through eternity,' disclaiming alliance with transience and decay."[11] What Shelley had grasped by 1815 was the importance of the intuitive faculty in Godwin's philosophy.

While Godwin is insistent that it is through the exercise of reason that man loses the self-regarding principle, he does not make it clear in his *Political Justice* that he is using the term reason in two distinct senses, which involve two separate modes of mental action. When he discusses reason in terms of reflection or "second thought," he is thinking of it in the analytical or discursive sense. When, however, he speaks of reason in terms of going out of oneself to become the impartial spectator of the universal order, he is thinking of reason not in its discursive, but in its intuitive sense. And it is this intuitive power that is necessary for the performance of voluntary acts. "Volition," he argues, "is an affair of foresight. 'No motion is voluntary, any further than it is accompanied with intention and design, and has for its proper antecedent the apprehension of an end to be ac-

[11]*On Life*, VI, 194.

complished. So far as it flows in any degree from another source [such as the "material automatism" of the *philosophes*], it is involuntary.' "[12] In a perfectly rational being this foresight or design is the good of the universal system. Intuition of the whole system, therefore, is prior to the fully voluntary action of the individual.

In his rereading of Godwin's *Political Justice* Shelley came to believe that this notion of intuition was at the very centre of Godwin's philosophy. His whole interpretation of Godwin is summed up in the following passage from his *Speculations on Morals* (c. 1815):

Imagination or mind employed in prophetically [imaging forth] its objects is that faculty of human nature on which every gradation of its progress, nay, every, the minutest change depends. Pain or pleasure, if subtly analysed, will be found to consist entirely in prospect. The only distinction between the selfish man, and the virtuous man, is that the imagination of the former is confined within a narrow limit, whilst that of the latter embraces a comprehensive circumference. In this sense, wisdom and virtue may be said to be inseparable, and criteria of each other. Selfishness is thus the offspring of ignorance and mistake; it is the portion of unreflecting infancy, and savage solitude, or of those whom toil or evil occupations have [blunted and rendered torpid;] disinterested benevolence is the product of a cultivated imagination, and has an intimate connexion with all the arts which add ornament, or dignity, or power, or stability to the social state of man. [VII, 75–6]

This identification of the faculty of imagination with the power of foresight is the source of Shelley's faith in all forms of visionary art. More than that, it partly dictated Shelley's choice of Prometheus as the hero of his lyrical drama. The name Prometheus means foresight; it is his imaginative power that ensures his victory over the forces of ignorance and mistake embodied in the figure of Jupiter. *Prometheus Unbound*, therefore, is Shelley's visionary re-creation of Godwin's implicit emphasis upon intuition.

In Godwin's system reason, as Professor Priestley points out, "not only judges the rightness of an action or the desirability of an end, but irresistibly urges towards that action or towards the pursuit of that end."[13] It is, therefore, not only a faculty which judges, but a force which compels. Reason, in this sense, includes feeling, but it is feeling divorced from its source in sensual pleasures and brought to the level

[12]Godwin, I, 423–4.
[13]Godwin, III, 13 (Professor Priestley's Introduction).

of consciousness, where it expresses itself in dispassionate benevolence. It is feeling disciplined and directed by reason. The power of reason to establish the state of anarchism reflecting in its ordered life the immutable laws of the universe rests for Godwin upon his belief that man's instinctive energies can be rendered serviceable to the pursuit of that ideal.

This redirection of instinctive power was for Shelley by 1815 the transformation of lust and sensuality into love of the good. He defines love in his *Speculations on Morals* as "disinterestedness . . . united with the natural propensities." "These propensities themselves," he continues, "are comparatively impotent in cases where the imagination of pleasure to be given, as well as to be received, does not enter into the account" (VII, 76–7).

By 1815, therefore, Shelley had evolved a doctrine of love and imagination which, while not precisely Godwinian in the emphasis which Shelley gave it, was certainly true to Shelley's own nature. What Shelley had done was to isolate in Godwin's philosophy what properly belongs to reason in its intuitive sense and ignore, almost entirely, the discursive. Godwin himself had assisted Shelley in arriving at this interpretation, first by showing him the limitations of materialism, and then by persuading him of the powers of the liberated human mind.

Shelley discovered the importance of the imagination by reading and rereading *Political Justice*, but it was not until he turned seriously to a study of Plato's dialogues between 1816 and 1817 that he discovered its creative power. In 1815, Shelley viewed the imagination as a power which both grasps the existing order of reality and makes it possible for man to conform his life to it. As a result of his conversion to Platonism, however, he came to believe that the imagination, in some sense, created that order. The objects with which man lives are not the existential objects of the external world, but the projected forms of his own psyche. The imagination recreates the universe into a human form.

Shelley was never particularly interested in Godwin's rather tedious arguments in defence of what was both to Godwin and himself intuitively self-evident. Godwin, therefore, could never completely persuade Shelley that it was better to analyse than to create. As a poet, Shelley believed that men must perceive the beauty of what they already know. By beauty, he simply meant the universe recreated by the imagination and perceived in the form of myth. In other words, he identified beauty with the mythological mode of perception which properly belongs to the imagination viewed as a creative power. That beauty, he found in Plato's dialogues.

Shelley's transition from Godwinism to Platonism, however, was not abrupt. When he returned from Ireland in April of 1812, he could not long endure the Stoical resignation which Godwin recommended. He quickly wearied of the endless discussions which Godwin, in the increasing conservatism of his later years, recommended. For this reason, Shelley identified himself in November of 1812 with an occult group headed by John Frank Newton, and including Thomas Love Peacock and possibly Thomas Taylor, some of whose translations of and commentaries on Plato he had read while at Oxford. Both Newton and Taylor were great admirers of Plato and interpreted him as an Orphic poet presenting in his dialogues a secret doctrine which the initiated alone could understand. Between 1812 and 1815, Shelley was initiated into the Orphic mysteries and it is out of that initiation that his later interpretation of Plato emerges.

In his "Dissertation on the Eleusinian and Bacchic Mysteries," Taylor accepts the historical existence of Orpheus as a prophet, and says that he taught the Greeks their sacred rites and mysteries from which "as from a perpetual and abundant fountain, the divine Muse of Homer, and the philosophy of Pythagoras and Plato flowed." He then goes on to deal with the secret doctrine in Plato's philosophy:

But not withstanding this important truth [man's true identity as divinity imprisoned in flesh] was obscurely shewn by the lesser mysteries, we must not suppose that it was generally known even to the initiated themselves: for as people of almost all descriptions were admitted to these rites, it would have been a ridiculous prostitution to disclose to the multitude a theory so abstracted and sublime. It was sufficient to instruct these in the doctrine of a future state of rewards and punishments, and in the means of returning to the principles from which they originally fell: for this last piece of information was, according to Plato in the Phaedo, the ultimate design of the mysteries. . . . Hence the reason why it was obvious to none but the Pythagoric and Platonic philosophers, who derived their theology from Orpheus himself, the original founder of these sacred institutions;

and why we meet with no information in this particular in any writer prior to Plotinus; as he was the first who, having penetrated the profound wisdom of antiquity, delivered it to posterity without the concealments of mystic symbols and fabulous narrations.[14]

Following the method of Plotinus, Taylor believed that Plato's dialogues were to be read allegorically in order to penetrate, through a knowledge of the Orphic rites, to "the profound wisdom of antiquity." Shelley's conviction that he had unveiled the imaginative form of Plato's philosophy and incorporated it into his own poetry places him within the Neo-Platonic tradition which he first understood in the translations and commentaries of Thomas Taylor. Although he began this study of the esoteric Plato at Oxford, he did not grasp its full significance until he directed his own creative powers to the shaping of a vision of the "divinity in Man" (VII, 137).

While Shelley was obviously enthralled by his esoteric studies and continued well into 1815 to live in close association with his occult friends, he had, as a rationalist, forsworn such activity. The conflict between rationalism and the occult is "writ large" in *Queen Mab*, which he completed before the summer of 1813. In his notes on the poem, Shelley is very much on the side of the rationalists and argues at some length that all forms of myth are but the expression of man's ignorance of the laws of Nature. At the same time, however, he makes tentative use of the Orphic myth of pre-existence in the poem and devotes some six pages in the notes to a defence of the Orphic and Pythagorean system of diet which he derived from Newton and further investigated in Plutarch.

By 1815, Shelley was extremely dissatisfied with the limitations of Godwin's philosophy and expressed that dissatisfaction with passionate intensity in *Alastor*, written in the autumn of that year. In the Preface to the poem, he describes a youthful poet who can no longer find satisfaction in the contemplation of the universe. As a result, the poet imaginatively recreates the objects of his contemplation into a vision of the being whom he loves, and then sets out to find her. "Blasted by his disappointment," Shelley writes (p. 15), "he descends to an untimely grave." The reason for the disappointment reveals at once the conflict in Shelley between rationalism and

[14]Thomas Taylor, *A Dissertation on the Eleusinian and Bacchic Mysteries* (Amsterdam: J. Weitstein, 1790), pp. 16–17.

the occult. The poet in *Alastor* searches throughout Nature for the object of his imagination, even though he knows that the object is a creature not of Nature, but of his own imagination. His epipsyche belongs in the world of psychic projection, which is the world of the occult, described by Shelley in the poem as "incommunicable dream" and "twilight phantasms" (39–40). She exists in the poet's imagination; "like an inspired and desperate alchymist" (31), the poet's "strange tears / Uniting with those breathless kisses" (34–5) have made "Such magic as compels the charmèd night / To render up [his] charge" (36–7). Thus, when he finally admits defeat, the poet cries out (681–6):

> O, that the dream
> Of dark magician in his visioned cave,
> Raking the cinders of a crucible
> For life and power, even when his feeble hand
> Shakes in its last decay, were the true law
> Of this so lovely world!

In 1815, Shelley could not yet submit to the dialectic of passion and discover the "true law" in the Orphic and Neo-Platonic occult tradition. At the same time, however, he could no longer live in the rationalist tradition, finding in the order of the universe the prototype of the psychic universe within himself.

The resolution of this impasse (which Shelley believed would destroy him) was found in turning independently and directly to Plato. In 1817, Shelley translated Plato's *Symposium*, in which he saw, or thought he saw, the poet's search for his epipsyche described in terms of intervention on the part of the gods. The poet's quest in *Alastor* was given a metaphysical status in the *Symposium*, leading, as it did in the *Symposium*, to the ultimate reality that transcends Nature. Shelley interpreted Plato's myth of Eros as a defence of the creative faculty in man. The object of the poet's imagination in *Alastor* was a revelation of the poet's "ideal prototype" requiring no sanction from the familiar world of Nature. Henceforth in Shelley's mind the dialectic of sacred passion transcends the dialectic of reason. The poet in creating his own objects is divinely inspired; the poet's mythical creations transcend the philosopher's argument. Shelley in translating the *Symposium* discovered what was lacking to the poet in *Alastor*: a metaphysical defence of the poet's creative power which liberated poetry from its radical dependence upon some external order.

While Godwin's notion of intuition allowed man to become the "impartial spectator" of the order of the universe, Plato's notion of divine intervention allowed him to recreate that order into a mythological vision. Eros, writes Plato in Shelley's translation, "fills up that intermediate space" between gods and men "so as to bind together, by his own power, the whole universe of things." Eros is a "great Daemon" who brings the messages of the gods to men "both whilst they sleep and when they wake"; the man who is "wise in the science of this intercourse . . . participates in the daemoniacal nature; whilst he who is wise in any other science or art, remains a mere ordinary slave."[15]

Here, for Shelley, is the radical distinction between the philosopher like Godwin and the poet like Plato. The philosopher observes; the poet participates. Not to participate is to remain an ordinary slave. Thus, in his Defence of Poetry (VII, 134), Shelley writes: "The cultivation of those sciences which have enlarged the limits of the empire of man over the external world, has, for want of the poetical faculty, porportionally circumscribed those of the internal world; and man, having enslaved the elements, remains himself a slave."

When Shelley wrote A Defence of Poetry in 1821, he was indebted not only to the Symposium, but even more directly to the Ion, which he also translated. Once again in the Ion Plato presents the notion of divine intervention; this time, however, he presents it with direct reference to the poet. Shelley's translation of the key passage (VII, 238–9) must be quoted at length, for echoes of it are to be found throughout his Defence.

It is not that you are master of any art for the illustration of Homer, but it is a divine influence which moves you, like that which resides in the stone called Magnet by Euripides, and Heraclea by the people. For not only does this stone possess the power of attracting iron rings, but it can communicate to them the power of attracting other rings; so that you may see sometimes a long chain of rings, and other iron substances, attached and suspended one to the other by this influence. And as the power of the stone circulates through all the links of this series, and attaches each to each, so the Muse, communicating through those whom she has first inspired, to all others capable of sharing in the inspiration, the influence of that first enthusiasm,

15VII, 197, 198.

creates a chain and a succession. For the authors of those great poems which we admire, do not attain to excellence through the rules of any art, but they utter their beautiful melodies of verse in a state of inspiration, and, as it were, *possessed* by a spirit not their own. Thus the composers of lyrical poetry create those admired songs of theirs in a state of divine insanity, like the Corybantes, who lose all control over their reason in the enthusiasm of the sacred dance; and, during this supernatural possession, are excited to the rhythm and harmony which they communicate to men. Like the Bacchantes, who, when possessed by the God draw honey and milk from the rivers, in which, when they come to their senses, they find nothing but simple water. For the souls of the poets, as poets tell us, have this peculiar ministration in the world. They tell us that these souls, flying like bees from flower to flower, and wandering over the gardens and the meadows and the honey-flowing fountains of the Muses, return to us laden with the sweetness of melody; and arrayed as they are in the plumes of rapid imagination, they speak truth. For a poet is indeed a thing ethereally light, winged, and sacred, nor can he compose anything worth calling poetry until he becomes inspired, and, as it were, mad, or whilst any reason remains to him. For whilst a man retains any portion of the thing called reason, he is utterly incompetent to produce poetry or to vaticinate. . . . The God seems purposely to have deprived all poets, prophets, and soothsayers of every particle of reason and understanding, the better to adapt them to their employment as his ministers and inter-preters; and that we, their auditors, may acknowledge that those who write so beautifully, are possessed, and address us, inspired by the God.

This doctrine of poetic inspiration became the focal point of Shel-ley's *Defence of Poetry*. When Peacock sent him a copy of *The Four Ages of Poetry* (in answer to which Shelley wrote his *Defence*), Shelley wrote back (Feb. 15, 1821) that Peacock ought to reconsider Plato's *Ion* (X, 234). The poet, says Shelley in his *Defence*, is, in the act of creation, possessed of a divine madness so that what he writes comes not from his own consciousness but from a realm above con-sciousness over which he has no control: "it is as it were the inter-penetration of a diviner nature through our own" acting "in a divine and unapprehended manner, beyond and above consciousness." It has, therefore, nothing to do with the will. "A man cannot say, 'I will compose poetry.' The greatest poet even cannot say it: for the mind in creation is as a fading coal, which some invisible influence, like an inconstant wind, awakens to transitory brightness . . . and the conscious portions of our natures are unprophetic either of its approach or its departure." The poet, when he "participates in the daemoniacal nature," ceases to be a man; it is only in the intervals between inspiration that "a Poet becomes a man, and is abandoned to the sudden reflux of the influences under which others habitually live."[16]

This "invisible influence" that awakens the mind "to a transitory brightness" and is compared to an "inconstant wind" is that hovering spirit that informs most of Shelley's poetry. Its first poetic incarnation is Queen Mab, the Daemon of the World, who visits Ianthe in sleep and carries her soul into a visionary world whose circumference contains within it the entire universe. The spirit reappears in *Alastor* as the veiled maiden who visits the poet in sleep and drives him to an untimely grave in his hopeless effort to find her counterpart in the world of reality. In the *Hymn to Intellectual Beauty*, it is that "awful shadow of some unseen Power" (1) to which, as a result of a momentary interpenetration, he has dedicated his powers. It is the beautiful lady in *The Sensitive Plant* whose presence is the source of life in Nature, and it is Asia in *Prometheus Unbound* whom Prometheus addresses as the "Shadow of beauty unbeheld" (iii, iii, 7). In *Adonais*, it is Urania, the muse of poetry, and in *The Triumph of Life* it is the informing spirit of the poets to which only Socrates and Christ remain faithful: when "they had touched the world with living flame" (130), they "fled back like eagles to their native noon" (131).

In his *Defence*, Shelley writes that, as a result of these visitations, the poet "creates anew the universe, after it has been annihilated in our minds by the recurrence of impressions blunted by reiteration" (VII, 137). Shelley is here speaking of the imagination as a creative power at work upon the chaos of man's familiar world, forcing it to assume a form which is the image of the "divinity in Man." That created image constitutes for Shelley the vision of apocalypse; it is the imaginative vision that releases man from the recurrent impressions "blunted by reiteration."

In the *Timaeus*, which he first read in Thomas Taylor's translation, Shelley thought he had found an account of the way in which man's creative faculty operates upon the world as habitually perceived. Using as his model the world of the Forms, the Demiurge in the *Timaeus* shapes his material much in the manner of a sculptor modelling clay. His material, however, is not completely amenable, so that he is limited in the extent to which order can be brought out of original chaos. Plato

[16]VII, 136, 116, 135, 139.

explains this recalcitrance of matter by the idea of Necessity or "erratic cause" which he describes (in Taylor's translation) as "the nurse of generation, fiery and moist" (p. 525). Being destitute of reason, Necessity cannot impose an order upon the elements of earth and air; as a result the motions of these elements remain altogether chaotic until they are persuaded by the Demiurge, which works with intelligence, to move in harmony. Plato's view of Necessity, therefore, is not to be confused with Godwin's view of Necessity as "the eternal chain of causes." Thus Plato concludes (p. 520):

For, the generation of the world being mingled, it was produced from the composition of intellect and necessity. But intellect ruling over necessity persuaded it to lead the most part of generated natures to that which is best; and hence necessity being vanquished by wise persuasion, from these two as principles the world arose. If, then, anyone truly asserts that the universe was generated according to these, he should also mingle with it the form of an erratic cause, which it is naturally adapted to receive.

Shelley interprets the Demiurge as performing the same creative function as the "one Spirit's plastic stress" which, in *Adonais* (382–5),

> Sweeps through the dull dense world, compelling there,
> All new successions to the forms they wear;
> Torturing th'unwilling dross that checks its flight
> To its own likeness, as each mass may bear.

Like Plato in the *Timaeus*, Shelley draws an analogy between the creative power of the "one Spirit's plastic stress" and the creative power of the poet. Keats in *Adonais* bears his part in the work of the one Spirit; he is, in this respect, "one with Nature" (370), a "portion of the loveliness / Which once he made more lovely" (379–80). Plato makes the same point in the *Timaeus* (pp. 519–20):

By us, indeed, it is asserted that Divinity bestowed sight on us for this purpose, that on surveying the circulations of intellect in the heavens we may properly employ the revolutions of our dianoëtic part, which are allied to their circulations; and may recall the tumultuous motions of our discursive energies to the orderly processions of their intellectual periods. That besides this, by learning these and participating right reason according to nature, and imitating the revolutions of Divinity which are entirely inerratic, we may give stability to the wanderings of our dianoëtic energy.

But concerning voice and hearing, we again assert that they were bestowed on us by the Gods on the same account. For the acquisition of speech pertains to these, and is of the greatest advantage to their possession.

And whatever utility musical voice brings to the sense of hearing, was bestowed for the sake of harmony. But harmony, possessing motions allied to the revolutions of our soul, is useful to the man who employs the Muses in conjunction with intellect. . . . Indeed, it was given us by the Muses for the purpose of reducing the dissonant circulation of the Soul to an order and symphony accommodated to its nature. . . . And thus far, a few particulars excepted, have we shown the fabrications of intellect.

In his mythical picture of man's condition within the cosmos, Plato describes it first under the control of the Demiurge and then under the control of Necessity. In the former condition, man lived in a paradise, which was a state of anarchism wherein he enjoyed the fruits of Nature without the expenditure of physical effort. In the latter condition, he lived in the midst of terrible convulsion which worked havoc among every race of living man. The temporal separation of these two conditions, however, is simply a mythical device; in reality the two coexist so that the work of persuading Necessity towards that which is good and desirable always confronts man. Creation, in the world of Becoming, is always being carried on. Continuous creation is the only answer to the threat of annihilation by which man is forever confronted in the realm of Necessity.

Returning again to the notion of divine inspiration which he had presented in the *Symposium* and the *Ion*, Plato says that man, in the world of Becoming, strives to recall the work and the instructions of the Demiurge. Memory, however, gives way to forgetfulness so that without divine intervention man would be in the direst straits. The evidence of divine intervention is to be found in the legendary gifts of the gods: fire from Prometheus, the arts and crafts from Hephaestus, and seeds and plants from other benefactors. In each of these mythical figures the work of the Demiurge is renewed: Prometheus, for example, brought fire from the realm of Necessity and converted it to the realm of intelligence by putting it at the service of man.

Viewing what Shelley has to say about reason and imagination in *A Defence of Poetry* in the light of Plato's mythical conception of Necessity and the Demiurge, it is possible to gain a clearer understanding of the apocalyptic nature of the creative imagination. Reason, says Shelley, is the "principle of analysis, and its action regards the relations of things, simply as relations; considering thoughts, not in their integral unity, but as the algebraical representations which conduct to certain general results" (VII, 109). Reason is Godwin's law of Necessity, the eternal chain of causes that determines the motions of the physical and mental universe. Shelley follows Godwin when, in his notes to *Queen Mab* (p. 809), he describes Necessity as the "constant conjunction of similar events, and the consequent inference of one from the other." It is this definition that reappears in *A Defence of Poetry* as a description of the world of recurrent impressions. Imagination, on the other hand, is the principle of synthesis which annihilates that "constant conjunction of similar events" (the product of mental fixation) and fuses them into a new harmony. Like Coleridge's conception of the secondary imagination, it "dissolves, diffuses, dissipates, in order to recreate; or where this process is rendered impossible, yet still, at all events, it struggles to idealize and to unify."[17]

On the basis of this distinction between reason and imagination, Shelley concludes in his *Defence* that poetry, as the expression of the imagination,

defeats the curse which binds us to be subjected to the accident of surrounding impressions. And whether it spreads its own figured curtain, or withdraws life's dark veil from before the scene of things, it equally creates for us a being within our being. It makes us the inhabitants of a world to which the familiar world is a chaos. It reproduces the common Universe of which we are portions and percipients, and it purges from our inward sight the film of familiarity which obscures from us the wonder of our being. . . . It creates anew the universe, after it has been annihilated in our minds by the recurrence of impressions blunted by reiteration. It justifies the bold and true word of Tasso: *Non merita nome di creatore, se non Iddio ed il Poeta*. [VII, 137–8]

The transmutation that Shelley here describes from the chaos of the familiar world, to which man is bound as by a curse, to a world that expresses "the wonder of our being" is the work, in Plato's terms, of the Demiurge in its persuasion of Necessity. The poet, as Plato points out, participates in this divine activity, and when Shelley says in his *Defence* that the poet participates in the infinite, the eternal and the one, he has in mind Plato's archetypal pattern as he understands it.

Shelley, therefore, developed under the influence of Plato a coherent conception of the nature of poetry which contained within itself the

17*Biographia Literaria*, ed. George Watson (London: J. M. Dent & Sons Ltd., 1956), p. 167.

principle of its own integrity. Identifying himself with the mytho-poeic poet in Plato to whom he subordinated the purely rational philo-sopher, he found his own centre in the world of the creative imagina-tion. He read into Plato's creation myth the type of all creative work on the part of poets. Man is engaged in a giant conflict with Necessity; his task is perpetually to renew the universe of which he is a part and thereby rid himself of all that binds him to surrounding impressions. For this labour of the ages (which is also the labour of the moment) imagination, quickened by the "visitations of the divinity in Man" (VII, 137) is needed. Without it, humanity perishes. Civilization finds its origin in the creative faculty; poets are the "unacknowledged legislators of the world" (VII, 140).

It is not the work of the poet, however, to make the application of his vision to society; that labour belongs to the "promoters of utility" in the limited sense, who have "their appointed office in society." Their task is to "follow the footsteps of poets, and copy the sketches of their creations into the book of common life" (VII, 132), while the poets, once they have discharged their Promethean fire, must, like Christ and Socrates, fly back to their "native noon" (*T.L.*, 131).

The implication is clear: Shelley's apocalyptic vision (i.e., the vision of a universe continuously created as distinct from a universe continuously perceived) belongs within a verbal universe; it is not an earthly kingdom that will one day be established among men. It is, like Plato's republic, a pattern set up in Heaven. In 1811 and 1812, Shelley confused the universe of poetic vision and the universe of men. Accepting Godwin's doctrine of progress and perfectibility, he thought that the process of Becoming would one day (by the law of Necessity) be absorbed into Being. His misplaced hope forced him to limit his apocalyptic vision to a coalescence of man with Nature, thus binding it to the "eternal chain of causes." In *Prometheus Unbound*, however, the apocalypse is a psychic event belonging not to time, but to eter-nity. In his victory over Jupiter, Prometheus defeats "the eternal chain of causes," though, of course, only in vision, not in reality. The vision of apocalypse is an *anagogia visionis* of the true apocalypse.

So long as Shelley remained under the direct influence of Godwin's doctrines he could not hope to escape the notion that poetry cannot contain within itself the principle of its own integrity; the judgment of poetry was referable to the moral progress of society. Society must be the ultimate judge. From this point of view, poetry must be didactic. In June 1811, Shelley argued in a letter to Elizabeth Hitchener (VIII, 100) that "poetical beauty ought to be subordinate to the inculcated moral," and that "metaphorical language ought to be a pleasing vehicle for useful and momentous instruction." Such statements reveal the restricted nature of Shelley's passion at that time.

Shelley's real break with Godwin, in favour of Plato, lies in the view of time which is implicit in *A Defence of Poetry*. The view of time in Godwin's system, as the doctrine of gradual progress shows, is linear: a fixed succession of events expressive of a gradual increase in human consciousness towards an ultimate state of perfection or pure intelligence. Now the difficulty involved for Shelley, as a poet, in this linear view of time was the fact that it was shapeless; the content of time could not be consolidated into formulated vision. The perfection of man, involved as it was in the passage of time, was an abstraction lost in the indefiniteness of future ages. The whole weakness of Godwin's system from the poet's point of view was that, while the strength of Godwin's argument lay in his faith in human perfectibility, the faith itself was devoid of the compelling power of vision. And without that vision, there was no incentive to moral improvement. Man, Shelley realized within himself, could not be motivated to the performance of benevolent acts by an abstraction called "distant ages." "We want," says Shelley in *A Defence of Poetry* (VII, 134) "the creative faculty to imagine that which we know."

In contrast to this linear conception of time, the limitations of which Shelley instinctively realized as early as 1812, is the conception of time presented in Plato's *Timaeus*. The Demiurge, says Plato, wished to create in the generation of the universe the likeness, so far as that was possible, of the eternal Form upon which it was modelled. The nature of the living Being serving as the model, however, is eternal and this character it was impossible to confer upon the generated thing. At best, the Demiurge could make a "movable image of eternity" (p. 490); accordingly, he "formed an eternal image flowing according to number, of eternity abiding in one; and receives from us the appellation of time" (pp. 490–1). To move according to number means to Plato that time is not a straight line of unlimited extent moving in both directions, but a circle which, though limited and circumscribed, is yet a symbol of eternity. It is the circular motion of time that makes it an image of eternity. Time means the complete circle in which the beginning is joined to the end. All of time constitutes the Great Year, the single period of the whole, which is the complete circle of life.

When Shelley speaks of time in *A Defence of Poetry*, he is thinking of it in terms of the single period of the whole whose form is a single cyclic poem to which all the poets since the beginning of the world have contributed an episode. Drawing his analogy from Plato's comparison of divine inspiration to the attracting power of a magnet, he writes:

The sacred links of that chain have never been entirely disjoined, which descending through the minds of many men is attached to those great minds, whence as from a magnet the invisible effluence is sent forth, which at once connects, animates and sustains the life of all. It is the faculty which contains within itself the seeds at once of its own and of social renovation. And let us not circumscribe the effects of the bucolic and erotic poetry within the limits of the sensibility of those to whom it was addressed. They may have perceived the beauty of those immortal compositions, simply as fragments and isolated portions: those who are more finely organised, or born in a happier age, may recognise them as episodes to that great poem, which all poets, like the co-operating thoughts of one great mind, have built up since the beginning of the world. [VII, 124]

This single great poem is the apocalyptic vision which contains all of time as the "movable image of eternity." It is not Godwin's far-off event. The visionary apocalypse, so far as it is in time, is the fusion of all time into an image of eternity quickened by divine inspiration and shaped by the creative imagination.

2

DIONYSUS

Between 1810 and 1812, Shelley was inspired by Godwin's ideal
of political justice. Following Godwin's example, he believed that in
Queen Mab he had "in imagination" gone out of himself and become
the impartial spectator of that eternal and immutable order which is
governed by the "most perfect intelligence." *Queen Mab* was Shelley's
first attempt both to give a visionary form to Godwin's ideal and, in
the interpenetration of the Fairy Queen, to dramatize the imaginative
process. Godwin, however, did not approve of the poem, quite apart
from the materialistic doctrine contained in the vision. He considered
it another example of Shelley's misguided passion for reforming the
world. Mankind, he argued, can only properly be assisted in its gradual
growth towards pure intelligence by science and reason. The mass
of mankind is not prepared for an apocalyptic vision, which must,
considering its present state, inevitably incite violent, abortive action.
Godwin therefore sought at all times to temper Shelley's enthusiasm.
"One principle that I believe is wanting in you, and in all our too
fervent and impetuous reformers," he wrote to Shelley on March 4,
1812, "is the thought that almost every institution and form of society
is good in its place and in the period of time to which it belongs. . . .
In this point of view nothing perhaps can be more worthy of our
applause than the English Constitution."[1]

[1]Quoted in C. Kegan Paul, *William Godwin: His Friends and Contemporaries*
(London: H. S. King and Co., 1876), II, 205–6.

If Shelley wished to write fiction, Godwin argued, he should devote his talents to a careful analysis of human motivation and demonstrate the way in which "the eternal chain of causes" operates in human behaviour. That is what he had done in his own novels, and, as his disciple, that is what Shelley should do. Shelley had, in fact, just such a novel in preparation. "Hubert Cauvin," which he hoped to have published while in Ireland, was designed, as he told Elizabeth Hitchener in his letter of January 2, 1812, "to exhibit the cause of the failure of the French Revolution, and the state of morals and opinions in France during the latter years of its monarchy" (VIII, 231).

Like his essay on the failure of the French Revolution, the novel was never completed. Instead, by 1817, Shelley appears to have incorporated both projects into a long poem of epic stature, *The Revolt of Islam*. On the one hand, the poem is a vision of an ideal revolution which, unlike the French Revolution, takes place primarily within the psyche; on the other, it is a picture of individual mind aspiring after excellence. Godwin's dislike of the poem (which he first read in its unrevised form as *Laon and Cythna*) was even more intense than his dislike of *Queen Mab*. Once again Shelley had substituted passion and vision for reason and science.

By 1817, however, Shelley had found his metaphysical defence of vision in Plato's *Symposium*. What he presented in the growth of individual mind in *The Revolt of Islam* was, as he wrote Godwin, a "genuine picture" of his own mind ruled not by the dialectic of reason, but the dialectic of sacred passion. Plato's Eros, rather than Godwin's supreme intelligence, governs the poem's action. Supported by Plato, Shelley was able to reject Godwin's criticism on the grounds that Godwin had no conception of the nature of Shelley's power as a poet. In his same letter to Godwin with reference to Godwin's attack on *The Revolt of Islam* (in its unrevised form) as well as in his Preface concerned with the education of the poet, Shelley expresses his poetic emancipation from the limitations of Godwin's philosophical method. "Nothing can be more satisfactory to me than the interest which your admonitions express," he writes (IX, 266). "But I think you are mistaken in some points with regard to the peculiar nature of my powers, whatever be their amount. I listened with deference and self suspicion to your censures of 'Laon and Cythna'; but the productions of mine [such as his review of *Mandeville*] which you commend hold a very low place in my own esteem, and this re-assured me, in some degree at least."

Between 1812 and 1817, Shelley transformed Godwin's view of reason into a creative power and his view of disinterested benevolence into the Platonic Eros. For the resigned Stoic, whom he saw as Godwin's ideal moral reformer, Shelley substituted Laon and Cythna: united lovers seeking to incarnate their psychic union in a recreated society. Shelley's heroes belonged not to Godwin's world of "science and improvement," but to that ideal world to which Plato's Eros led them.

In his imaginative re-creation of Godwinism under the influence of Plato, Shelley believed that he had restored Godwin's philosophy to its original mythical form. "The resolution of objects into their simple elements," Godwin writes with reference to the act of perception, "is an operation of science and improvement; but it is altogether foreign to our first and original conceptions. *In all cases, the operations of our understanding, are rather analytical than synthetical,* rather those of resolution than composition. We do not begin with the successive perception of elementary parts till we have obtained an idea of the whole; but, beginning with a whole, are capable of reducing it into its elements."[2] In his poetic vision, Shelley sought to restore to Godwin's philosophy those "first and original conceptions" which constitute the "idea of the whole." All knowledge may require reducing that whole to "the successive perception of elementary parts"; unless, however, the whole is present to the mind no such rational resolution is possible. Shelley therefore argues in his *Defence* that poetry is the circumference of all knowledge, that upon which all knowledge depends. Poetry is a vision of the intuitive, pre-conscious, Gestalt experience which science reduces "into its elements."

By 1817, Shelley recognized what he considered the true Platonic foundation of Godwin's ideal of political justice. Godwin's ideal was not the product of his analytical powers; it was the product of an intuition of the cosmic order, seen as the "antitype" of the divinity within him. It could therefore only be imaged in its ideal form (as opposed to its elementary parts) when presented as the object of the prophetic imagination. And this is the way that Shelley chose to

[2]Godwin, I, 407 (italics not in original).

present it in *Prometheus Unbound*. His lyrical drama is a vision of the community of life, governed not by the scientific 'principle of causality, but by the psychic principle of sympathy. The poet, argues Shelley, is not a scientist; he is a magician. His obvious analogy for the poet was the alchemist. The imagination, Shelley writes in his *Defence* (VII, 137), "transmutes all that it touches, and every form moving within the radiance of its presence is changed by wondrous sympathy to an incarnation of the spirit which it breathes; its secret alchemy turns to potable gold the poisonous waters which flow from death through life." Thus the poet in *Alastor* whose imagination has waned yearns for "Medea's wondrous alchemy" (672) and desires to believe that the "dark magician in his visioned cave" (682) is the "true law" (685) of life. Too much a rationalist to accept the lore of the magician in *Alastor*, Shelley, by 1819, had finally submitted to the occult. His Prometheus is in fact the "dark magician" who, once released, retires to a "visioned cave" to create "arts, though unimagined, yet to be" (III, iii, 56).

The re-creation of Godwinism in *Prometheus Unbound* shows the extent to which the occult tradition to which he had been introduced by Taylor, Newton, and Peacock had supplanted Shelley's earlier rationalism. Under their influence, Shelley, as early as 1813, had returned to his study of "ancient books of Chemistry and Magic" which even at Oxford he had "perused with an enthusiasm of wonder, almost amounting to belief," as he recalled in writing to Godwin early in January, 1812 (VIII, 239). In 1813, Shelley was translating two essays of Plutarch which, among other things, dealt with Orphism. "They are very excellent," Shelley wrote to Hogg on November 26, 1813 (IX, 81–2). "I intend to comment upon them, and to reason in my preface concerning the Orphic and Pythagoric system of diet." In *Queen Mab*, this system of diet is the means by which the golden age will be restored. The method is prophetic of the vision to come: Shelley is already suggesting that Godwin's Utopia will be established by a universal conversion to Orphism.

Orphism, destined to provide the mythological framework for Shelley's view of the creative imagination and the archetypal pattern of his apocalyptic vision, is essentially a refinement of the primitive Dionysian cult, the history of which reveals three fairly distinct phases. The first phase is one of primitive, orgiastic rite brought on by extreme intoxication; here Dionysus appears as the decadent wine-god. The second phase demonstrates the transforming power of Orphism in which mere madness is elevated to divine madness. The cult of Dionysus becomes a religion of purification and spiritual rebirth. In the final phase, evident in the dialogues of Plato, *mythos* is replaced by *logos,* and myth is rejected as a revelation of ultimate reality. Each of these phases of the Dionysian myth will be examined with reference to Shelley's attitude to it. On the basis of this examination, Shelley's conception of the myth and its importance for an understanding of his poetry should become clear.

Shelley's knowledge of the primitive phase of the Dionysian religion derives in part from his reading of Nonnos' *Dionysiaca* and Euripides' *Bacchae.* Nonnos treats the legendary conquests of Dionysus in the epic manner. He presents Dionysus as a world conqueror like Alexander going from country to country subduing the people in huge and bloody battles and converting them through the intoxicating powers of wine. Nonnos' description of the conquest of India, for example, is an orgy of blood and slaughter climaxed by Dionysus turning "a bubbling bloodbath mingled with Indian gore" (xiv, 410) into wine. This miracle, says Nonnos, Dionysus performed because the "god pitied his foes in his heart of merry cheer" (xiv, 412). The Indian warriors drink the wine, and, "driven by the gadfly of mind-robbing drink" (xv, 27), attack a herd of cattle believing it to be the fierce warriors of Dionysus. Reduced to madness, they then imitate the Corybantes and the Satyrs in a wild and frenzied dance until they fall into a stupor "tormented in mind by immoderate wine, doing grace to Pasithea's father, Dionysos" (xv, 91–2). Shelley recreates this kind of orgy in his vision of the perverted Bacchanalia in *The Triumph of Life.*

The conquest of Thebes, as depicted by Euripides in the *Bacchae,* shows the same abandoned frenzy issuing in brutal and inhuman acts. When Pentheus, King of Thebes, resists the advance of the Dionysian cult in his own city, the fierce Maenads, led by Agave his mother, turn upon him and tear him limb from limb (p. 63)

> But she, with lips a-foam and eyes that run
> Like leaping fire, with thoughts that ne'er should be
> On earth, possessed by Bacchios utterly,
> Stays not nor hears. Round his left arm she put

> Both hands, set hard against his side her foot,
> Drew . . . and the shoulder severed!—Not by might
> Of arm, but easily, as the God made light
> Her hand's essay.

After dismembering the body of Pentheus in this manner, Agave places his head upon her thyrsus and bears it aloft, while leading her sisters in their Maenad dance.

The loathsome brutality of this act brought on by wine is characteristic of the Dionysian cult in its first stage of orgiastic rite. Shelley, as might be expected, completely rejects it in this form. Describing a statue of Bacchus by Michelangelo, he says (VI, 329): "The countenance of this figure is the most revolting mistake of the spirit and meaning of Bacchus. It looks drunken, brutal, and narrow-minded, and has an expression of dissoluteness the most revolting. . . . It is altogether without unity, as was the idea of the Deity of Bacchus in the conception of a Catholic. . . . It wants as a work of art unity and simplicity; as a representation of the Greek Deity of Bacchus it wants every thing."

Shelley is here viewing this primitive conception of Bacchus in the light of the radical transformation brought about by Orphism. Not only did Orphism change the conception of the god, but also the means by which the godhead could be attained. The means was no longer physical intoxication, but spiritual ecstasy through abstinence and rites of purification. In the peace-loving figure of Orpheus, whose music could tame the wildest beast, the Dionysian cult underwent a metamorphosis. Shelley considered this transfiguration similar in many respects to the one he thought he saw from the Old Testament Jehovah to the New Testament Christ. Here, for example, is his description (VI, 319–20) of one of the Ampelus-Bacchus group which he saw in Florence. It is quoted at some length because Shelley obviously had it in mind when he composed his self-portrait in *Adonais*.

He is crowned with vine leaves laden with their crude fruit, and the crisp leaves fall as with the inertness of a lithe and faded leaf over his rich and over-hanging hair, which gracefully divided on his forehead falls in delicate wreaths upon his neck and breast. . . . The countenance of Bacchus is sublimely sweet and lovely. . . . It has a divine and supernatural beauty, as one who walks through the world untouched by its corruptions, its corrupting cares; it looks like one who unconsciously yet with delight confers pleasure and peace. The flowing fulness and the roundness of the breast and belly, whose lines fading into each other, are continued with a gentle motion as it were to the utmost extremity of his limbs. Like some fine strain of harmony which flows round the soul and enfolds it, and leaves it in the soft astonishment of a satisfaction, like the pleasure of love with one whom we most love, which having taken away desire, leaves pleasure, sweet pleasure. The countenance of the Ampelus is in every respect inferior . . . but the Bacchus is immortal beauty.

Shelley is here describing the Orphic Bacchus, who is only remotely connected to the Dionysus of the primitive cult. Yet there is a connection. Orphism pictured man as engaged in a giant conflict of spirit and flesh which can only be resolved by the descent of the god, or more properly, the ascent of man to a state of divine possession in which he becomes the god. The primitive Dionysus was required adequately to define that struggle. Together, the primitive and the Orphic Bacchus present the struggle in the process and the ideal calm in the resolution. Shelley had seen this pattern in the *Bacchae*. In the choral odes the figure of Dionysus is quite distinct from the vengeful god inspiring the Maenads to lead Pentheus to his horrific death. He is presented as a god of joy, a bringer of new life to Thebes, evoking in his followers a peace that surpasses human understanding (pp. 24–5).

> A God of Heaven is he,
> And born in majesty;
> Yet hath he mirth in the joy of the Earth,
> And he loveth constantly
> Her who brings increase,
> The Feeder of Children, Peace.
>
> No grudge hath he of the great;
> No scorn of the mean estate;
> But to all that liveth his wine he giveth,
> Griefless, immaculate;
> Only on them that spurn
> Joy, may his anger burn.

Shelley's apocalyptic vision presents the same pattern of destruction and re-creation. In his *Ode to the West Wind*, for example, the destructive power of the wind is compared to "the bright hair uplifted from the head / of some fierce Maenad." Precisely the same Dionysian image is used in Shelley's vision of the universe recreated by love in the last act of *Prometheus Unbound*. The revolutions of the Moon and Earth are (473–5)

> Like a Maenad, round the cup
> Which Agave lifted up
> In the weird Cadmaean forest.

The "fierce Maenad" in *Ode to the West Wind* suggests the orgiastic, destructive power of the primitive Dionysian cult. The Maenad in the last act of *Prometheus Unbound* suggests the recreative power of divine possession which Shelley found in Plato's *Ion*. The former is Bacchic; the latter is Orphic.

Unlike Dionysus, Orpheus was known as the author of a religion based on the written word; he is the *theologos* and when, in the epic of Apollonius, he raises his voice to sing, the theme of his lay is cosmogonical. Shelley's knowledge of the Orphic cosmology derives primarily from his reading of Plato's dialogues, the Neo-Platonic commentaries of Thomas Taylor, and a wide range of occult books, which, in the dedication stanzas of *The Revolt of Islam*, he describes as the "knowledge from forbidden mines of lore" (38) with which he armed his spirit. Any attempt to describe the Orphic myth must invariably be an over-simplification which ignores many or most of the endless variations that grew out of the retelling. For the purposes of clarity, however, it may be presented in a simplified form in order to explain Shelley's understanding of it. Just as Shelley read into the account of the Demiurge in the *Timaeus* the type of the creative imagination as a shaping power at work upon its materials, so into the Orphic myth he read the mythopoeic form of visionary art, to the making of which he was but one contributor.

In the Orphic myth, Dionysus undergoes three distinct incarnations. In his first incarnation, he is Dionysus-Phanes, the first born of the gods (Protagonos). He is born from the egg fashioned by Chronos and identified with Eros—"a figure of shining light, with golden wings on his shoulders, four eyes and the heads of various animals"[3]— by the Orphic theologians. The account of the birth of Eros (Dionysus-Phanes) in the Orphic myth finds its parallel in the account of the birth of Venus from the shell made by Proteus and it is in this

[3]W. K. C. Guthrie, *Orpheus and Greek Religion* (London: Methuen Co., 1952), p. 80.

latter form that Shelley uses it in *Prometheus Unbound*. To announce to the world the restoration of the original reign of love, Ione, at the command of Prometheus, gives to the Spirit of the Hour "that curvèd shell, which Proteus old / Made Asia's [Venus'] nuptial boon" (III, iii, 65–6). This shell contains within it "a voice to be accomplished" (III, iii, 67) which is, of course, the prophecy of renewal.

In his second incarnation, Dionysus is born from the thigh of Zeus and is known as Dionysus-Zagreus (son of Zeus). Zeus then sets him upon his throne and places his own sceptre in his hands. But the Titans, having found a new life under the rule of Zeus, and being therefore jealous of Dionysus, with the help of Hera, the lawful wife of Zeus, plot to kill him. The infant tries to protect himself by assuming the form of a bull, but the Titans divert him with a mirror and various playthings, and then slay and devour him. But the heart of Dionysus is saved by Athene who brings it to Zeus. Zeus cuts open his thigh and within the male womb of Zeus the god is reconstituted and brought back to life. Dionysus is thus called by the Orphics the thrice-born: Dionysus-Phanes, Dionysus-Zagreus, and Dionysus the resurrected. And it is this third birth of Dionysus that is celebrated in the central Orphic rite.

The devouring of Dionysus-Zagreus provides the explanation not only of man's creation but of his condition in this world. When Zeus sees that the Titans have tasted the flesh of Dionysus, he launches a thunderbolt at them and burns them. Out of the smoking remnants of the Titans arises the new race of men. Man's nature, therefore, is twofold. He is born from the Titans, the wicked sons of earth, but these Titans contain fragments of the body of Dionysus, son of Zeus. Man is, consequently, both mortal and divine; his chief purpose here on earth is to liberate himself from the evil nature of his mortality and assume that immortality which is the recovery of his own divinity. It is for this reason that the Orphic rites of rebirth reach their climax in calling upon the god to descend upon them and release them from their Titanic selves: Dionysus, in his third incarnation, is the vision of a divine humanity restored to unity after being scattered into multiplicity. The words ascribed to Orpheus by his pupil Musaios sum up the whole significance of the myth: "Everything comes to be out of the One and is resolved into the One."

For Shelley, the words ascribed to Musaios are a statement of what art reveals. It should not be concluded, however, that Orphism was the "source" of Shelley's vision or of his view of art. That "source" was within himself. He saw in Orphism the mythical analogue of his own creative spirit and, as will now be examined, the creative spirit that informs Greek tragedy. Orphism was to Shelley what the Bible was to Blake: the great code of art.

Shelley believed that the true significance of the Dionysian myth was revealed in Greek tragedy. Here the struggle in man between his Titanic nature and his Dionysian divinity was dramatized, but always with the Titanic nature acting as a "thin disguise of circumstance" behind which the "ideal perfection" could be seen. The presence of that perfection behind the mask of crime and suffering produced the "exalted calm" of the audience. "The tragedies of the Athenian poets," he writes,

are as mirrors in which the spectator beholds himself, under a thin disguise of circumstance, stript of all but that ideal perfection and energy which everyone feels to be the internal type of all that he loves, admires, and would become. The imagination is enlarged by a sympathy with pains and passions so mighty, that they distend in their conception the capacity of that by which they are conceived; the good affections are strengthened by pity, indignation, terror and sorrow; and an exalted calm is prolonged from the satiety of this high exercise of them into the tumult of familiar life: every crime is disarmed of half its horror and all its contagion by being represented as the fatal consequence of the unfathomable agencies of nature; error is thus divested of its wilfulness; men can no longer ∗cherish it as the creation of their choice. In a drama of the highest order there is little room for censure or hatred; it teaches rather self-knowledge and self-respect. Neither the eye nor the mind can see itself, unless reflected upon that which it resembles. [VII, 121]

What Shelley saw in Greek tragedy is essentially what Nietzsche was later to see: "the one truly real Dionysus appears in a variety of forms, in the mask of a fighting hero and entangled, as it were, in the net of individual will." Identifying itself with the ideal image of its inner nature, the audience undergoes catharsis. Shelley believed that all imaginative art is, in some sense, a purification rite. He believed, again to use Nietzsche's words, that art teaches that "individuation [is] the primal cause of evil, and art . . . [a] joyous hope that the bonds of individuation may be broken as in augury of restored oneness."[4]

[4]F. Nietzsche, *The Birth of Tragedy*, trans. Clifton Fadiman, in *The Philosophy of Nietzsche* (New York: Modern Library, 1927), pp. 1001–2.

Shelley accepted this account of Greek tragedy as one form of the archetypal vision of all art, which was best defined in Plato's Orphic myths.

In Plato's dialogues, Socrates emerges as the philosopher who has gained self-knowledge. Although he feigns ignorance, it is merely a pretence necessary to his dialectical method of teaching. How did Socrates find truth? Shelley found his answer in the *Symposium*: through Diotima, the Orphic prophetess. By what method did he find it? The answer is implicit in Socrates' own method of teaching: dialectic. The question, however, needs to be pushed one step further. Who taught the truth to Diotima so that she might pass it on to Socrates? And precisely at this point the limit of reason has been reached; Plato must revert to the Orphic myths to provide an answer.

Plato argues that knowledge is recollection, and proceeds to prove it in the *Meno* by eliciting from the Greek slave, who was previously ignorant of geometry, the proof of one of Euclid's theorems. Plato explains this doctrine of knowledge as recollection by means of the Orphic myth of pre-existence. In the *Phaedrus*, he describes the soul in its previous existence where it had been in the presence of the Forms and had been so impressed by the sight of the true, the beautiful, and the good that even after it had fallen and become immersed in body, it still had some recollection of those Forms and was drawn, by the sight of beautiful objects, to them.

This myth is a variation of the Orphic myth of Dionysus-Zagreus. Man in his original divinity is Dionysus. That divinity, however, has fallen into matter as a result of the devouring of Dionysus by the Titans. Yet even in the form of flesh, man is still aware of the divinity within him and may by the performance of purification rites climaxing in a state of divine possession re-establish his oneness with the god. Plato's theory of knowledge, therefore, rests upon a mythical base.

The restoration of myth in the Romantic movement, its acceptance as a revelation of psychic truth, lies in the fact that Romantic poets considered it the expression of a realm beyond the reach of normal consciousness. It was a revelation of the secret springs of human thought and feeling. In the philosophy of the Enlightenment those secret springs had been buried beneath a vast rational structure. To uncover them was to return to the origins in the imagination, and from those origins recreate human society. Thus, in his Preface to *The Revolt of Islam*, Shelley condemns the neo-classical critics who daily murder imagination and defends the mythopoeic poets who write without regard for their censure.

The locating of myth within the unconscious portion of the human psyche produced in English Romanticism what may be called the cult of childhood. In his *Defence of Poetry*, Shelley argues that the child is to years what primitive man is to ages. The world of myth and rite characteristic of primitive man is also the world of the child. In this sense, the ideal world is the recovery of the lost childhood in every man. Before examining this view held by Shelley, however, it may be worth while to examine it in its most explicit form in the poetry of Wordsworth.

It is not without significance that Wordsworth in his account of the process of growing up describes the child in terms of the Platonic and Orphic doctrine of pre-existence. In his "Intimations of Immortality" ode he says that the child is a "Mighty Prophet" and "Seer blest" (114) because he enters the world "not in utter nakedness" (63) but "trailing clouds of glory" (64) from the ideal world in which he previously existed. Those "clouds of glory" are his memory of pre-existence. In childhood, however, "Shades of the prison-house" (67) begin to descend and the glory is soon lost in the light of common day. Through the imagination, however, this lost glory can be momentarily restored. He describes these moments in "Tintern Abbey": they are the gifts of "aspect more sublime" (37) in which, as in the Orphic state of divine possession, "we are laid asleep / In body, and become a living soul" (45–6). The eye is made quiet "by the power / Of harmony, and the deep power of joy" (47–8) so that we "see into the life of things" (49). And what precisely is it that is seen? Wordsworth comes closest to an answer in *The Prelude* (vi, 634–9):

> The unfettered clouds and region of the Heavens,
> Tumult and peace, the darkness and the light—
> Were all like workings of one mind, the features
> Of the same face, blossoms upon one tree;
> Characters of the great Apocalypse,
> The types and symbols of Eternity.

What Wordsworth saw was an augury of restored oneness, a vision of the "Mighty Prophet" within the self.

From this point of view, poetry is the articulation of the inarticulate vision of childhood. It is a return to origins, recreating in the adult mind the eternal childhood of the race. For this reason Shelley says in his *Defence* that "poetry is connate with the origin of man." And he illustrates this view with reference to both primitive man and the child. Primitive man, he says, dances and sings, gaining an intense and pure pleasure from his "sense of an approximation" to the eternal order of Nature which these rites provide. What is characteristic of primitive man is also characteristic of the child (for "the savage is to ages what the child is to years").

A child at play by itself will express its delight by its voice and motions; and every inflexion of tone and every gesture will bear exact relation to a corresponding antitype in the pleasurable impressions which awakened it; it will be the reflected image of that impression; and as the lyre trembles and sounds after the wind has died away, so the child seeks, by prolonging in its voice and motions the duration of the effect, to prolong also a consciousness of the cause.[5]

In his essay, *On Life*, Shelley again expresses this view of childhood and follows the Wordsworthian view of the process of growing up.

Let us recollect our sensations as children. What a distinct and intense apprehension had we of the world and of ourselves! Many of the circumstances of social life were then important to us which are now no longer so. But that is not the point of comparison on which I mean to insist. We less habitually distinguished all that we saw and felt, from ourselves. They seemed as it were to constitute one mass. There are some persons who, in this respect, are always children. Those who are subject to that state called reverie, feel as if their nature were dissolved into the surrounding universe, or as if the surrounding universe were absorbed into their being. They are conscious of no distinction. And these are states which precede, or accompany, or follow an unusually intense and vivid apprehension of life. As men grow up this power commonly decays and they become mechanical and habitual agents. Thus feelings and then reasonings are the combined result of a multitude of entangled thoughts, and of a series of what are called impressions, planted by reiteration.

What Shelley is here describing is the state of *participation mystique* which is characteristic both of individual childhood and racial childhood. Childhood has within it the archetypal patterns of myth lost to consciousness in the process of growing up, and yet capable of

[5]VII, 109, 111, 110.

being reclaimed by the "visitations of the divinity in Man." In Words-worth's "Mighty Prophet," Shelley sees the Dionysian archetype. When, therefore, Shelley presents himself not as a man "abandoned to the sudden reflux of the influences under which others habitually live," but as a poet redeeming "from decay the visitations of the divinity in Man," he emerges as Dionysus, "the pardlike Spirit beautiful and swift," carrying "a light spear topped with a cypress cone, / Round whose rude shaft dark ivy-tresses grew."[6]

In his letter of June 5, 1821, to Gisborne, Shelley writes of *Adonais* that it is "perhaps better in point of composition than any thing [he has] written" (X, 270). It presents him at the height of his genius, at a time when his creative vision achieves that ultimate form toward which his powers have been tending. The poem, however, is both a climax and a crisis for Shelley. In his image of the "dome of many-coloured glass" he recognizes that however beautiful the image of the One in poetry may be, it is only an image and as such "stains the white radiance of Eternity." The conclusion is inevitable: "Die, / If thou wouldst be with that which thou dost seek" (464–5). Such a conclusion means the rejection of the image, and with the rejection of the image the rejection of the poet. "The deep truth is imageless," he had written in *Prometheus Unbound* (II, iv, 116); the realization as a conscious being of this intuition beyond the reach of consciousness is beginning to dawn upon him. In his last un-completed poem, *The Triumph of Life*, Shelley sees all the heroes of his lifetime trapped on the wheel of life; only two, both of them martyrs, remain companions to his thoughts: Socrates and Christ. The real apocalypse is not the vision of an ideal world, the vision of the community of life created by the imagination, but the vision-less world beyond imagination—the God without creation standing alone in the void. The other is but an "augury" of the ultimate apocalypse. Not eternity, but the "movable image of eternity," is the best that Plato's Demiurge can shape. It is the limit of poetry as well. All his life, Shelley, in poetry, tried to outreach the limitations of what is inherently limited. Speaking of that invisible influence that quickens the poet's imagination, he says in *A Defence of Poetry* (VII, 135): "Could this influence be durable in its original purity and force, it is impossible to predict the greatness of the results; but when

[6]VI, 195–6; VII, 139, 137; *Adonais*, 280–92.

composition begins, inspiration is already on the decline, and the most glorious poetry that has ever been communicated to the world is probably a feeble shadow of the original conception of the Poet."

To understand this last insight on the part of Shelley, it is necessary to pick up the thread of Plato's argument where it was left. Plato is reaching for a truth beyond the image. While it is true that he does revert to myth in order to provide an answer to those questions which cannot be answered within the limits of reason, he is careful to explain what he means by myth. Shelley, as it were, fails to wait for an answer. He plunges in and proclaims, along with the philosophers of the Romantic movement, that myth is a revelation of ultimate truth. And his Platonic justification is to be found in both the *Ion* and the *Timaeus*. What Plato says of the creation myth in the *Timaeus*, however, is that it is a "likely account." And it is a "likely account" because no true account is possible.

Nowhere in his philosophy does Plato attempt to present the object of truth as such. His whole concern as a philosopher is to present the method by which true knowledge about that object may be attained. There is a real distinction, however, between knowledge of the object and the object of knowledge. In his seventh Epistle, Plato makes this fact clear:

One statement at any rate I can make in regard to all who have written or who may write with a claim to knowledge of the subjects to which I devote myself no matter how they pretend to have acquired it, whether from my instruction or from others or by their own discovery. Such writers can in my opinion have no real acquaintance with the subject. I certainly have composed no work in regard to it, nor shall I ever do so in the future, for there is no way of putting it into words like other studies. Acquaintance with it must come rather after a long period of attendance or instruction in the subject itself and of close acquaintance when suddenly like a blaze kindled by a leaping spark, it is generated in the soul and at once becomes self-sustaining. [341C–D]

The subject to which he devotes himself and about which he has never written, he goes on in the Epistle to explain: it is the actual object of knowledge as distinct from knowledge of the object. Of one thing Plato is quite certain: dialectic may provide knowledge of the object one is after, but it does not provide the seeker with the object itself. The question is: can the actual object be attained? Plato's answer is in the affirmative, although he has written no work about it. Nevertheless, wordless and silent, "it is generated in the soul and at once becomes self-sustaining."

This generation in the soul is the true hieromania of Orphism in which the soul's object is achieved. Plato, then, is not altogether ironic when he speaks of "divine madness" for, properly understood, it is the soul's recovery of its original and divine form. That the poets have generated this object—what Shelley (*On Love*) calls the "soul within our soul" (VI, 202)—he is quite willing to concede. So far, therefore, Shelley in his view of Plato appears to be on solid ground. Yet Shelley is precisely the type of poet that Plato would expel from his republic. And the reason is that, while Plato does not reject the experience of the poet, he does reject the forms of myth which that experience assumes in poetry.

Poets write in a state of "divine madness," having no knowledge of what they are writing about. They argue, therefore, and the citizens accept, that what they write is the revelation of the god. And here Plato and the poets part company. What they experience, Plato argues, may be the revelation of the god, but what they write is that experience seen, to use Shelley's phrase, through a "dome of many-coloured glass." What is given to the reader is not the "white radiance" but its reflection. The poets fail to make this distinction; instead of presenting what is so obviously a "likely account," they present what they think to be, or those who read it think to be, the object itself. It is as if the Demiurge were to identify the world he creates with the model upon which it is constructed so that no distinction whatsoever remains between them. The result is that poets delude and thereby undermine the search for the object of truth by presenting a false object. Cassirer's explanation of Plato's expulsion of the poets from his republic provides some support for this point of view:

What is combated and rejected by Plato is not poetry in itself, but the myth-making function. To him and to every other Greek both things were inseparable. From time immemorial the poets had been the real myth-makers. As Herodotus said, Homer and Hesiod had made the generations of the gods; they have portrayed their shapes and distinguished their offices and powers. Here was the real danger for the Platonic *Republic*. To admit poetry meant to admit myth, but myth could not be admitted without frustrating all philosophical efforts and undermining the very foundations of Plato's state. Only by expelling the poets from the ideal state could the philosopher's state be protected against the intrusion of subversive hostile forces.[7]

Here, then, in Plato's attitude to myth, is the explanation of the last brief phase of Shelley's career. He too came to realize that "the deep truth is imageless." In the last stanza of *Adonais* he is "borne darkly, fearfully afar," following the soul of Adonais, which "like a star / Beacons from the abode where the Eternal are." There is for the poet, Shelley realizes in *The Triumph of Life*, the danger of being destroyed by his own vision if that vision becomes for the poet the object itself.

If myth transforms the world of the discursive reason into an imaginative form, then death transforms both the worlds of reason and imagination. This ultimate transfiguration, which is the true object of apocalypse, can only be presented in a moving image such as *Prometheus Unbound* reveals.

[7]Ernest Cassirer, *Myth of the State* (New York: Doubleday & Co., 1955), p. 79.

3

EROS

The Dionysian character of Shelley's apocalyptic vision explains the
presence of a scheme of salvation in his poetry in terms of which he
defines his opposition to institutional Christianity. Salvation, in the
Orphic religion, lies in the recovery of the lost god within the self. For
Shelley, the creative imagination is the instrument of this recovery.
Professor Grierson, in his valuable essay, "Classical and Romantic,"
says that "in Romantic poetry the spirit of man found an outlet for
feelings that Christianity condemned and strove to repress, for ideals
which the church might and did strive to annex and to modify, but
which are essentially anti-Christian."[1] Shelley's poetry provides ample
evidence to support this statement. He was throughout his life the
implacable foe of orthodox Christianity. In 1812, this opposition
briefly included Christ Himself. As his own vision clarified, however,
his conception of Christ changed until He became an object of venera-
tion, one of the greatest human spirits the world had ever failed to
know. The vision of Christ that emerges in Shelley's poetry is that
of a Dionysian hero.

Shelley's view of the creative imagination is the logical starting
point for an understanding of this view of Christ and the part which it
plays in his poetic vision. The imagination, says Shelley, is that faculty

[1]In his *The Background of English Literature, Classical and Romantic, and
Other Collected Essays and Addresses* (London: Chatto and Windus, 1934), p. 279.

in man whereby, out of the ruins of his fallen self, he reshapes and recreates his own inherent divinity. Viewed in terms of Christian orthodoxy, therefore, the imagination is a daemonic (in the Christian rather than the Greek sense) force that would persuade man that he is God. This conception of the imagination is found in the New Testament. Paul, for example, in his Epistle to the Romans (1:21–3) condemns the vanity of imagination because it leads men to assert that God is created in their image. "Because that, when they knew God, they glorified him not as God, neither were thankful; but became vain in their imaginations, and their foolish heart was darkened. Professing themselves to be wise, they became fools, and changed the glory of the uncorruptible God into an image made like to corruptible man. . . ."

The Church Fathers were even more explicit in their condemnation of this daemonic influence at work in men. In the Bacchic rites they saw the worship of the Devil. "The Bacchoi," writes Clement of Alexandria,

hold orgies in honour of mad Dionysos, they celebrate a divine madness by Eating of Raw Flesh [a reference to the devouring of a bull, the form in which Dionysus had been slain by the Titans], the final accomplishment of their rite is the distribution of the flesh of the butchered victims, they are crowned with snakes, and shriek out the name of Eva, that Eve through which sin came into the world, and the symbol of their Bacchic orgies is a consecrated serpent.[2]

Clement is here describing the Maenads who, as in Euripides' *Bacchae*, weave serpents through their hair and cry out "Evoe," the name of the Evian goddess which became one of the names of Dionysus. One of the animal forms of Dionysus was the snake. When he was reborn from the thigh of Zeus, the god wound living serpents around his horned head to signify his release from his fallen condition.

As might be expected, this conception of the serpent symbol finds its way into some of Shelley's poetry. "Among the Greeks the Serpent," says Shelley in his essay *On the Devil, and Devils* (VII, 103) "was considered as an auspicious and favourable being. He attended on Aesculapius and Apollo. In Egypt the Serpent was an hieroglyphic of eternity." Thus, in *The Revolt of Islam* the struggle between the

[2]Quoted in Jane Harrison, *Prolegomena to the Study of Greek Religion* (New York: Meridian Books, 1955), p. 483.

forces of good and evil is symbolized in the first canto by a battle between a serpent and an eagle. The serpent, "hieroglyphic of eternity" and symbol of man's ultimate victory over the forces of evil, comes to Cythna in answer to her song (the language is "his native tongue and hers") and coils itself in her embrace. The serpent here is the spirit form of Cythna depicting her role in the poem as the instigator of a bloodless revolution against the forces of darkness.

Milton's use of the serpent symbol to describe Satan in the ninth book of *Paradise Lost* fits Shelley's Dionysian conception of Satan as hero. Satan persuades Eve to eat of the Tree of Knowledge by telling her that she will, as a result of eating the fruit, assume divinity. Eve, according to Shelley, is being "tempted" by her buried creative power to establish her birthright and assume a Promethean role, which she has sacrificed in submitting to a power conceived of as external to herself.

As a Dionysian poet, Shelley believed that Satan was the real hero of *Paradise Lost*. To what extent did he believe that Milton also thought so? In his essay *On the Devil, and Devils* (VII, 91) he suggests the possibility that Milton was not a Christian at the time he composed the epic, for, had he been a Christian, he could not, in all likelihood, have written it. "The writer who would have attributed majesty and beauty to the character of victorious and vindictive omnipotence," Shelley writes,

must have been contented with the character of a good Christian; he never could have been a great epic poet. It is difficult to determine, in a country where the most enormous sanctions of opinion and law are attached to a direct avowal of certain speculative notions, whether Milton was a Christian or not, at the period of the composition of Paradise Lost. . . . Thus [this] much is certain that Milton gives the Devil all imaginable advantage; and the arguments with which he exposes the injustice and impotent weakness of his adversary are such as had they been printed, distinct from the shelter of any dramatic order, would have been answered by the most conclusive of syllogisms—persecution.

What Shelley is saying here of Milton, he says elsewhere of other poets. To some extent every poet is the expression of his age, and therefore of those oppressive superstitions by which it is bound. These superstitions, however, are but the thin veil of circumstance which the poet wears as a mask or mantle to hide his real intention. Had the poet dared to remove the disguise so that his apocalyptic perception stood forth in its naked purity the vision would be too dazzling to contemplate. Thus Shelley writes in his *Defence of Poetry* (VII, 117):

But a poet considers the vices of his contemporaries as the temporary dress in which his creations must be arrayed, and which cover without concealing the eternal proportions of their beauty. An epic or dramatic personage is understood to wear them around his soul, as he may the antient armour or the modern uniform around his body; whilst it is easy to conceive a dress more graceful than either. The beauty of the internal nature cannot be so far concealed by its accidental vesture, but that the spirit of its form shall communicate itself to the very disguise, and indicate the shape it hides from the manner in which it is worn. A majestic form and graceful motions will express themselves through the most barbarous and tasteless costume. Few poets of the highest class have chosen to exhibit the beauty of their conceptions in its naked truth and splendour; and it is doubtful whether the alloy of costume, habit, &c., be not necessary to temper this planetary music for mortal ears.

Among these "poets of the highest order," Shelley by 1815 includes Christ. By that peculiar fusing power of imaginative perception in which individual forms participate in archetypal form, the figure of Christ merges with the figure of Milton's Satan. In *Prometheus Unbound*, Shelley quite explicitly identifies his Prometheus with Christ and Milton's unacknowledged hero. Prometheus is the Christ-figure released from the restrictions of Christian orthodoxy, and, at the same time, a purified Satan.

Milton's Satan, according to Shelley, is the real hero of the epic because of the justice of his cause in attempting to overthrow the tyranny of Heaven. The God of Milton's poem is the vengeful Jehovah of the Old Testament and the role of Satan is that of a liberator. Shelley assigns the same function to the New Testament Christ. Not only does Shelley see an identity between the two figures in terms of function; he also sees an identity in terms of the methods of persuasion which Milton uses in presenting Satan and which Christ uses in presenting His doctrines. Milton, says Shelley, was required, by virtue of the religious opinions legally upheld in his own day, to disguise his real intention by an apparent acquiescence to the popular forms of belief. According to Shelley, Christ also wears the mask of orthodoxy in His appeal to the Jewish people. As he writes in his *Essay on Christianity* (VI, 242–3),

Jesus Christ did what every other reformer who has produced any considerable effect upon the world has done. He accommodated his doctrines to the preposessions [sic] of those whom he addressed. He used a language for this view sufficiently familiar to our comprehensions. He said—However new or strange my doctrines may appear to you, they are, in fact only the restoration and re-establishment of those original institutions and antient customs of your own law and religion. . . . Thus like a skilful orator (see Cicero de Oratore), he secures the prejudices of his auditors, and induces them by his professions of sympathy with their feelings to enter with a willing mind into the exposition of his own. . . . All reformers have been compelled to practise this misrepresentation of their own true feelings and opinions. It is deeply to be lamented that a word should ever issue from human lips which contains the minutest alloy of dissimulation, or simulation, or hypocrisy, or exaggeration, or anything but the precise and rigid image which is present to the mind, and which ought to dictate the expression. But this practice of entire sincerity towards other men would avail to no good end, if they were incapable of practising it towards their own minds.

Having pointed out that Christ was practised in the art of misrepresentation in order that his real intention might be communicated at all, Shelley goes on to say (p. 243) that Christ rejected the vengeful Jehovah of the Old Testament on grounds that recall Satan's defiance of God in *Paradise Lost*. "The conclusion of the speech [words missing]," he writes,

is in a strain of most daring and most impassioned speculation. He seems emboldened by the success of his exculpation to the multitude to declare in public the utmost singularity of his faith. He tramples upon all received opinions, on all the cherished luxuries and superstitions of mankind. He bids them cast aside the chains of custom and blind faith by which they have been encompassed from the very cradle of their being, and become the imitators and ministers of the Universal God.

Nor do the parallels cease at this point. Milton, he says in *A Defence of Poetry*, was "deeply penetrated with the antient religion of the civilized world." By " antient religion," Shelley, judging from the context, refers to the religion of Greece, for he is associating Milton with Dante, who was the "Lucifer of that starry flock" presiding over the "resurrection of learning." Christ too was the inheritor (and perpetuator) of this ancient religion. Thus Shelley writes: "Plato, following the doctrines of Timaeus and Pythagoras, taught also a moral and intellectual system of doctrine, comprehending at once the past, the present, and the future condition of man. Jesus Christ divulged the sacred and eternal truths contained in these views to mankind, and Christianity, in its abstract purity, became the exoteric expression of the esoteric doctrines of the poetry and wisdom of antiquity."[3]

Out of his conception of the archetypal identity of the New Testament Christ and Milton's Satan emerged Shelley's Prometheus. In Prometheus' defeat of Jupiter in *Prometheus Unbound*, Shelley presents both his interpretation of Christ's rejection of the Old Testament Jehovah and the apocalyptic form of Satan's struggle with God. Restricted by the legalized superstitions of his age, Milton in *Paradise Lost* could not give the ultimate victory to Satan. For this reason, he had to encumber Satan with those vices which would dramatically justify his defeat. Shelley removes these vices from his Prometheus, substituting for them the virtues of love and forgiveness, which properly belong to the figure of Christ. Thus in his Preface to the poem (p. 205) he writes:

The only imaginary being resembling in any degree Prometheus, is Satan; and Prometheus is, in my judgement, a more poetical character than Satan, because, in addition to courage, and majesty, and firm and patient opposition to omnipotent force, he is susceptible of being described as exempt from the taints of ambition, envy, revenge, and a desire for personal aggrandisement, which, in the Hero of *Paradise Lost,* interfere with the interest. The character of Satan engenders in the mind a pernicious casuistry which leads us to weigh his faults with his wrongs, and to excuse the former because the latter exceed all measure. In the minds of those who consider that magnificent fiction with a religious feeling it engenders something worse. But Prometheus is, as it were, the type of the highest perfection of moral and intellectual nature, impelled by the purest and the truest motives to the best and noblest ends.

The imperfect realization of Satan in *Paradise Lost* is, for Shelley, indicative of the weakness of the epic as a whole. What he finds in Milton's poem is an arrested vision of man's divinity. The epic finds its centre not in an apocalypse, but in a fall. The whole purpose of the visionary poet is to recreate, out of the ruins of that fall (which is the world of a paralysed subject confronting a universe of fixed objects), man's original divinity. Milton's God, like Shelley's Jupiter, is the archetypal image of the fallen world. Had the apocalyptic vision been realized within the poem, this image of God would have been

[3]VII, 130, 131, 127.

transfigured by the shaping power of Milton's imagination, so that, like Shelley's Jupiter, He would have completely disappeared, and the reborn Satan, freed from the tyranny of external omnipotence, would have emerged purified and victorious. Prometheus, like Satan, is the victim of an external God so long as his inner being mirrors that figure of vengeance and wrath. Not until Prometheus recalls his curse and replaces it with his love for Asia is he freed of the Jupiter figure within himself. This inner transformation is what distinguishes Shelley's Prometheus from Milton's Satan; hence Shelley considers his Prometheus a "more poetical figure." The change in Prometheus constitutes an internal apocalypse which then finds its objective counterpart in the reunion of Asia and the hero.

In terms of the contrast between the two poems, it is possible to define Shelley's opposition to orthodox Christianity. The God of the theologians and Christian institutions, Shelley believed, was the archetypal image of the fallen world. "Every epoch," he writes in *A Defence of Poetry*, "under names more or less specious, has deified its peculiar errors." The theological, institutional God of Christianity is just such a deification and He finds His place in Milton's poem because "a poet considers the vices of his contemporaries as the temporary dress in which his creations must be arrayed." The consolidation of this perverted vision of God ("the Mammon of the world" or deification of the "principle of Self") is to be found in the Old Testament image of Jehovah. Christ came into the world to destroy that image and replace it with a genuine poetic vision of the "divinity in Man." "The perfection of the human and the divine character is thus asserted to be the same," says Shelley of Christ's vision of God. "God is a model thro which the excellence of man is to be estimated, whilst the *abstract* perfection of the human character is the type of the *actual* perfection of the divine."[4] Against this conception of God, the Hebrew and Roman world rose in revolt and put the visionary poet to death. The death of Christ, type of all activity on the part of fallen man, soon became a central symbol in Christianity, so that the God the Christians worship is a dead God upon the dead Tree of Life. This worship, says Shelley, is nothing more than the worship of the "principle of Self." It is the rejection of vision and imagination.

Institutional Christianity, from Shelley's point of view, is the

4*Defence of Poetry*, VII, 117, 134, 137; *Essay on Christianity*, VI, 239.

consolidated form of the fallen world. Its counterpart in his own poetry is the image of Prometheus bound to a precipice of icy rocks. To the Christians, the crucifixion of Christ is directly attributable to God Who offered Him as a vicarious atonement for man's rebellion against His decree. The people, therefore, who actually forced this sacrifice by condemning Christ to die upon the cross were acting under the instructions of their God. The purpose of the act, Shelley believed, was to perpetuate the worship of Jehovah (and therefore error) by annihilating those visionaries who would dare to usurp His power. Far from being a redemptive act, its purpose was to destroy all possibility of redemption through the annihilation of man's creative faculty. Hence the identification of the serpent with evil, when, in reality, its proper symbolic function is that of a "hieroglyphic of eternity." "The Christians," says Shelley in *On the Devil, and Devils*, "have turned this Serpent into their Devil [the invention of the writers of the Bible], and accommodated the whole story to their new scheme of sin and propitiation, &c." (VII, 104).

The myth of Prometheus, essentially Dionysian in its spirit and form, had an obvious attraction for Shelley, for here was a mythical hero who dared to challenge the authority of the gods by stealing their fire (symbol of creative power) and giving it to men. The concept of original sin, therefore, takes on an entirely different significance in the Promethean myth. Sin, as rebellion against God, becomes a virtue. The suffering that results from rebellion is no longer simply punishment that must lead men ultimately to bend the knee and "sue for grace," but the inner struggle towards re-creation. The pain endured is the labour of rebirth. Man's emergence from Eden is the emergence from the womb of Nature into the life of the spirit. Nietzsche's contrast of the Promethean myth and the Hebraic myth provides a fair summing up of Shelley's position on Christianity.

The story of Prometheus is an original possession of the entire Aryan race, and is documentary evidence of its capacity for the profoundly tragic. Indeed, it is not entirely improbable that this myth has the same characteristic significance for the Aryan genius that the myth of the fall of man has for the Semitic, and that the two are related like brother and sister. The presupposition of the Promethean myth is the transcendent value which a naive humanity attaches to *fire* as the true palladium of every rising culture. That man, however, should not receive this fire only as a gift from heaven, in the form of the igniting lightning or the warming sunshine, but should, on the contrary, be able to control it at will—this appeared to the reflective primitive man as sacrilege, as robbery of the divine nature. And thus the first philosophical problem at once causes a painful, irreconcilable antagonism between man and God, and puts as it were a mass of rock at the gate of every culture. The best and highest that men can acquire they must obtain by a crime, and then they must in turn endure its consequences, namely, the whole flood of sufferings and sorrows with which the offended divinities *must* requite the nobly aspiring race of man. It is a bitter thought, which, by the *dignity* it confers on crime, contrasts strangely with the Semitic myth of the fall of man, in which curiosity, deception, weakness in the face of temptation, wantonness,— in short, a whole series of preeminently feminine passions,—were regarded as the origin of evil. What distinguishes the Aryan conception is the sublime view of *active sin* as the essential Promethean virtue. . . .[5]

Nietzsche's distinction between the Aryan and Semitic traditions indicates the character of Shelley's imaginative transplanting of Christ out of one tradition into another. While Christ poses as One who has come to fulfil the laws of the prophets, He is, in reality, attacking those conceptions to which the Jewish people have been accustomed "from the very cradle of their being." Inspired and emboldened by His apparent success in placating His audience, Christ goes on to present the "utmost singularity of his faith." That singularity lies in the fact that "Christianity, in its abstract purity, became the exoteric expression of the esoteric doctrines of the poetry and wisdom of antiquity." The specific doctrines to which Shelley refers are "the doctrines of Timaeus and Pythagoras," which found their way into the philosophy of Plato. The tradition to which Christ belongs is the esoteric tradition of Orphism.

Shelley believed that the most characteristic poetical expression of Christ's teachings (especially His teaching concerning love) is to be found in the courtly love tradition, which finds its purest utterance in Dante's love for Beatrice. Shelley's account of the emergence of this tradition shows again the way in which he grafted Christ's teachings to the Aryan myth. In his *Defence of Poetry*, Shelley describes the way in which he believed Christ's teachings fused with the mythology of the Celtic nations. "The incorporation of the Celtic nations with the exhausted population of the south," he writes,

impressed upon it [the poetry of Christ's doctrines] the figure of the poetry existing in their mythology and institutions. The result was a sum of

[5]*The Birth of Tragedy*, trans. Clifton Fadiman, in *The Philosophy of Nietzsche* (New York: Modern Library, 1927), pp. 997–8.

the action and reaction of all the causes included in it; for it may be
assumed as a maxim that no nation or religion can supersede any other
without incorporating into itself a portion of that which it supersedes.
The abolition of personal and domestic slavery, and the emancipation of
women from a great part of the degrading restraints of antiquity, were
among the consequences of these events. [VII, 127]

Shelley here implies that Christ's teaching of human equality
liberated woman, with the result that the ideal love of the *Symposium*
could now become the expression of the spiritual relation between
man and woman. "It was not until the eleventh century," he writes,

that the effects of the poetry of the Christian and Chivalric systems began
to manifest themselves. . . . Love became a religion, the idols of whose
worship were ever present. It was as if the statues of Apollo and the Muses
had been endowed with life and motion, and had walked forth among their
worshippers; so that earth became peopled by the inhabitants of a diviner
world. The familiar appearance and proceedings of life became wonderful
and heavenly; and a paradise was created as out of the wrecks of Eden.
. . . Love, which found a worthy poet in Plato alone of all the antients, has
been celebrated by a chorus of the greatest writers of the renovated world;
and the music has penetrated the caverns of society, and its echoes still
drown the dissonance of arms and superstition. [VII, 127, 127–8]

Professor Milton Wilson's contention that Shelley attempted in his
poetic vision to remake the history of Western thought is substantiated
in Shelley's identification of Christ's conception of love with the pagan
Eros of Plato's *Symposium*.[6] The struggle to supplant pagan thought
by Christianity is reversed in Shelley's poetic vision. The proper antecedent of Christ's teaching is not the Old Testament; it is pagan
literature. Platonism, De Rougemont argues in *Love in the Western
World*, entered Europe as esoteric wisdom and, with the forcing of
Christianity upon the peoples of the West, this esoteric wisdom became an underground movement that flourished "in the guise of
secret heresies more or less orthodox in appearance."[7] In the nineteenth century that movement still flourished among Neo-Platonists like
Thomas Taylor, and with it Shelley identified himself. In the category
of "secret heresies more or less orthodox in appearance" Shelley places
the two great Christian epics, Dante's *Divine Comedy* and Milton's
Paradise Lost. The latter poem has already been examined from this

[6]Milton Wilson, *Shelley's Later Poetry* (New York: Columbia University Press,
1959), p. 281.
[7]Denis de Rougemont, *Love in the Western World*, trans. M. Belgion (New
York: Harcourt, Brace, 1940), p. 69.

point of view, and, while Shelley is not quite so explicit about Dante's epic, it is evident that he considers the poem equally heretical. "The distorted notions of invisible things which Dante and his rival Milton have idealized," he writes,

> are merely the mask and the mantle in which these great poets walk through eternity enveloped and disguised. It is a difficult question to determine how far they were conscious of the distinction which must have subsisted in their minds between their own creeds and that of the people. Dante at least appears to wish to mark the full extent of it by placing Riphaeus, whom Virgil calls *justissimus unus,* in Paradise, and observing a most heretical caprice in his distribution of rewards and punishments. [VII, 129]

The opposition between Shelley's conception of love and that of orthodox Christianity lies in the difference between Eros and Agape. The distinction between these two concepts will serve further to clarify Shelley's opposition to Christianity and his pagan view of the apocalypse.

The Christian concept of Agape takes for its premise the fact of original sin. Having, by an act of deliberate disobedience, chosen to separate himself from God, man is incapable of engendering within himself that love for God by which the breach may be healed. He cannot, on the basis of his own initiative alone, hope to reassemble his own psychic forces and redirect them from a love of the self to a love of God. To suggest that man, of himself, can "regain the blissful seat" is to be the victim of pride and find in Satan's attempt in *Paradise Lost* the type or pattern of his own efforts. This being man's condition as a result of the fall, the initiative, if man is to be redeemed, must be taken by God. The whole meaning of the New Testament, from this point of view, is the evidence in Christ of God's initiative. This initiative is taken because it is the nature of God to love; it does not depend upon man's worthiness or unworthiness. Grace is initially indifferent to human merit.

The extent to which man's natural powers can co-operate with Agape in the act of salvation depends upon the view of the fall held by various schools of theology. Professor Nygren in *Agape and Eros* presents what is an essentially Calvinistic view of man's natural depravity, and hence upholds a radical distinction between natural love (Eros) and divine love (Agape). Eros cannot co-operate in

Agape; man is totally dependent upon God.[8] Father D'Arcy, on the other hand, defends an essentially Roman Catholic position in *The Mind and Heart of Love*, and argues that Agape co-operates with Eros, directing it to a supernatural end.[9] Shelley's approach to Christianity reveals a Calvinistic bias which fails to recognize the possibility of a co-operative relation between Agape and Eros. His whole attack upon Christianity focuses on the notion of man's radical dependence upon a Being external to himself that allows little place for man's natural powers.

In the pagan conception of Eros, the divinity that lives within man is man's own archetypal form. The Christian belief in incarnation in which God assumes the form of flesh is, from the point of view of Eros, not the first act in the drama of redemption, but the last act in the drama of the fall. This fact is clear from an examination of the myth of Dionysus-Zagreus. In the myth, Eros is the first creation of Dionysus, the Dionysus-Phanes "with the golden wings on his shoulders, four eyes and the heads of various animals." This same Dionysus, in his second birth, is Dionysus-Zagreus who is devoured by the Titans. Out of the ashes of the Titans, whom Zeus destroyed for killing his son, was created the race of men. The descent, therefore, of Dionysus into the form of flesh is an account of man's condition in his present fallen state.

The second act of the Christian drama of redemption is the crucifixion of Christ. The counterpart of this redeeming act in the Orphic myth is the devouring of the god by the Titans, which again symbolizes not the rebirth of man but the fall of archetypal man. In other words, the Christian drama of salvation is the Orphic drama of the fall.

The point where Christianity and Orphism come closest to agreement is in the resurrection of Christ. The counterpart of the resurrection in Orphism is man's reassumption, through the rites of purification, of his inherent divinity. This reassumption, however, is an event possible in the here and now. The resurrection of Christ, on the other hand, is what Paul calls the "first fruits" of the revelation. It pertains to Christ alone during His dispensation; only with His return will all believers be resurrected and assume a spiritual body.

[8] Anders Nygren, *Agape and Eros*, trans. P. S. Watson (London: S.P.C.K., 1953), pp. 53–8.
[9] *The Mind and Heart of Love* (London: Faber and Faber, 1945). See esp. pp. 308–30.

On the basis of these radical differences between the Agape and Eros dramas it is possible to discover the opposition not only between two views of man, but also between two views of matter. Matter from the Christian point of view is good; from the Orphic point of view it is evil. The Christian concept of a spiritual body suggests that Christ came not only to redeem the soul but also to redeem the flesh. The dualism of flesh and spirit, the central struggle within the Orphic drama, is present also in the Christian drama, but in a very different sense. Flesh of itself is not evil; it has not the curse of the Titans upon it. It is evil only if it comes between man and his consciousness of God. Since it belongs to a lower order of creation, it must be subject to the higher order, which is the living soul created to worship God and have dominion over all other created things.

For the Orphics, as for Plato, evil is inherent in matter, and is therefore never entirely susceptible to the shaping power of the spirit. The Demiurge is limited in the expression of its creative power. Out of matter the Demiurge cannot create things-in-themselves, but only their imperfect appearance. The image of reality, by virtue of being dependent on the senses, partakes of the nature of evil. For Plato, the artistic image is at two removes from reality. No matter how refined the image, how symbolic it may be of ultimate reality, it must stain "the white radiance of Eternity."

Plato makes this fact clear in the *Symposium*. In his account of man's ascent to the contemplation of the Form of Beauty he uses the image of a ladder. This ladder, as C. S. Lewis points out, is a ladder in the real sense: every step requires removing oneself from the rung immediately below it.[10] To attain to the ultimate goal towards which Eros leads requires the loss of the sensible world entirely, for it subsists in itself and in no other thing which seeks to participate in it. Here is Shelley's translation of the key passage in Plato:

" 'It is eternal, unproduced, indestructible; neither subject to increase nor decay: not, like other things, partly beautiful and partly deformed; not at one time beautiful and at another time not; not beautiful in relation to one thing and deformed in relation to another; . . . nor can this supreme beauty be figured to the imagination like a beautiful face, or beautiful hands, or any portion of the body, nor like any discourse, nor any science. Nor does it subsist in any other that lives or is, either in earth, or in heaven, or in any other place; but it is eternally uniform and consistent, and

10C. S. Lewis, *The Allegory of Love* (London: Oxford University Press, 1953), p. 5.

monoeidic with itself. All other things are beautiful through a participation of it, with this condition, that although they are subject to production and decay, it never becomes more or less, or endures any change. When any one, ascending from a correct system of Love, begins to contemplate this supreme beauty, he already touches the consummation of his labour. For such as discipline themselves upon this system, or are conducted by another beginning to ascend through these transitory objects which are beautiful, towards that which is beauty itself, proceeding as on steps from the love of one form to that of two, and from that of two, to that of all forms which are beautiful; and from beautiful forms to beautiful habits and institutions, and from institutions to beautiful doctrines; until, from the meditation of many doctrines, they arrive at that which is nothing else than the doctrine of the supreme beauty itself, in the knowledge and contempation of which at length they repose.

" 'Such a life as this, my dear Socrates,' exclaimed the strange Prophetess, 'spent in the contemplation of the beautiful, is the life for men to live; which if you chance ever to experience, you will esteem far beyond gold and rich garments, and even those lovely persons whom you and many others now gaze on with astonishment, and are prepared neither to eat nor drink so that you may behold and live for ever with these objects of your love! What then shall we imagine to be the aspect of the supreme beauty itself, simple, pure, uncontaminated with the intermixture of human flesh and colours, and all other idle and unreal shapes attendant on mortality; the divine, the original, the supreme, the self consistent, the monoeidic beautiful itself? What must be the life of him who dwells with and gazes on that which it becomes us all to seek? Think you not that to him alone is accorded the prerogative of bringing forth, not images and shadows of virtue, for he is in contact not with a shadow but with reality; with virtue itself, in the production and nourishment of which he becomes dear to the Gods, and if such a privilege is conceded to any human being, himself immortal.' " [VII, 206–7]

The soul's contemplation of beauty-in-itself is the goal of Eros. Behind this notion of the ladder, describing the soul's journey of ascent from the sensible to the supersensible, is Plato's doctrine of pre-existence and of true knowledge as the recollection of it. Viewed outside the discipline of Platonic dialectic, it is, as De Rougemont says,

complete Desire, luminous Aspiration, the primitive religious soaring carried to its loftiest pitch, to the extreme exigency of purity which is also the extreme exigency of Unity. But absolute unity must be the negation of the present human being in his suffering multiplicity. The supreme soaring of desire must end in non-desire. The erotic process introduces into life an element foreign to the diastole and systole of sexual attraction —a desire that never lapses, that nothing can satisfy, that even rejects and flees the temptation to obtain its fulfillment in the world, because its demand is to embrace no less than the All. It is *infinite transcendence*, man's rise into his god. And this rise is *without return*.[11]

Eros freed of *logos* and incarnate in myth and poetry belongs to a mystical tradition that is foreign to Christianity. It belongs to the tradition of the Orient. In Hindu mysticism, for example, the transcendental experience is the union of the soul (Atman) with the undifferentiated One (Brahman). The way to this union is the cessation of all desire ending in enlightenment (Satori), which is not only an annihilation of the self in the fallen form of matter but also the annihilation of the material universe. This process of purification takes place through a series of incarnations in which the soul is gradually released from the cyclic round of the wheel of life. This same image of a wheel to explain the various incarnations of the soul is used in Orphic theology. Plato, following the Orphics, incorporates it into his myth in the *Phaedrus*. Whether or not Orphism has its origin in Oriental mysticism cannot be proved. It is worth pointing out, however, that Newton, from whom Shelley derived much of his knowledge of Orphism, assumes the Oriental origin of the cult; he identifies the Orphic scheme of salvation with the esoteric meaning of the Hindu Zodiac.

From the Christian point of view, Oriental mysticism is an irrational plunge into an abyss of nothingness. The goal of Eros is death. Agape, on the other hand, gives a new integrity to the human personality. God's assumption of human form in the person of Christ redeems both flesh and spirit and makes of flesh the temple of an indwelling presence. God's gift of love makes it possible for man to love himself and his neighbour as himself. The apocalypse, therefore, is not absorption into the One but the assumption of a spiritual body.

Blake, who found in the Bible the great code of art, viewed the apocalypse essentially in Christian terms, that is, as the assumption of a spiritual body. His giant Forms are the figures of the Christian apocalypse. He belongs, as Professor Frye points out, to the tradition of Christian Platonism in the Italian Renaissance in which the imaginative approach to God lies through love and beauty.[12] The beauty of Beatrice, for example, is the image of the beauty of God. Shel-

---

[11]*Love in the Western World*, p. 56.
[12]Northrop Frye, *Fearful Symmetry: A Study of William Blake* (Princeton: Princeton University Press, 1947), p. 155.

ley's Platonism, on the other hand, is, in its final phase at least, Pythagorean and Orphic rather than Christian. Blake, with his characteristic
intuitive grasp of traditions he had never bothered to explore in any
rational manner, recognized at once the danger in the Pythagorean
and Orphic aspect of Platonism for the poet. Blake would allow no
notion of the soul as distinct from the body; the imaginative enlargement of the soul has the form of a spiritual body.

So long as Shelley identified Eros with the creative imagination,
he too was able to create the spiritual bodies of the apocalypse. In the
end, however, Eros led him beyond the world created by the imagination to the One. This process has already been explored with reference
to Plato's rejection of myth. It must now be explored with reference
to Plato's doctrine of Eros.

Between 1815 and 1817 Shelley wrote a brief essay on the subject
of love in which he defines what he means by love. "It is that powerful attraction," he writes,

towards all that we conceive, or fear, or hope beyond ourselves, when we
find within our own thoughts the chasm of an insufficient void, and seek
to awaken in all things that are, a community with what we experience
within ourselves. . . . We are born into the world, and there is something
within us which, from the instant that we live, more and more thirsts
after its likeness. It is probably in correspondence with this law that the
infant drains milk from the bosom of its mother; this propensity develops
itself with the development of our nature. We dimly see within our intellectual nature a miniature as it were of our entire self, yet deprived of
all that we condemn or despise, the ideal prototype of everything excellent
or lovely that we are capable of conceiving as belonging to the nature of
man. . . . a soul within our soul that describes a circle around its proper
paradise, which pain, and sorrow, and evil dare not overleap. To this we
eagerly refer all sensations, thirsting that they should resemble or cor-
respond with it. The discovery of its antitype; the meeting with an understanding capable of clearly estimating our own; . . . this is the invisible
and unattainable point to which Love tends. [VI, 201–2]

This statement contains within it the germ of much of Shelley's later
poetry. He speaks, first of all, of the archetype within the soul which
assumes imaginative form in the figure of Prometheus. He speaks
also of the correspondence between this prototype and its antitype
(all those sensations which are referable to the prototype). This correspondence finds its imaginative form in the reunion of Prometheus

and Asia. And he speaks, finally, of the imposssibility of finding that antitype in another person. This latter point finds poetic expression in *Alastor*, and remained, in his personal life, an insoluble problem. Love, therefore, as here described, is the infinite yearning of the soul for its antitype, a yearning that cannot be fulfilled in the relation between man and woman, and must, as a result, find its visionary fulfilment in the ideal world of poetry. Hence, in his Preface to *Prometheus Unbound* (p. 207), he describes poetry as "beautiful idealisms of moral excellence." As early as 1815, Shelley recognized that Eros is, as Professor Nygren defines it, a real force driving the soul upwards to seek the world of the Forms.[18] And these Forms are for Shelley the antitype of the prototype within man, or, in terms of the myth, the god behind the mask.

The revelation of the archetypal figure within man, says Shelley in his *Speculations on Morals* (probably written in 1815), lies in the shaping power of the imagination. Imagination he defines as mind "prophetically [imaging forth] its objects" (VII, 75). This power to image forth the objects of the mind is a vicarious imagistic fulfilment of desire. Imagination is the form or vision of Eros. The more refined and intense the passion, the more beautiful its imaginative form. For Shelley, the supreme image of Eros in modern literature is Dante's Beatrice because of the spiritual passion that dictated it. "His apotheosis of Beatrice in Paradise," he writes in *A Defence of Poetry*, "and the gradations of his own love and her loveliness, by which as by steps he feigns himself to have ascended to the throne of the Supreme Cause, is the most glorious imagination of modern poetry" (VII, 128).

Yet, because Eros longs for the infinite, it must destroy the very forms which seek to embody Eros. The poet, possessed by Eros, must perpetually bring into existence new configurations of form. Eros forever outreaches the power of the imagination to confine it within a given shape. Like a flame, it is forever consuming and, at the same time, forever refining. That ultimate refinement is the recovery of pure Being in which prototype and antitype become one and both disappear. The principle of opposition which makes objects or images to appear out of the Heraclitean flux is stilled into a motionless Nirvana. How clearly Shelley perceived this ultimate unpredicated

---

[18]Nygren, *Agape and Eros*, p. 170.

state can be seen in his essay, *On Life*. Associating Eros with life itself, he says:

The mist of familiarity obscures from us the wonder of our being. We are struck with admiration at some of its transient modifications, but it is itself the great miracle. What are changes of empires, the wreck of dynasties, with the opinions which supported them; what is the birth and the extinction of religious and of political systems, to life? What are the revolutions of the globe which we inhabit, and the operations of the elements of which it is composed, compared with life? What is the universe of stars, and suns, of which this inhabited earth is one, and their motions, and their destiny, compared with life? Life, the great miracle, we admire not, because it is so miraculous. It is well that we are thus shielded by the familiarity of what is at once so certain and so unfathomable, from an astonishment which would otherwise absorb and overawe the functions of that which is its object. [VI, 193]

This statement by Shelley echoes, in a curious way, the last words of Diotima to Socrates in the *Symposium*. Once again, however, it is important to note that Shelley in his reading sought (as probably most poets do) analogues for those interior experiences which were peculiar to his nature. That these analogues helped him to shape his vision is evident; but the assistance took the form of confirmations of what was already present within himself. He was in this sense the true Platonist; all his knowledge was a form of reminiscence. Plato, more than any other author, was the midwife who assisted at its birth. In other words, after all the so-called sources have been examined and related to Shelley's apocalyptic vision, one is forced back to something like Plato's own myth to provide not the real account, but the likely account, of its origin. When Jung was confronted with the extraordinary recurrence of the archetypal figures and patterns of primitive myth in the dreams of his patients he was led to posit a racial unconscious to explain it. The materials that Shelley shaped into an imaginative pattern cannot be accounted for by a series of footnotes as in Eliot's *The Waste Land*. It is evident that literary criticism, when it is confronted by a poet like Shelley, is still in a primitive stage. Shelley's prose works are full of suggestions that have been taken up by anthropologists, archaeologists and psychologists. It may very well be, as Professor Frye suggests, that these related fields of investigation are the groundwork for a science of literary criticism.[14]

[14]Northrop Frye, "The Language of Poetry," *Explorations*, IV (1955), 87.

Shelley's prose works attributed to the period around 1815 present a constellation of ideas, the implications of which were to be worked out in the poetry of his maturity. Shelley's evolution as a poet, moving spirally not linearly, follows, under the propulsion of Eros, a pattern that reveals four fairly distinct phases: love as a cosmic principle making for harmony in the universe (*Queen Mab* and *Prometheus Unbound*); love as the personal desire of the prototype for its antitype (*Alastor* and *Epipsychidion*); love as the sole law governing the moral world (*The Revolt of Islam*); love as mystical union with the One (*Adonais*). The poems listed in parentheses, of course, cannot be limited to any one of these phases; they present, rather, the more characteristic expression of a particular phase.

These poems present two aspects of Shelley's apocalyptic vision: the personal and erotic, the racial and Promethean. The evolution of both aspects shows Shelley moving from partial failure to partial success; from *Alastor* to *Epipsychidion* on the one hand, and from *Queen Mab* to *Prometheus Unbound* on the other. In *The Revolt of Islam*, he made his first attempt to combine the erotic (Laon and Cythna) with the Promethean (human regeneration); not until *Prometheus Unbound*, however, were the two apocalyptic themes successfully fused into a single organic vision.

To trace the growth of Shelley as a poet is to examine the gradual clarification of his central and controlling vision of the wholeness of the cosmos embracing both Nature and man. Propelled by Eros, he sought to resurrect the entire universe into the form of a spiritual body which would be the antitype of that prototype within himself. This imaginative re-creation Shelley described as the desire within the poet to arrest from decay "the visitations of the divinity in Man" (VII, 137). As an apocalyptic poet, he could not rest until the entire cosmos had been transfigured into an image of that inner divinity.

In the *Hymn to Intellectual Beauty*, which is, as it were, his manifesto, Shelley dedicates himself to the task. He speaks, in the opening lines of the poem, of that "awful shadow of some unseen Power" which visits this "various world with an inconstant wing," and goes on to say how, in the midst of his quest to resolve the riddle of existence, that shadow fell upon him. This visitation, he continues, led him to dedicate his powers to that mysterious force, to become the incarnation of that shadow, the redeemer who would lift the veil of familiarity from the world and reveal its "awful Loveliness."

The disciple of Eros, however, cannot, as Plato says, be content with shadows. He must ultimately penetrate beyond the shadow world of images, beyond the *analogia visionis*, to beauty itself. Whatever is created in the name of Eros does not partake of true Being, for Eros is not a god, but a daemon who shows the way in the world of Becoming to the world of Being. Poetry, while a "movable image of eternity," is, above all, an image. It is complete in itself as a pattern of words and images, and, at the same time, it is the reflected shadow of that which casts it.

This dual nature of poetry, like the dual nature of Eros who is the offspring of Plenty and Want, can be illustrated with reference to Keats's *Ode on a Grecian Urn* in which both the completeness and the incompleteness of a work of art are shown not so much in statement as in the images themselves. The function of art, says Keats, is to arrest a moment of beauty in order that it may be released from mutability (which Shelley calls the "accident of surrounding impressions") by giving it permanent form. To the extent to which any work of art is an eternal form, it participates in Form itself (in the Platonic sense) and therefore is the image of truth or truth knowable on earth. Hence: "Beauty is truth, truth beauty,—that is all / Ye know on earth, and all ye need to know." The phrase "on earth," however, is an important qualification. The "silent form" of the Grecian urn, Keats says, "dost tease us out of thought / As doth eternity." Does this statement mean that art adumbrates a truth beyond the reach of art? There is evidence within the images themselves to suggest that it does. The bride on the urn is "still unravish'd," the lover can never kiss "though winning near the goal," and the urn itself is a "Cold Pastoral," where boughs can never shed their leaves (or bear fruit) and spring is eternal (allowing no harvest). It would appear that the images, complete within the total pattern of the poem, suggest or evoke a truth beyond their reach. That truth is Being itself where the bride is ravished and yet chaste, the lover enjoys his love without the satiety of love, and the trees shed their leaves and yet do not die. A world, in other words, where eternity is not something arrested, nor, on the other hand, a wheel making its endless cyclic round of death and regeneration.

Plato would explain the ambiguity of the poetic image in terms of the nature of Eros. Eros, he says, is neither a mortal nor an immortal, but a daemon who acts as a mediator between the world of

Becoming and the world of Being. The soul, in its fallen condition of flesh, yearns to behold once again the world of the Forms. Eros is the personification of that yearning, the principle of generation which, out of the memory of pre-existence, brings forth images of immortality. These images are the expression of something immortal and eternal in mortality, approximations of that state of Being which the soul originally enjoyed and to which it longs to return.

These images approximate Being in the realm of Becoming because they find their source in the memory of the Forms. At the sight of beautiful objects, these images, lying dormant in the unconscious, are, as it were, awakened and assume a life of their own. Hence Plato defines memory as the science of escape. Ultimately it is possible to resurrect all the images from the fallen state of forgetfulness, at which time the total pattern of images reflects the soul's original condition. When this occurs—and for Plato it requires the method of dialectic—the soul beholds itself in the creation of its antitype. At that moment, says Plato, the image, as it were, dissolves, and the soul is left in the contemplation of itself in a state of total recollection.

In the essay, On Love, Shelley is moving in the direction of the Platonic idealism outlined above. "We dimly see," he says, "within our intellectual nature a miniature as it were of our entire self, yet deprived of all that we condemn or despise, the ideal prototype of everything excellent or lovely that we are capable of conceiving as belonging to the nature of man . . . a soul within our soul that describes a circle around its proper paradise" (VI, 201–2). This circle around the paradise of the prototype within the soul is the form of his apocalyptic vision. The content of that circle was, between 1815 and 1817, but dimly perceived. Gradually, however, the "film of familiarity" was lifted until he achieved in Prometheus Unbound a total perception of its content. The imagination had revealed the "divinity in Man." And with that total perception, he met, like the Magus Zoroaster in Prometheus Unbound (i, 192), his own image and was united with himself. He had discovered the imageless truth, the real apocalypse of which his own created vision was the analogue. In Adonais he brought this final dimension into focus. The "dome of many-coloured glass" was smashed and his "spirit's light" (418) satiated "the void circumference" (420).

4

APOCALYPTIC
VISION

On the basis of the previous three chapters it is possible to gather together various threads of the argument of this book and define the nature of Shelley's apocalyptic vision. The word ἀποκάλυψις means an unveiling or an uncovering. For Shelley, this unveiling is a revelation of the "divinity in Man." Within man, he says, there exists potentially an ideal self which he variously describes as the "ideal prototype," "a soul within our soul," "a being within our being," and the "archetype [which] forever exists in the mind."[1] Outside the mind of man there exists a mass of sensations which impress themselves upon the mind and assume a certain order that reflects the inner nature of the perceiver. The ideal self within man, viewed in terms of its potential, is a shaping spirit and it is this shaping spirit or imagination that reduces the mass of sensations from without to *a kind* imaginative order which Shelley calls the "antitype" (VI, 202) of the prototype within man. Imagination is therefore a creative power because it transforms what is merely potential both within man and in Nature into a realized form. It is this realized form that is the revelation of the "divinity in Man."

[1] VI, 202 (*On Love*); VII, 137 (*A Defence of Poetry*); VII, 228 (*A Discourse on the Manners of the Ancients*).

There is, however, Shelley says, a danger inherent in the realization of an imaginative vision. When the prototype emerges in the creation of its object, that object tends with time to break loose from its source and take on an autonomous existence. When this happens the universe of created objects is conceived as something separate from the mind of the perceiver and therefore, in some sense, is set over against man as object to subject, thing to thought. Shelley identifies this mode of perception with reason, which, he says, stands in relation to the imagination "as the body to the spirit, as the shadow to the substance" (VII, 137). When imagination fails and reason assumes control, the spirit that informs body is lost, and the substance that casts its shadow is forgotten. Men live in a world that resembles Plato's cave in the *Republic*.

The visionary forms of poetry, therefore, must be continuously recreated from their source in the prototype within man. Unless this process of re-creation is continuous, poetry descends to dogma. The revelation of man's divinity separates itself from man and becomes a god whose authority is imposed from without through a set of institutions erected in his name. As soon as this separation occurs, poets must arise, and, like Prometheus, steal the creative fire from the gods and return it to men where it properly belongs. Thus, for Shelley, all poetry written since the dawn of human history is a single cyclic poem to which all poets have contributed in their effort continuously to recreate its single archetypal form.

The apocalyptic nature of poetry, therefore, lies in its unveiling of man's divinity through a continuous process of recreating its archetypal vision. Poetry, writes Shelley (VII, 137), "reproduces the common Universe of which we are portions and percipients, and it purges from our inward sight the film of familiarity which obscures from us the wonder of our being." It "withdraws life's dark veil from before the scene of things"; once that "dark veil" is removed, the prototype (the "wonder of our being") is revealed in the creation of its antitype, which is the entire universe transfigured by a moment of imaginative perception. "It transmutes all that it touches," writes Shelley of the creative faculty, "and every form moving within the radiance of its presence is changed by wondrous sympathy to an incarnation of the spirit which it breathes; its secret alchemy turns to potable gold the poisonous waters which flow from death through life; it strips the veil of familiarity from the world, and lays bare the naked and sleeping beauty, which is the spirit of its forms."

The universe presented "as an incarnation of the spirit" assumes the form of a mythological vision. As soon as Shelley became aware of the importance of the creative imagination (in the period between 1812 and 1817), he became a poet in search of a myth within which he could express his own apocalyptic vision. No poet, of course, simply incorporates another poet's myth into his own poetry: myth stands in need of continuous re-creation. What myth does is to define a poetic tradition through its allegiance to a single archetypal form. Towards the discovery of that form Shelley was guided by his reading of Plato (interpreted in the Neo-Platonic manner of Taylor, Newton and Peacock), whose mythical foundations were in Orphism. In the Orphic interpretation of Plato, Shelley rediscovered the poetic value of the Dionysian myth and set to work to recreate it out of his own imagination. The choice of the Dionysian myth, however, was governed by factors other than his reading of Plato, and these factors must now be considered.

Shelley's reading covered a wider range than that of any other English Romantic poet with the possible exception of Coleridge. His early reading during the period around 1812 was centred in the philo-sophy of the Enlightenment, both French and English. Between 1812 and 1815, his interest shifted from the philosophers of the Enlighten-ment to the Greek poets. In addition, he developed a new enthusiasm for the literature of the Bible, especially the New Testament and "portions of the Old Testament—the Psalms, the Book of Job, the Prophet Isaiah, and others, the sublime poetry of which filled him with delight."[2] Viewed imaginatively, each of these literary traditions presented to Shelley, either implicitly or explicitly, an apocalyptic vis-ion: in the philosophy of the Enlightenment, a secular apocalypse rooted in a doctrine of Nature; in Greek literature, a pagan apocalypse rooted in the doctrine of Eros; in the literature of the Bible, a Christian apocalypse rooted in the doctrine of Agape. Shelley's attitude to each of them, already suggested in the foregoing chapters, will serve to bring into closer focus the nature of his own poetic vision.

The philosophy of the Enlightenment, which Shelley believed was summed up in Godwin's *Political Justice*, assumes the existence of an

[2] Mrs. Shelley's note on *The Revolt of Islam*, p. 156.

external and immutable order which is knowable by the exercise of reason. For the proper functioning of that faculty, however, man is obliged to give up all forms of irrational activity which find their source in his ignorance of natural causes. Christianity, with its faith in a personal God and the efficacy of miracles, is the supreme example of this sort of ignorance. In 1812, Shelley was convinced that when men learn to use their rational powers they "will laugh as heartily at grace, faith, redemption, and original sin, as they now do at the metamorphoses of Jupiter, the miracles of Romish saints, the efficacy of witchcraft, and the appearance of departed spirits." In place of these superstitions, men will substitute the "hypothesis of a pervading Spirit co-eternal with the universe" and bring their lives into conformity with its dictates as manifest in the "eternal chain of causes."[3] Shelley has here in mind the secular apocalypse of the Enlightenment, which consists in a perfect correspondence between the rational life of human society and the rational order of the universe.

The origins of this apocalyptic outlook can, in part, be traced to the writing of Francis Bacon, whom Shelley describes in *The Triumph of Life* (271–3) as compelling,

> "The Proteus shape of Nature, as it slept
>
> To wake, and lead him to the caves that held
> The treasure of the secrets of its reign."

In *Advancement of Learning* Bacon argues that God has revealed Himself in two scriptures: the written word and the created universe. The two revelations, however, must be studied independently of each other in order that the truths of religion may be kept separate from the truths of science. His purpose, as Professor Willey points out, was not so much to preserve the Christian faith as to "keep science pure from religion."[4] He sought to shift the emphasis in men's minds from Grace to Nature.

Bacon believed that once the shift was achieved there was virtually no limit to the possible extension of men's power. Contemplating that extension, men need not wait upon the direct intervention of God to establish the New Jerusalem; by focusing their attention upon the operations of Nature, men could bring its secular counterpart, the

[3]His notes on *Queen Mab*, pp. 821, 812.
[4]Basil Willey, *Seventeenth-Century Background* (Cambridge: Cambridge University Press, 1933), p. 29.

New Atlantis, within their rational grasp. In this grand undertaking, Bacon says in the *Novum Organum* (read by Shelley in 1815), men should not give way to despair "considering with themselves the obscurity of nature ... the deceitfulness of the senses, the weakness of the judgment, the difficulty of experiment and the like"; rather, men's minds should be brought to particulars, "especially to particulars digested and arranged in my Tables of Discovery ... since this is not merely the promise of the thing but the thing itself." At the same time, men should have faith in God, "for the business which is in hand, having the character of good so strongly impressed upon it, appears manifestly to proceed from God, who is the author of good, and the Father of Lights." The work of rehabilitating Nature is a divine operation; "the smallest beginnings lead of a certainty to their end." Bacon then concludes:

And as it was said of spiritual things, "The kingdom of God cometh not with observation," so it is in all the greater works of Divine Providence; everything glides on smoothly and noiselessly, and the work is fairly going on before men are aware that it has begun. Nor should the prophecy of Daniel be forgotten, touching the last ages of the world: "Many shall go to and fro, and knowledge shall be increased"; clearly intimating that the thorough passage of the world (which now by so many distant voyages seems to be accomplished, or in course of accomplishment), and the advancement of the sciences, are destined by fate, that is, by Divine Providence, to meet in the same age.[5]

Bacon here presents the beginnings of a secular apocalypse in which the Christian archetypal pattern of a creation, a fall and a redemption is transferred to the world of science. God's original creation has become obscured to men by the "deceitfulness of the senses and the weakness of judgment." By the patient gathering and classifying of particulars, that obscurity can be removed, and Nature, as it were, restored to its unfallen condition in the minds of men. As a result of this labour, the kingdom of God, as prophesied by Daniel, will gradually emerge and the apocalypse be a matter of "the advancement of the sciences."

Bacon, however, was not a scientist in the modern sense. To turn from him to such scientists as Galileo and Kepler is to see how a scientific view of Nature. could, and did, evoke a very different

[5]*The New Organon and Related Writings*, ed., with Introduction, by F. H. Anderson (New York: Liberal Arts Press, 1960), pp. 90, 91, 91-2, 92.

response, which the church was quick to recognize. Bacon's distinction between the two orders of truth, the word of God revealed in scripture and the works of God revealed in Nature, finds its counterpart in Kepler's and Galileo's distinction between primary and secondary qualities. Primary qualities are those characteristics properly belonging to matter; secondary qualities are those characteristics properly belonging to mind. It is the scientist's duty, Kepler argues, to isolate the primary qualities of matter and deal with them in isolation from the secondary. The works of God revealed in Nature are His government not of man, but of things. Science deals with natural phenomena, the material stuff of the universe seen in terms of the forces which govern it. The word of God revealed in scripture, on the other hand, is concerned not with matter, but with man, and man, not as material stuff, but as a living soul, a special creation of God in some sense outside the order of Nature.

This separation of primary and secondary characteristics produced a new picture of Nature which Whitehead describes as "a dull affair, soundless, scentless, colourless: merely the hurrying of material, endlessly, meaninglessly." "However you disguise it," he continues by way of comment,

this is the practical outcome of the characteristic scientific philosophy which closed the seventeenth century.... No alternative system of organizing the pursuit of scientific truth has been suggested.... And yet it is quite unbelievable.... The enormous success of the scientific abstractions yielding on the one hand *matter* with its *simple location* in space and time, on the other hand *mind* perceiving, suffering, reasoning, but not interfering, has foisted on to philosophy the task of accepting them as the most concrete rendering of fact.[6]

So long as man continued to define his nature within a Christian framework that transcended the order of Nature, he was not particularly threatened by the implications of the new philosophy. When, however, as in the case of the more radical aspects of the Enlightenment, that Christian framework was rejected and man was conceived of as belonging entirely within the order of Nature, man found himself, as a spiritual being, alienated in a purely material universe. Shelley was reduced to this position in 1812.

[6]A. N. Whitehead, *Science and the Modern World* (New York: Macmillan, 1925), pp. 77-8.

Shelley in 1812 had arrived at the impasse in which many of the *philosophes* had found themselves. Professor Becker points out, for example, that Diderot reached the conclusion in *La Physiologie* that "the world is mechanically determined, that man is an accident, the soul is 'nothing without a body,' good will is nothing but 'the last impluse of desire and aversion,' and vice and virtue are mere names signifying nothing." At the same time, Diderot wished to demonstrate that the *philosophes* could place moral virtue on a sounder foundation than religious faith. " 'It is not enough,' " he wrote with reference to the theologians, " 'to know more than they do: it is necessary to show them that we are better, and that philosophy makes more good men than sufficient or efficacious grace.' " But how, as an atheist, could he prove it? To the end of his days, Becker continues, Diderot was "unable to find any sufficient reason for virtuous conduct, his heart unable to renounce the conviction that nothing is better in this world than a good man."[7] Shelley faced precisely the same problem in 1812. In his notes on *Queen Mab* (p. 814) he argued, paraphrasing Bacon, that "atheism leaves to man reason, philosophy, natural piety, laws, reputation, and everything that can serve to conduct him to virtue." He even attempted to persuade Godwin that materialism and virtue were not at odds. Finally, however, he was forced to conclude that the aspirations of mind find no support in the indifference of matter. The universe of the *philosophes* was inhospitable to man; it would have to be conceived anew.

The effort to recreate the view of Nature that emerged out of the new philosophy defines, in part, the Romantic movement. Romanticism tended to reject the distinction between primary and secondary qualities set up by the scientific outlook and attributed to Nature those qualities with which the mind endows it in the act of perception. The following passage from *Dejection: An Ode* (47–58) best describes this Romantic viewpoint:

> O Lady, we receive but what we give
> And in our life alone does Nature live;
> Ours is her wedding garment, ours her shroud:
> And would we ought behold of higher worth
> Than that cold, inanimate world allowed

[7] Carl L. Becker, *The Heavenly City of the Eighteenth-Century Philosophers* (New Haven: Yale University Press, 1951), pp. 79, 81, 80.

> To the poor, loveless, ever-anxious crowd,
> Ah from the soul itself must issue forth
> A light, a glory, a fair luminous cloud
> Enveloping the earth.

The "cold, inanimate world" of matter in a state of motion is all that
the "poor, loveless, ever-anxious" *philosophes* could conceive of because for them there was no soul from which issued forth the light
and glory that enveloped the earth of the Romantics. That earth was
the product of the Romantic imagination and its validity lay in the
fact that the imagination is the divine faculty in man by which he
perceives the divine order.

Shelley's rejection both of dualism and materialistic monism is
evident in his essay *On Life* (VI, 194). "The shocking absurdities of
the popular philosophy of mind and matter," he writes, "its fatal
consequences in morals, and their violent dogmatism concerning the
source of all things, had early conducted me to materialism. This
materialism is a seducing system to young and superficial minds." In
its place he substituted, in the first instance, Godwin's immaterialism
which had its source in Plato and Berkeley. On the basis of that
immaterialism he was able to locate the active powers of the mind
within a mental, as distinct from material, universe. He was able
to envision mankind aspiring through a gradual increase of consciousness to an ultimate condition of pure intelligence in which the
human mind was one with the mind of the universe. And this vision
he considered the imaginative form of Godwinism, the secular apocalypse of the Enlightenment whose origins were to be found in the
works of Bacon viewed, as in his *Defence*, not as science but as poetry.

In his analysis of Bacon's rehabilitation of Nature, Professor Willey
argues that within the framework of Pauline and Augustinian
theology Bacon's undertaking was Satanic. What Professor Willey
has to say is worth quoting because it adequately sums up Shelley's
own view of Bacon as poet and atheist and also helps to explain his
rejection of the Christian myth in favour of the Promethean one as
a mythological framework for his vision. "Both the myth-making
instinct of paganism and the Stoic yearning for the Universe as the
City of God," writes Professor Willey,

were checked by the Pauline and Augustinian theology, which represented
Nature (including man) as depraved since the Fall, and as groaning

under the divine malediction. The divine order, the order of Grace, was felt to be wholly separate from, and in a sense opposed to, "Nature." The sense which above all marks the Christian consciousness, of sin in man and of imperfection in Nature, expressed itself in a virtual dualism, the Satanic forces being as real as the divine, if less powerful. The "beggarly elements" of Nature, as St. Paul calls them, were handed over to the Prince of the Air and his fallen angels, who were soon identified with the dethroned divinities of the heathen pantheons. . . . Since earth, water, air and fire were the allotted spheres of the several hierarchies of evil spirits, to study nature meant to repeat the original sin of Adam; it meant a compact with the devil and the death of the soul.[8]

Shelley's conviction that the European advancement of knowledge which began with Bacon was opposed to all forms of organized Christianity made it impossible for him to shape his myth, as Blake had done, on the foundation of the Biblical vision of the fall and the redemption. While he would admit that Bacon paid lip service to the Christian religion, he would argue that, like Milton's vision, it was but a thin disguise behind which his real purpose as a visionary lay hidden. Bacon, the poet, was Promethean rather than Christian. Bacon's "eagle spirit" lept "like lightning out of the darkness," says Shelley in *The Triumph of Life* (270). Curiously enough, this is precisely the view of Professor Willey. Having explained the Christian opposition to science (ignoring, it should be pointed out, the theology of Aquinas and Hooker), Professor Willey concludes: "On the other hand, that it had at any rate once been possible to think of science quite differently, the Promethean myth was there to testify. The purveyor of knowledge and civilisation might be the friend, and not the Adversary of man. Bacon's task, it may be said, was to prove that natural science was Promethean and not Mephistophelean."[9]

Admiring as he did the New Testament image of Christ, Shelley had to remove Christ from the context of the Old Testament Jehovah and enlist His support under the banner of Prometheus. He had to penetrate Christ's disguise and reveal His true identity. "It is of importance, therefore," he writes in his notes on *Queen Mab* (p. 820),

to distinguish between the pretended character of this being as the Son of God and the Saviour of the world, and his real character as a man, who,

8*Seventeenth-Century Background*, pp. 33–4.
9*Ibid.*, p. 33.

for a vain attempt to reform the world, paid the forfeit of his life to that overbearing tyranny which has since so long desolated the universe in his name. Whilst the one is a hypocritical Daemon, who announces Himself as the God of compassion and peace whilst He stretches forth His blood-red hand with the sword of discord to waste the earth, having confessedly devised this scheme of desolation from eternity; the other stands in the foremost list of those true heroes who have died in the glorious martyrdom of liberty, and have braved torture, contempt, and poverty in the cause of suffering humanity.

The distinction which Shelley here makes between the "pretended" and "real" character of Christ at once reveals his rejection of the Christian view of the apocalypse rooted in the idea of Agape. Behind that conception of love, Jehovah is lurking; the "blood-red hand with the sword of discord" is stretched forth in the guise of "compassion and peace."

Thus, as early as 1812, Shelley had dissociated Christ from the Christian apocalypse as he conceived it. By 1815 he had placed Him firmly in the Promethean camp by interpreting His teachings as an effort to persuade men to aspire to the condition of divinity as Milton's Satan had persuaded Eve. In his *Essay on Christianity* (VI, 231), he attributes the following sentiments to Christ: "Whoever has maintained with his own heart the strictest correspondence of confidence, who dares to examine and to estimate every imagination which suggests itself to his mind, who is that which he designs to become, and only aspires to that which the divinity of his own nature shall consider and approve—he, has already seen God." And he has seen God because, according to Shelley, God is the "divinity in Man" which the poet's imagination reveals. Shelley's Christ restored divinity to what Shelley considered its proper place. Like Prometheus, He brought back to man the creative fire of the gods that man might shape his own universe.

The Promethean myth is a variation of the myth of Dionysus. Its fundamental assertion is that the creative power of the gods properly belongs to man and that through the recovery of this power man can restore his lost divinity. In Orphism that creative power is Eros, the infinite yearning in man to recover his own divine form, to remove all the veils which separate him from Dionysus, the archetype of his own divine nature. All of Christ's teachings, according to Shelley, focus upon that yearning in man and reveal to him the way to its fulfilment. Christ, like Plato, is an Orphic poet revealing the Orphic scheme of salvation. Within the Orphic vision, as opposed to the Christian, Shelley's apocalypse is defined. As early as 1812, under the influence of Taylor and Newton, Shelley sought to relate Orphism to the philosophy of the Enlightenment, embodied in Godwin and the *philosophes*. While in *Queen Mab* rationalism and the occult made strange bedfellows, by 1819, in the composition of *Prometheus Unbound*, an extraordinary fusion had been achieved. Such was the power of Shelley's creative imagination, and such was the nature of his apocalyptic vision.

Shelley's apocalyptic vision declares the triumph of an occult paganism over Christianity. As such, it stands outside the major tradition of European poetry to which such poets as Dante, Spenser and Milton belong. These poets shared Shelley's admiration for classical art. That admiration, however, did not include an acceptance of the vision of life which classical art expressed. They viewed themselves as Christian poets and sought in all their major works to subordinate the pagan vision which they inherited as poets to the Christian vision which they accepted as men. Shelley rejected from the outset this rather obvious fact. His *Defence of Poetry*, in the final analysis, must be interpreted as a defence of his own poetry. He foisted his own hostility to Christianity on his favourite poets and argued that what is distinctly Christian in their poetic vision is simply "the mask and mantle" in which they walk through eternity "enveloped and disguised." He argued that the poet and the man are two distinct natures and that, in all cases, the poet must take priority over the man. Shelley, in fact, rejected human nature, accepting in the final analysis only what he described as the "divinity in Man." This attitude led him to affirm Plato's doctrine of divine inspiration in the *Ion* in which the poet is described as casting off his human nature and assuming the powers of divinty. "Poets," Shelley writes in his *Defence* (VII, 140), "are the hierophants of an unapprehended inspiration; the mirrors of the gigantic shadows which futurity casts upon the present; the words which express what they understand not; the trumpets which sing to battle, and feel not what they inspire; the influence which is moved not, but moves." Finally, by the peculiar logic of his apocalyptic imagination, his rejection of man in favour of divinity led him to smash the "dome of many-coloured glass" that he might be absorbed into the "white radiance of Eternity." In *The Hymn to Intellectual Beauty*, Shelley argues that if man's creative power were not subject to periods of waxing and waning, he would be omnipotent. He returns to the same point at the end of the third act of *Prometheus Unbound*. Jupiter has been dethroned; man is "sceptreless, free, uncircumscribed." But, and here is the limitation, he is still man (197–204):

>   but man:
> Passionless? no: yet free from guilt or pain,
> Which were, for his will made or suffered them,
> Nor yet exempt, though ruling them like slaves,
> From chance, and death, and mutability,
> The clogs of that which else might oversoar
> The loftiest star of unascended heaven,
> Pinnacled dim in the intense inane.

In *Adonais* this "loftiest star" beckons Shelley. Only life can divide him from that "unascended heaven." Death will restore him to the "intense inane" which is the goal of his Orphic quest. The apocalyptic vision itself becomes but the feeble shadow of that "deep truth" which is "imageless." As such it contains within itself the source of its own annihilation.

Part Two

THE UNFOLDING OF THE
VISION

All but the sacred few who could not tame
Their spirits to the conquerors—but as
soon
As they had touched the world with living
flame,

Fled back like eagles to their native noon.

The Triumph of Life

5

QUEEN MAB

The idea for *Queen Mab* seems to have occurred to Shelley towards the end of 1811. On December 11 he wrote to Elizabeth Hitchener (VIII, 213): "I have now my dear friend in contemplation a Poem. I intend it to be by anticipation a picture of the manners, simplicity, and delights of a perfect state of society, tho' still earthly. Will you assist me? I only thought of it last night." The poem, however, was postponed because of Shelley's plan to go to Ireland.[1]

Queen Mab is a vision of the past, present and future condition of human society viewed through the eyes of that pure intelligence embodied in the figure of the Fairy Queen. In writing the poem, Shelley had no particular audience in mind. He wrote it primarily to clarify his own mind, to resolve, if possible, the conflicting demands of Godwin's immaterialism, D'Holbach's materialism, and Taylor's and Newton's Orphism.

Godwin's immaterialism was based on the belief that the universe is governed by a perfect intelligence, which man in some sense can comprehend by his reason, thereby bringing his life into conformity with its will. Shelley presents this belief in the figure of the Fairy Queen, the pure intelligence who has the power to rend the "veil of mortal frailty" and allow man to comprehend her dictates (i, 167–85):

> "I am the Fairy Mab: to me 'tis given
> The wonders of the human world to keep:

[1] See above, chap. 1, pp. 4–6.

The secrets of the immeasurable past,
In the unfailing consciences of men,
Those stern, unflattering chroniclers, I find:
The future, from the causes which arise
In each event, I gather: not the sting
Which retributive memory implants
In the hard bosom of the selfish man;
Nor the ecstatic and exulting throb
Which virtue's votary feels when he sums up
The thoughts and actions of a well-spent day,
Are unforeseen, unregistered by me:
And it is yet permitted me, to rend
The veil of mortal frailty, that the spirit,
Clothed in its changeless purity, may know
How soonest to accomplish the great end
For which it hath its being, and may taste
The peace, which in the end all life will share."

D'Holbach, as opposed to Godwin, believed that all reality consists
of matter in a state of motion, without cause, from eternity and of
necessity. Man himself is simply a highly complex form of matter, and
has, as a function of matter, no freedom of the will, no soul distinct
from the body. To argue either for the freedom of the will or for the
immortality of the soul is to deny both reason and the witness of the
senses. It is to escape into a world of the imagination that has no
foundation in the inexorable order of Nature. Man, therefore, must
destroy the false gods of his imagination and substitute for them
correct ideas of Nature. Shelley presents this opposite belief in his
description of Necessity:[2]

"Nor the events enchaining every will,
That from the depths of unrecorded time
Have drawn all-influencing virtue, pass
Unrecognized, or unforeseen by thee, . . .
                              the slave,
Whose horrible lusts spread misery o'er the world,
And the good man, who lifts, with virtuous pride,
His being, in the sight of happiness,
That springs from his own works; . . .
                      are equal in thy sight:
No love, no hate thou cherishest; revenge
And favouritism, and worst desire of fame

2Q.M., vi, 186–9, 203–7, 211–19.

> Thou know'st not: all that the wide world contains
> Are but thy passive instruments, and thou
> Regard'st them all with an impartial eye,
> Whose joy or pain thy nature cannot feel,
>   Because thou hast not human sense,
>   Because thou art not human mind."

The Orphic viewpoint of Taylor and Newton presents a vision of man as a divinity imprisoned in flesh, gradually releasing himself from the restless wheel of life, and finally, when purified, returning to his original state. This doctrine, somewhat confused with his two other attitudes, is presented by Shelley in the following passage (IX, 149–63):

> For birth and life and death, and that strange state
> Before the naked soul has found its home,
> All tend to perfect happiness, and urge
> The restless wheels of being on their way,
> Whose flashing spokes, instinct with infinite life,
> Bicker and burn to gain their destined goal:
> For birth but wakes the spirit to the sense
> Of outward shows, whose unexperienced shape
> New modes of passion to its frame may lend;
> Life is its state of action, and the store
> Of all events is aggregated there
> That variegate the eternal universe;
> Death is a gate of dreariness and gloom,
> That leads to azure isles and beaming skies
> And happy regions of eternal hope.

A more adequate presentation of this doctrine, however, is offered in a passage in which Shelley radically distinguishes between the soul and the body (I, 144–56):

> 'twas a sight
> Of wonder to behold the body and the soul.
>   The self-same lineaments, the same
>   Marks of identity were there:
> Yet, oh, how different! One aspires to Heaven,
> Pants for its sempiternal heritage,
> And ever-changing, ever-rising still,
>   Wantons in endless being.
> The other, for a time the unwilling sport
> Of circumstance and passion, struggles on;
> Fleets through its sad duration rapidly:

> Then, like an useless and worn-out machine,
> Rots, perishes, and passes.

While, as might be expected, Shelley fails to bring together these three points of view, he nevertheless manages to indicate the general direction of his evolving outlook. He infuses D'Holbach's materialism with Godwin's faith in a governing spirit of the universe and identifies that spirit with the Orphic doctrine of man's latent divinity yearning to escape the limitations of flesh. This pattern, however, exists only in some fragmentary form; it is neither sustained nor coherent. Since, however, *Queen Mab* is Shelley's first attempt in poetry "to rend / The veil of mortal frailty" (i, 180–1) and reveal man's eternal nature, his failure deserves to be explored at length. The materials contained in *Queen Mab* are those which Shelley shaped in future years into a genuine and coherent vision of man's struggle to transcend the world of his senses and discover that ideal world to which he properly belongs. Thus, what is implicit in *Queen Mab* becomes explicit in *Prometheus Unbound*.

D'Holbach's *Système de la nature*, which Shelley quotes in defence of atheism in his notes on *Queen Mab*, represents the extreme form of eighteenth-century radical thought, and, although it was widely read and discussed, it made few converts among the *intelligentzia*. Critics were quick to expose its inner contradictions. Godwin, for example, who was one of the severest critics of D'Holbach, did his best to persuade Shelley that no moral reformer could base his philosophy upon a doctrine of materialism. Since in D'Holbach's system the mind is enslaved to "material automatism" no voluntary action is possible. It is mere folly to attack the injustices of human society if those injustices are dictated by a blind and fatalistic Necessity. Shelley, however, as he explained in a letter to Godwin on July 29, 1812 (IX, 11), could not "conceive how the loftiest disinterestedness is incompatible with the strictest materialism." Thus, he falls into D'Holbach's trap. In *Queen Mab*, after condemning all priests, monarchs and statesmen, he goes on (vi 171–90) to describe how Necessity rules every passion, thought, and act, chained as they are "from the depths of unrecorded time."

> No atom of this turbulence fulfils
> A vague and unnecessitated task,
> Or acts but as it must and ought to act.

Even the minutest molecule of light,
That in April sunbeam's fleeting glow
Fulfils its destined, though invisible work,
The universal Spirit guides; nor less,
When merciless ambition, or mad zeal,
Has led two hosts of dupes to battle-field,
That, blind, they there may dig each other's graves,
And call the sad work glory, does it rule
All passions: not a thought, a will, an act,
No working of the tyrant's moody mind,
Nor one misgiving of the slaves who boast
Their servitude, to hide the shame they feel,
Nor the events enchaining every will,
That from the depths of unrecorded time
Have drawn all-influencing virtue, pass
Unrecognized or unforeseen by thee,
Soul of the Universe!

In this passage, Shelley has in mind not only D'Holbach's determinism, but also Pope's *Essay on Man*. Pope, however, is arguing a very different point from the one that Shelley is making in *Queen Mab*. Pope argues that because man is ignorant of the total pattern of the universe, his point of view is inevitably limited. What appears evil to man is really "universal good." For this reason "Whatever is, is right." Here are the lines (i, 155–64) which Shelley probably had in mind in composing the above passage:

If plagues or earthquakes break not Heav'n's design,
Why then a Borgia, or a Catiline?
Who knows but he, whose hand the light'ning forms,
Who heaves old Ocean, and who wings the storms,
Pours fierce Ambition in a Caesar's mind,
Or turns young Ammon loose to scourge mankind?
From pride, from pride, our very reas'ning springs;
Account for moral as for nat'ral things:
Why charge we Heav'n in those, in these acquit?
In both, to reason right is to submit.

Shelley, however, argues that to reason right is to rebel, although on the basis of D'Holbach's materialistic determinism, the reasoning is quite illogical.

In *Queen Mab*, Shelley attempts to avoid this contradiction by equating D'Holbach's Necessity with the Neo-Platonic World Soul.

The result is even more confusing. The World Soul, which Shelley encountered in his reading of the *Timaeus* in Taylor's translation, is mystically conceived as the animating power of the universe of which the individual soul is the microcosmic form. According to this doctrine, the soul, by means of spiritual discipline, is able to comprehend its identity with the "Soul of the Universe." In a state of divine illumination, man is able to view the universe as contained within himself. He is able to experience what Shelley, in a letter to Elizabeth Hitchener dated October 18, 1811, describes as "omnipotence of mind" (VIII, 160). Shelley, therefore, partially transforms man's passive submission to D'Holbach's Necessity into the active acquiescence of the mystic. In *Queen Mab*, rebellion against the existing order of society is the result of spiritual penetration into the universal World Soul. In 1812, however, Shelley was unable completely to locate himself within this metaphysical framework which alone could justify his Promethean impulse. And that failure defines the failure of the poem.

When, under the influence of Godwin's immaterialism and further training in the occult, Shelley finally clarified the radical difference between D'Holbach's Necessity and the Neo-Platonic World Soul, he was able to equate D'Holbach's materialism with the habitual world of recurrent impressions to which the unimaginative man is subject. D'Holbach's universe by 1815 became to Shelley a symbol of the "curse" from which the poet's creative imagination releases humanity.

Shelley nevertheless anticipates this later development in his account of the visionary process in *Queen Mab*. When Ianthe is released from her body to become a "living soul," she is able, to use the wording of the *Defence*, to "defeat the curse which binds [man] to be subjected to the accident of surrounding impressions" (VII, 137). She becomes, as a result, the inhabitant of an ideal world in contrast to which D'Holbach's world is chaos. While Ianthe's soul "wantons in endless being" (ɪ, 151), matter endures simply, as "the unwilling sport / Of circumstance and passion" (ɪ, 152–3). Shelley presents this conception of matter, radically opposed to D'Holbach's materialism, in his description of the ruin of past civilizations.

As Ianthe surveys the past, the Fairy Queen comments on what she sees (ɪɪ, 111–20):

> "Behold! where grandeur frowned;
> Behold! where pleasure smiled;

> What now remains?—the memory
> Of senselessness and shame—
> What is immortal there?
> Nothing—it stands to tell
> A melancholy tale, to give
> An awful warning: soon
> Oblivion will steal silently
> The remnant of its fame."

This image of the world's body, like the body of Ianthe, moving towards its inevitable ruin is, however, redeemed in part by the process of cyclic renewal. Nature is continuously revived from the inevitable decay of matter by the presence of the World Soul. The "generations of the earth" which "go to the grave" also "issue from the womb," so that life survives "the imperishable change / That renovates the world" (v, 1–4).

Implicit in Ianthe's ascent into a visionary world is the Promethean vision of human renewal. Her experience describes in miniature the death and rebirth of civilization. Shelley, however, fails to make explicit in the poem the close identification between the process of creation in the poet and the process of creation in Nature. Although the daemon tells Ianthe the golden age must be restored "when man, with changeless Nature coalescing / Will undertake regeneration's work" (vi, 42–3), Shelley, it would seem, barely understands the import of the statement. He does not identify Ianthe with the Promethean archetype of his mature vision and see in her ascent the poet's creative process out of which the universe is recreated. By focusing on the Fairy Queen rather than Ianthe, by making Ianthe the passive observer of an impersonal order rather than a poet who transforms that order into a human form, Shelley fails to fuse the contradictory elements of his poem or find his creative centre in the poet's psyche. Shelley, as it were, explores in *Queen Mab* the elements of a genuinely apocalyptic vision without synthesizing them. He describes the creative process; he recognizes the need for a coalescence with Nature; he views Nature as a potential human form ("There is not one atom of yon earth / But once was living man"—ii, 210–11); he describes the daemon's power to endow D'Holbach's Nature with "manner, being and reality": the elements are all there. What is lacking is the mythological form within which the imagination could unite them into a poetic vision that revealed the divinity within man. Ianthe, like Shelley in 1812, is not a poet, but a potential poet; she is unable to impose an imaginative form upon that vast amount of material which Shelley in 1812 was struggling to control.

Perhaps for this reason, Professor Baker in his analysis of *Queen Mab* is unable to see in the visionary machinery anything more than "a considerable amount of second-hand lumber, on which the stamp of the eighteenth-century was prominent."[3] He identifies the Fairy Queen with the "usual hierophant," and argues that the vision granted to Ianthe follows the usual pattern of eighteenth-century moral allegory popular among the Augustan and post-Augustan imitators of Spenser. What he fails to recognize is that Shelley turned everything he borrowed to his own use. The machinery of the poem may be "second-hand lumber," like most of the ideas; both, however, undergo in the vision a partial transformation. In the interpenetration of the "usual hierophant" into the soul of Ianthe, Shelley is presenting for the first time the creative process which he later describes in *A Defence of Poetry*. In turning, therefore, to an examination of two, among many, of the Orphic sources of Shelley's vision, this fact must be kept in mind. The two sources selected are Erasmus Darwin and John Frank Newton.

On July 28, 1811, Shelley wrote to Hogg to say that he was amusing himself with reading Darwin, and on December 24, 1812, he ordered from Clio Rickman, the bookseller, a copy of Darwin's *Temple of Nature*.[4] He met John Frank Newton in November of 1812 and refers at some length to Newton's *Return to Nature* in his notes on *Queen Mab*. Both of these authors presented an Orphic vision of the universe and provided Shelley with an insight into the way in which his early enthusiasm for the occult, arising out of his reading at Oxford of Taylor's translations of Plato, could be incorporated into his poem.

As the disciple of Godwin and the *philosophes*, Shelley considered myth simply the expression of man's ignorance of the laws of Nature. Darwin, on the other hand, argued that myth and science were not natural enemies. It was the poet's function to present the world of the natural sciences in mythical terms. The possibility of describing the natural world in terms of a mythological vision must have appealed

---

[3]Carlos Baker, *Shelley's Major Poetry: The Fabric of a Vision* (Princeton: Princeton University Press, 1948), p. 23.
[4]VIII, 135; IX, 35–6.

to Shelley, resolving as it did the conflicting demands within himself of reason and imagination.

In his Advertisement to *The Botanic Garden*, Darwin writes:

The general design of the following sheets is to inlist Imagination under the banner of Science; and to lead her votaries from the looser analogies, which dress out the imagery of poetry, to the stricter ones which form the ratiocination of philosophy. While their particular design is to induce the ingenious to cultivate the knowledge of Botany, by introducing them to the vestibule of that delightful science, and recommending to their attention the immortal works of the celebrated Swedish Naturalist, Linneus.[5]

In this passage, Darwin is thinking of the imagination in the neo-classical sense. The function of poetry is to present a truthful representation of the nature of reality; to this extent reason and judgment must be the guide. The purpose of the imagination is to create those fictions whereby the representation is rendered pleasing. Darwin, however, takes the imagination more seriously than most neo-classical theorists. By suggesting that the votaries of imagination can be led "from the looser analogies, which dress out the imagery of poetry, to the stricter ones, which form the ratiocination of philosophy," he is implying that the dichotomy of reason as the organ of truth and imagination as the organ of fiction can be broken down. At the same time, he still subordinates imagination to reason: his purpose in *The Botanic Garden* is "to induce the ingenious to cultivate a knowledge of Botany." There is no suggestion of the Romantic view of the creative imagination as the organ of a higher truth than the truth of reason. Nevertheless, he demonstrated to Shelley the way in which myth and imagination could be used to support, rather than oppose, science and reason.

In *The Temple of Nature*, Darwin makes use of the Orphic cosmogony to present a biological account of the origin and evolution of life. "In the Eleusinian mysteries," he writes, "the philosophy of the works of Nature, with the origin and progress of society, are believed to have been taught by allegoric scenery explained by the Hierophant to the initiated, which gave rise to the machinery of the following Poem."[6] Shelley uses precisely the same technique in *Queen*

[5]*The Botanic Garden* (London: J. Johnson, 1791), p. v.
[6]*The Temple of Nature; or, The Origin of Society* (London: J. Johnson, 1803), n.p. (Preface).

Mab, with this difference, however: the "machinery" becomes a statement of a metaphysical doctrine destined in later works to supplant the "particular design" of the poem.

In the opening section of *The Temple of Nature*, Darwin invokes Immortal Love, who holds the entire cosmos in her embrace. He then proceeds (15–26) to describe the birth of Nature in terms of the emergence of Eros from the Orphic egg:

> Immortal Love! who ere the morn of Time,
> On wings outstretch'd, o'er Chaos hung sublime;
> Warm'd into life the bursting egg of Night,
> And gave young Nature to admiring Light!—
> You! whose wide arms, in soft embraces hurl'd
> Round the vast frame, connect the whirling world!
> Whether immers'd in day, the Sun your throne,
> You gird the planets in your silver zone;
> Or warm, descending on ethereal wing,
> The Earth's cold bosom with the beams of spring;
> Press drop to drop, to atom atom bind,
> Link sex to sex, or rivet mind to mind.

This vision of Nature held in the embrace of Love is the same vision that Queen Mab reveals to the soul of Ianthe (I, 264–77):

> Spirit of Nature! here!
> In this interminable wilderness
> Of worlds, at whose immensity
> Even soaring fancy staggers,
> Here is thy fitting temple.
> Yet not the lightest leaf
> That quivers to the passing breeze
> Is less instinct with thee:
> Yet not the meanest worm
> That lurks in graves and fattens on the dead
> Less shares thy eternal breath.
> Spirit of Nature! thou!
> Imperishable as this scene,
> Here is thy fitting temple.

Darwin goes on to describe the temptation of Eve and her exclusion from the Temple of Nature, arguing, however, that her fall must be viewed in terms of her inevitable restoration. It must be understood as an allegorical picture of the perpetual pattern of death and renewal in Nature. "When we reflect on the perpetual destruction of organic life," he points out in his footnote on the cave of Trophonius, "we should also recollect, that it is perpetually renewed in other forms by the same materials, and thus the sum total of the happiness of the world continues undiminished; and that a philosopher may thus smile again on turning his eyes from the coffins of nature to her cradles."[7] Man's salvation, in other words, lies in coalescing with Nature to undertake regeneration's work. Shelley incorporates this vision of Nature's perpetual renewal into his own poetry, drawing from it Darwin's conclusion. Clearly anticipating the vision of his *Ode to the West Wind*, he says in *Queen Mab* that just as the dead leaves fertilize with their own "loathsome rottenness" (v, 8) the land "they long deformed" (v, 12), so also out of "suicidal selfishness . . . shall spring all virtue, all delight, all love" (v, 16, 19). In other words, "All things are recreated, and the flame /Of consentaneous love inspires all life" (viii, 107–8). The renewal of Nature is a symbol of human regeneration. Darwin's Orphic vision in *The Temple of Nature* provided Shelley with a mythological method for the expression of that faith.

John Frank Newton was as knowledgeable in "secret lore" as Darwin was. Himself a votary of the Orphic mysteries, his cosmological myth embraced the four ages of man pictured on the Hindu Zodiac, from which he believed the Orphic cosmogony derived. Unlike Darwin, however, Newton was in some sense committed to the Orphic religion. Darwin's fanciful "machinery" was for Newton almost a way of life. Included among the purification rites of Orphism was abstinence from the eating of animal flesh. In the Orphic myth, the fall of man was the result of the Titans' devouring the body of Dionysus-Zagreus. The eating of flesh, therefore, symbolizes the entrance of sin into the world. Newton argues in *The Return to Nature* that to abstain from the eating of flesh is to usher in the golden age. Shelley spends nearly six pages in his notes on *Queen Mab* defending this curious notion. The important thing, however, is not that Newton reinforced Shelley's vegetarianism, but that, like Darwin, he showed him how Orphism could be enlisted in support of his radical hopes for the renovation of the world. Darwin's Orphic vision of the great community of Nature and Newton's Orphic concept of the way in which man will be reabsorbed into it are fundamental to an under-

[7]*Ibid.*, p. 12.

standing of Shelley's vision in *Queen Mab*. In some sense, Queen Mab is the Orphic hierophant explaining the "Eleusinian mysteries" to the initiated Ianthe. She teaches her (ix, 149–51) that

> ". . . birth and life and death, and that strange state
> Before the naked soul has found its home,
> All tend to perfect happiness."

She teaches that in death the soul will be restored to its original naked condition, and that to prepare herself for it, Ianthe must abstain from animal diet. But Queen Mab also teaches many other doctrines which find their source in D'Holbach's materialism and are totally alien to the Orphic rejection of the body of man and the body of the world when accepted in and for themselves. No Orphic hierophant would suggest that the "naked soul" finds its "home" in Nature. Such a statement reveals Shelley's confusion between idealism and materialism. It is this confusion that destroys the inner consistency of the poem.

When *Queen Mab* is studied in relation to Shelley's whole development as a poet, it is possible to see his mature vision adumbrated in it. The view of the transforming power of the imagination is there. The Orphic myth underlying his apocalyptic vision is present. The doctrine of Eros derived from Plato's *Symposium* is suggested. However crudely and diffidently, Shelley in *Queen Mab* is moving into that psychic domain which he was destined to accept as his "proper post." Nor can it be said that he left the rationalism of such men as Godwin behind; rather, he transformed it into an imaginative vision. Shelley's quest was, in part, a search for the imaginative form of his early radical ideas. His *Prometheus Unbound* cannot be divorced from the doctrines which he found in Godwin's *Political Justice*.

Ultimately, of course, much of what he learned from Godwin had to be left behind. Godwin's hopes rested with the future condition of man on earth. Shelley, who lived all his life in the shadow of death, placed his lasting hopes elsewhere. In a letter to John Gisborne dated April 10, 1822 (X, 371) he rejects as absurd Wordsworth's sentiment that this earth is the place where "we find our happiness, or not at all." While he believed that there was no rational proof for the immortality of the soul, he nevertheless accepted the idea of an "inextinguishable thirst for immortality" within men. The poet's function was to give expression to that thirst without resorting to the dogmatism of religion. In this sense, Shelley agreed with Sidney's conviction that the poet "nothing affirmeth." "That there is a true solution of the riddle," he writes in his notes on *Hellas* (pp. 478–9) from which the above excerpt is taken,

and that in our present state that solution is unattainable by us, are propositions which may be regarded as equally certain: meanwhile, as it is the province of the poet to attach himself to those ideas which exalt and ennoble humanity, let him be permitted to have conjectured the condition of that futurity towards which we are all impelled by an inextinguishable thirst for immortality. Until better arguments can be produced than sophisms which disgrace the cause, this desire itself must remain the strongest and the only presumption that eternity is the inheritance of every thinking being.

Even in *Queen Mab*, in which his apocalyptic vision is marred by materialism, his thoughts are, in part at least, on death and immortality. Before Ianthe fell asleep, she had been walking along the beach talking to Henry about death. The poem opens with a meditation on death in which Shelley compares it to sleep. And later in the poem he implies that what is revealed to Ianthe in sleep is analogous to what she will know in death. The poem, therefore, not only adumbrates *Prometheus Unbound*; it adumbrates *Adonais* as well.

Finally, in this first attempt at an apocalyptic poem, it is possible to discern those various levels of meaning which provide the structural pattern of Shelley's mature vision. The cycles of death and rebirth in Nature are the analogue of the death and rebirth of civilization. In *Ode to the West Wind*, the cyclic pattern of Nature dominates the poem; the analogy to man is developed in the last section. In *Prometheus Unbound*, on the other hand, the death and rebirth of humanity dominates, the rebirth of Nature providing the analogue. Shelley's vision, however, does not stop here. The death and resurrection of man is but the analogue of man's descent from the One and his ultimate return to the One. This essentially Orphic dimension, already suggested in *Queen Mab*, comes into clearer focus in *Adonais*. It is, in fact, in *Adonais* that the total pattern of meaning is finally worked out. Before Shelley could achieve this, however, he had to see it in operation in such works as Dante's *Divine Comedy*. He had to immerse himself in a literary tradition and then set about to revive it in his own works.

6

THE REVOLT OF ISLAM

In *Queen Mab* Ianthe asks the daemon when the "universal Spirit" will "revivify this withered limb of Heaven" (vi, 20-1). The daemon replies (vi, 33-8):

> Some eminent in virtue shall start up,
>   Even in perversest time:
> The truths of their pure lips, that never die,
> Shall bind the scorpion falsehood with a wreath
>   Of ever-living flame,
> Until the monster sting itself to death.

These "eminent in virtue," quickened by "consentaneous love" which "inspires all life" (viii, 108), will recreate the earth into the form of Heaven. Such a one is Ianthe herself who, says the daemon, is "judged alone worthy of the envied boon, / That waits the good and the sincere" (i, 123-4). Her supremacy among all the dwellers of the earth is suggested by the adoration of Henry who lies sleepless by her side and "waits to catch / Light, life and rapture from her smile" (i, 29-30). And when the vision is complete, and the soul of Ianthe has reunited with her body, Henry is described kneeling "in silence by her couch, / Watching her sleep with looks of speechless love" (ix, 237-8).

The kind of leadership which will gradually transform the natural and human world, therefore, is to be found in those who are united in love such as that shared by Ianthe and Henry. The truths which they utter can never die because they find their source in that animating spirit which sustains all life and binds the universe together in harmony and joy. *The Revolt of Islam*, begun four years after the completion of *Queen Mab*, focuses upon this theme which was undeveloped in the earlier poem.

The significance of this focus in *The Revolt of Islam* for an understanding of Shelley's development as a poet between 1812 and 1817 is of the utmost importance. When Shelley wrote *Queen Mab* he considered himself more a political reformer than a poet. He consciously attempted in the poem to present a logical argument, based upon the doctrine of Necessity derived from Godwin and the *philosophes*, showing the inevitability of moral reformation attendant upon the rational progress that man has made through the advancement of the sciences. He is careful to reject this approach in *The Revolt of Islam*, not because it is not valid in itself, but because it is not the method of the poet. "I have made no attempt," he writes in the Preface (p. 32), "to recommend the motives which I would substitute for those at present governing mankind, by methodical and systematic argument." On the contrary, he will "awaken the feelings, so that the reader [shall] see the beauty of true virtue." "It is the business of the Poet," he continues (p. 33), "to communicate to others the pleasure and the enthusiasm arising out of those images and feelings in the vivid presence of which within his own mind consists at once his inspiration and his reward."

In the early part of 1812, Shelley was convinced that, as a disciple of Godwin, he must forsake the world of romance in order to devote his life to the cause of moral reform. Placing his faith in man's future and rejecting the past as the history of superstition and barbarism, Shelley could see in classical literature nothing more than the record of tyranny and injustice. He writes to Godwin on July 29, 1812 (IX, 12): "And what do we learn from [classical] poets? As you have yourself acknowledged somewhere, 'they are fit for nothing but the perpetuation of the noxious race of heroes in the world.'" By 1817, however, Shelley had completely reversed his position. He had given up the cause of moral reform as he had practised it in 1812 and returned to poetry. As for the poets of ancient Greece and Rome, they had become "a passion and an enjoyment." More than that, he intended to devote the rest of his life to the study of their works in an attempt to recreate their vision in his own poetry. When Godwin objected, Shelley replied on December 11, 1817 (IX, 266–7) that he thought Godwin "mistaken in some points with regard to the peculiar nature of my powers, whatever be their amount." His real powers, he told Godwin, lay in sympathy and imagination which were the prerequisites of a poet. When, therefore, Godwin cited Shelley's Chancery paper—"a cold, forced, unimpassioned, insignificant piece of cramped and cautious argument"—as a specimen of his peculiar genius, Shelley concluded: "surely I must feel that in some manner, either I am mistaken in believing that I have any talent at all, or you in the selection of the specimens of it."

This profound change in his attitude to Godwin was partly the result of his discovery of the literature of Italy, England, Rome and Greece, and certain portions of the Bible, and partly the result of the new group of friends which he had made in 1812. In his *Memoirs of Shelley*, Peacock describes a visit to Shelley at Bracknell in the summer of 1813. "At Bracknell," he recounts, "Shelley was surrounded by a numerous society, all in a great measure of his own opinions in relation to religion and politics, and the larger portion of them in relation to vegetable diet. But they wore their rue with a difference. Every one of them adopting some of the articles of the faith of their general church, had each nevertheless some predominant crotchet of his or her own, which left a number of open questions for earnest and not always temperate discussion."[1]

Other than Shelley, the most memorable member of this society was John Frank Newton, whose ideas appear to have been the main inspiration of the group. Peacock, therefore, goes on to give a rather exact account of Newton's ideas, judging from the latter's own writings. "He was," says Peacock,

an estimable man and an agreeable companion, and he was not the less amusing that he was the absolute impersonation of a single theory, or rather of two single theories rolled into one. He held that all diseases and all aberrations, moral and physical, had their origin in the use of animal food and of fermented and spirituous liquors; that the universal adoption of a diet of roots, fruits, and distilled water, would restore the golden age of universal health, purity and peace; that this most ancient and

[1]Thomas Love Peacock, *Memoirs of Shelley* (London: Henry Frowde, 1909), pp. 29–30.

sublime morality was mystically inculcated in the most ancient Zodiac, which was that of Dendera; that this Zodiac was divided into two hemi-spheres, the upper hemisphere being the realm of Oromazes or the prin-ciple of good, the lower that of Ahrimanes or the principle of evil; that each of these hemispheres was again divided into two compartments, and the four lines of division radiating from the centre were the prototype of the Christian cross. The two compartments of Oromazes were those of Uranus or Brahma the Creator, and of Saturn or Veishnu the Preserver. The two compartments of Ahrimanes were those of Jupiter or Seva the Destroyer, and Apollo or Krishna the Restorer. The great moral doctrine was thus symbolized in the Zodiacal signs:—In the first compartment, Taurus the Bull, having in the ancient Zodiac a torch in his mouth, was the type of eternal light. Cancer the Crab was the type of celestial matter, sleeping under the all-covering water, on which Brahma floated in a lotus-flower for millions of ages. From the union, typified by Gemini, of light and celestial matter, issued in the second compartment Leo, Primo-genial Love, mounted on the back of a Lion, who produced the pure and perfect nature of things in Virgo, and Libra the Balance denoted the coincidence of the ecliptic with the equator, and the equality of man's happy existence. In the third compartment, the first entrance of evil into the system was typified by the change of celestial into terrestrial matter— Cancer into Scorpio. Under this evil influence man became a hunter, Sagittarius the Archer, and pursued the wild animals, typified by Capri-corn. Then, with animal food and cookery, came death into the world, and all our woe. But in the fourth compartment, Dhanwantari or Aescu-lapius, Aquarius the Waterman, arose from the sea, typified by Pisces the Fish, with a jug of pure water and a bunch of fruit, and brought back the period of universal happiness under Aries the Ram, whose benignant ascendancy was the golden fleece of the Argonauts, and the true talisman of Oromazes.[2]

When Shelley speaks in the dedication to *The Revolt of Islam* of heaping "knowledge from forbidden mines of lore" (38) he has in mind, among other things, Newton's Zodiacal mythology. In this vastly complicated myth, which Newton, writing in the *Monthly Magazine* in March, 1812, regards "as the basis of all heathen mytho-logy and poetry,"[3] Shelley was offered a vision of the past, present and future condition of men, which, at the same time, was revolu-tionary in its implications. In that same article Newton argues that, although the world is at present under the control of Sagittarius in

[2]*Ibid.*, pp. 30ff.
[3]John F. Newton, "Hindoo Zodiac," *Monthly Magazine*, XXXIII (March, 1812), 109.

the third compartment of the Zodiac, the spirit of good in the fourth compartment continues to influence certain minds so that men are not destitute of hope. This hope, symbolized by Aquarius rising from the sea, is an augury of a new golden age soon to be ushered in. More important than the revolutionary implications of the myth, however, was the fact that it provided Shelley with an archetypal structure which allowed him to reduce all visionary poetry to a single cyclic pattern, and, on the basis of that pattern, shape a vision of his own. Newton declares that "the four heads of Brahma, Vishnu, Siva and Krishnu" embody the "four principal ideas, which have descended in triumph down the stream of Time, transfusing themselves through man's intellectual horizon." Those ideas are "Creation, Preservation, Destruction, Renovation." From Newton's myth emerged Shelley's conception, expressed in his *Defence of Poetry*, of "that great poem, which all poets, like the co-operating thoughts of one great mind, have built up since the beginning of the world" (VII, 124). On the basis of this conception, Shelley was able to identify his own vision with the eternal and unchanging pattern of poetry, to shape it according to the dictates of that archetypal structure. Newton, rather than Godwin, placed Shelley as a poet on the "pinnacle of the ages."

To understand Newton's influence upon the mythological framework of *The Revolt of Islam*, it is first necessary to compare Shelley's poem with Peacock's fragment, *Ahrimanes*. Peacock's poem, as he himself points out, derives primarily from Newton's articles in the *Monthly Magazine*.[4] In the finished sixteen stanzas of the first version, he presents the four phases of Newton's Hindu Zodiac: El Oran, the Creator, unfurls his banner of light over chaos and brings forth the glowing infant world ruled by the heavenly lion, Primordial Love. When the destined period of his rule is over, Oromazes, the Preserver, assumes control, and man, not yet doomed to toil, wanders free upon the earth. Then follows the reign of Ahrimanes in which man becomes a hunter and the earth is laid waste. Meanwhile, Oromazes retires to the southern extremity of the globe and, from its impenetrable bowers, sends forth his genii to quicken hope and prepare the way for the coming of Mithra, the Renovator.

---

[4]Peacock acknowledges his source in a footnote to the second stanza of the first canto of *Ahrimanes*. See *The Works of Thomas Love Peacock*, ed. H. F. B. Brett-Smith and C. E. Jones (10 vols., London: Constable, 1931), VII, 423.

Here the first version breaks off. The larger prose outline repeats the same Zodiacal myth and goes on to describe the catastrophic adventures of two lovers, Darassah and Kelasris, who are messengers of Oromazes bringing hope to the world under the control of Ahrimanes. From the prose outline, it is evident that the epic adventures of these two lovers was meant to provide the larger narrative portion of the poem. After surviving shipwreck, volcanoes, imprisonment, famine and pestilence, they are deemed worthy to participate in the happiness of the southern world. The poem, therefore, was to end with an account of the journey to the southern climes and a prophecy of the new age which must inevitably follow.

The identification of Utopia with the climate of the southern world stems from Newton's astrological notion that during the reign of Primogenial Love the ecliptic was coincident with the equator. With the fall of man, Nature underwent a radical change and the temperate climate of the original Eden was replaced by an arctic wasteland. Shelley, who was familiar with Newton's Zodiacal myth by the end of 1812, makes use of this curious notion in describing his Utopia in *Queen Mab* (viii, 58–69):

> "The habitable earth is full of bliss;
> Those wastes of frozen billows that were hurled
> By everlasting snowstorms round the poles,
> Where matter dared not vegetate or live,
> But ceaseless frost round the vast solitude
> Bound its broad zone of stillness, are unloosed;
> And fragrant zephyrs there from spicy isles
> Ruffle the placid ocean-deep, that rolls
> Its broad, bright surges to the sloping sand,
> Whose roar is wakened into echoings sweet
> To murmur through the Heaven-breathing groves
> And melodize with man's blest nature there."

And he returns again to this idea in *Prometheus Unbound*. The drama opens with Prometheus bound to a ravine of icy rocks. As the time of his release approaches, spring bursts upon the earth (ii, i, 1–11):

> *Asia.* From all the blasts of heaven thou hast descended:
> Yes, like a spirit, like a thought, which makes
> Unwonted tears throng to the horny eyes,
> And beatings haunt the desolated heart,
> Which should have learnt repose: thou hast descended

> Cradled in tempests; thou dost awake, O Spring!
> O child of many winds! As suddenly
> Thou comest as the memory of a dream,
> Which now is sad because it hath been sweet;
> Like genius, or like joy which riseth up
> As from the earth, clothing with golden clouds
> The desert of our life.

Peacock's second version of *Ahrimanes* is an expansion of the earlier one. Instead of thinking in terms of two parts, he now outlined a plan for twelve cantos, of which he finished the first (thirty stanzas) and about half the second (fourteen stanzas). He simplified the mythological framework of the first version by reducing the four Zodiacal phases to two: Oromazes and Ahrimanes. The first canto opens with Darassah standing by a moonlit sea out of which emerges a beautiful female genius. In his description of her rising from the sea, holding a wand in her right hand, Peacock has in mind the Zodiacal symbol of Aquarius who rises from the ocean depths bearing a jug of pure water and a bunch of fruit. Her emergence from the sea symbolizes the return to universal happiness. Thus, he compares the female genius to the "primordial love" which "sprang o'er the infant sphere."[5]

The female genius proceeds to explain to Darassah that Ahrimanes is now in control of the world, while Oromazes has found a nameless grave. She then describes his reign (xxvii):

> "Favor to few, to many wrath he shews:
> None with impunity his power may brave.
> Two classes only of mankind he knows,
> The lord and serf—the tyrant and the slave.
> Some hermit-sage, where lonely torrents rave,
> May muse and dream of Oromazes still:
> Despised he lives, and finds a nameless grave.
> The chiefs and monarchs of the world fulfil
> Great Ahrimanes' behests—the creatures of his will."

Nevertheless, she urges Darassah to become a votary of Oromazes and "blaze forth conspicuous in the fields of fight" (xxviii). In return, she will reunite him with Kelasris, from whom he has been separated by the intervention of her father. Darassah accepts the offer, is reunited with Kelasris, and the two of them sail from the Araxian isle.

A complete reversal takes place in the second canto. Darassah grows

[5]*Works*, VII, 267.

ambitious and the female genius turns out to be an evil spirit in the guise of a votary of Mithra. Kelasris, on the other hand, turns out to be an Oromazian sub-deity in disguise. Apart from these added complications, the prose outline of the second version follows, more or less, the prose outline of the first. Apparently, however, the radical inversion of good and evil was too complicated for Peacock to work out and he simply gave up. It was left to Shelley to start again and bring the vision to completion.

In the over-all pattern of *The Revolt of Islam*, Shelley is indebted to Peacock's fragments. He follows Peacock in recounting the adventures of two lovers, culminating (as in Peacock's first version) with their spiritual victory over the forces of evil. He also sets his narrative within the mythological framework of Peacock's second version so that the conflict is reduced to a struggle between the spirit of good and the spirit of evil. And in the actual detail of the poem, Shelley is again indebted to Peacock. *The Revolt of Islam* opens with a youth who climbs a promontory to mourn the failure of the French Revolution. The parallel with Darassah mourning the passing of Oramazes' reign is evident. As Shelley's youth stands on the promontory, he observes an air battle between an eagle and a snake, and then descends to the seashore where he encounters a beautiful maiden who explains to him the significance of the battle. Her explanation parallels the female genius's account of the conflict between Oromazes and Ahrimanes in Peacock's poem. Both speakers conclude that the spirit of evil is now in control. Peacock's disguised votary of Ahrimanes, like Shelley's Jupiter in *Prometheus Unbound*, cannot, being evil, prophesy the ultimate triumph of the spirit of good. Hence, the author himself, in the second stanza of the second canto, voices some of the sentiments that Shelley attributes to the beautiful maiden who wears no disguise.

Unlike Peacock's first canto of his second version, Shelley's first canto is purely introductory. The youth joins the beautiful maiden in "a boat of rare device" (1, 200) and travels with her and the snake (which has come up out of the water, like Aquarius, and coiled in her embrace) to a magnificent temple where the departed heroes of the world sit upon thrones, one of which stands vacant. As the youth looks on, the maiden dissolves into a darkness that fills the temple. In that darkness the eyes of a serpent move along the floor, then merge and glow like the light from a mighty planet. Beneath that light sits a male form on the erstwhile empty throne. As will become evident later, the serpent, despised spirit of good, has been restored to his original form as Lucifer, the Morning Star. And in his divine presence, Laon and Cythna, transported to this Temple of the Spirit after meeting a martyr's death, tell the youth their story. Their purpose is to offer consolation by showing him both why the French Revolution failed and how, through love, the ideals which it embraced must ultimately be accomplished.

Shelley makes this latter point clear in his Preface to the poem. "But, on the first reverses of hope in the progress of French liberty," he writes (pp. 33–4),

the sanguine eagerness for good overleaped the solution of these questions, and for a time extinguished itself in the unexpectedness of their result. Thus, many of the most ardent and tender-hearted of the worshippers of public good have been morally ruined by what a partial glimpse of the events they deplored appeared to show as the melancholy desolation of all their cherished hopes. Hence gloom and misanthropy have become the characteristics of the age in which we live, the solace of a disappoint-ment that unconsciously finds relief only in the wilful exaggeration of its own despair. This influence has tainted the literature of the age with the hopelessness of the minds from which it flows. . . . But mankind appear to me to be emerging from their trance. I am aware, methinks, of a slow, gradual, silent change. In that belief I have composed the following Poem.

The youth in the first canto awakening "from visions of despair" (129) embodies Shelley's belief that "mankind appear . . . to be emerging from their trance." And in the adventures of Laon and Cythna, through which the youth is instructed, Shelley pictures "the slow, gradual, silent change." The tedious polemic of *Queen Mab* has, in *The Revolt of Islam*, been transformed into "a succession of pictures illustrating the growth and progress of individual mind aspiring after excellence, and devoted to the love of mankind" (p. 32).

Peacock, who did not share Shelley's radical ideas, simply turned Newton's Zodiacal myth into a literary exercise of which he soon wearied. Shelley, on the other hand, made it the vehicle of his own passionate faith. It provided him with a universal framework, such as Milton found in the Christian myth, for the expression of a republican ideal, which, he believed, Milton had also shared. For this reason he states in his Preface (p. 36) that his ideal "Public" is "the tribunal from which Milton received his crown of immortality." And it is with his view of Milton's epic in mind that he makes use of the serpent symbol to stand for the eternal spirit of good.

Shelley believed (as has already been pointed out) that Satan was the real hero of *Paradise Lost*, and that, owing to the prejudices of the age, Milton's vision was obscured by his being forced to make use of the Hebrew-Christian myth. As Shelley explains in his *Defence of Poetry*, the "thin disguise of circumstance" which veils without obscuring the "ideal perfection" of the heroes of Greek tragedy is more opaque in the case of Milton's Satan (VII, 121). By rejecting the Christian myth and substituting for it Newton's Hindu and Orphic mythology, Shelley believed that he had removed Milton's "mask" and "mantle" to reveal the true Promethean form of his Satan (VII, 129). This partial metamorphosis, completed in *Prometheus Unbound*, was begun in *The Revolt of Islam*. Viewed mythologically, the theme of *The Revolt of Islam* is the rehabilitation of Milton's Satan to his unfallen condition as Lucifer. That process must now be explored with reference to the influence of Peacock's *Ahrimanes* upon the composition of *The Revolt of Islam*.

In the second version of *Ahrimanes*, Peacock presents a complete inversion of good and evil. The messenger of Ahrimanes first appears in the guise of a "votary of Mithra," for which Darassah at first mistakes her. While the people appear to call upon God in the name of Oromazes, they are, in reality, calling upon Ahrimanes, the avenging god. Priests and prophets do precisely the same thing (xxv–xxvi):

> "For him on earth unnumbered temples rise,
> And altars burn, and bleeding victims die:
> Albeit the sons of men his name disguise
> In other names, that choice or chance supply,
> To him alone their incense soars on high.
> The god of armies—the avenging god—
> Seeva or Allah—Jove or Mars—they cry:
> 'Tis Ahrimanes still that wields the rod;
> To him all nature bends, and trembles at his nod.

> "Yea, even on Oromazes' self they call,
> But Ahrimanes hears their secret prayer.
> Not in the name that from the lips may fall,
> But in the thought the heart's recesses bear,
> The sons of earth the power they serve declare.
> Wherever priests awake the battle-strain,

And bid the torch of persecution glare,
And curses ring along the vaulted fane—
Call on what name they may—their god is Ahrimane."

This inversion of good and evil, in which Ahrimanes is triumphant and rules in the name of religion, while the follower of Oromazes "finds a nameless grave," parallels Shelley's own myth in *The Revolt of Islam*. In the first canto, the maiden tells the youth that when the first man stood alone "on the verge of chaos" (353), two meteors—"a blood-red Comet and the Morning Star" (356)—mingled their beams in battle, and the sole dweller, "in dreadful sympathy" (359), became a centre of conflict within himself, one thought warring with another. Finally the Morning Star fell and the "earliest dweller" (352) killed his brother. The blood-red Comet, spirit of evil, thus assumed control and "the new race of man went to and fro, / Famished and homeless, loathed and loathing" (365–6). The Morning Star was changed from "starry shape, beauteous and mild, / To a dire Snake" (368–9) so that all men cursed the spirit of good, believing it to be evil. None henceforth knew good from evil, for the natural order had been reversed. Out of this monstrous perversion arose kings and priests, filling the earth with tyranny and war. In calling upon God, men called upon a tyrant.

Shelley's favourite prophet in the Old Testament was Isaiah, and, as his essay *On the Devil, and Devils* proves, he was familiar with the prophet's account of the Babylonian king which Isaiah compares to the fall of Lucifer, the Morning Star. Shelley interprets this passage in terms of the transition from the second to the third compartment in Newton's Zodiac. In *Isaiah* there is no suggestion that Lucifer is Satan; Shelley says that this identification was the invention of the Church Fathers, who equated the fall of Satan in *Revelation* with the fall of Lucifer in *Isaiah*, and then identified the resultant composite figure with the serpent who tempts Eve in *Genesis*. "The Christians," he writes, "have turned this Serpent into their Devil, and accommodated the whole story to their new scheme of sin and propitiation, &c." (VII, 104). The Serpent in reality, however, is an "auspicious and favourable being" and an "hieroglyphic of eternity" (VII, 103).

The rise of the Christian church, therefore, is the reign of the spirit of evil and their God is the Ahrimanes of Peacock's poem. The snake, on the other hand, is the debased form which this tyrant God forces the Morning Star—the light-bearing Taurus of Newton's Zodiac—to assume. The restoration of the serpent to his original form, therefore, symbolizes the triumph of good over evil. And restore him is precisely what Shelley does in the first canto of *The Revolt of Islam* (622–30):

> Then first, two glittering lights were seen to glide
>   In circles on the amethystine floor,
> Small serpent eyes trailing from side to side,
>   Like meteors on a river's grassy shore,
>   They round each other rolled, dilating more
> And more—then rose, commingling into one,
>   One clear and mighty planet hanging o'er
> A cloud of deepest shadow, which was thrown
> Athwart the glowing steps and the crystalline throne.

In a passage that adumbrates the ascension of Keats at the conclusion of *Adonais*, Lucifer, restored to his unfallen condition, assumes his place on the throne that has awaited his return. This event takes place in the "Temple of the Spirit," which is to say man's "invisible nature," where, says Shelley in his *Defence*, the throne of "that imperial faculty," the imagination, is "curtained" (VII, 113). Before that throne and in the presence of the Morning Star, Laon and Cythna begin their story. Allegory and narrative fuse, the myth of Lucifer being the eternal type of all that their adventures reveal. 134132

Shelley's Morning Star is an archetypal image of Eros, the Primogenial Love of Newton's Hindu Zodiac and the hero of Plato's *Symposium*. The two lovers, Laon and Cythna, are the votaries of Lucifer. In his conception of them, Shelley anticipates his later discovery in the *Paradiso*: "the apotheosis of Beatrice in Paradise, and the gradations of [Dante's] own love and her loveliness, by which as by steps he feigns himself to have ascended to the throne of the Supreme Cause." Shelley[6] goes on to describe Dante as "the Lucifer of that starry flock" and to declare that the account of his ascension in the *Divine Comedy* "is the most glorious imagination of modern poetry." Shelley's association of Dante with Lucifer may thus be understood in terms of the Lucifer myth in *The Revolt of Islam*. It also explains Shelley's use of Dante, rather than the Promethean Milton, as a model for his later vision.

The Revolt of Islam, therefore, reveals the "education peculiarly fitted for a Poet" (p. 34) which Shelley describes in detail in his Preface, ignoring entirely his earlier training in the radical philosophy

[6]*Defence of Poetry*, VII, 128, 131.

of the Enlightenment. The difference between *The Revolt of Islam* and *Queen Mab* can be judged by contrasting Shelley's Preface to the former poem with his notes on the latter. When Godwin condemned the poem, Shelley defended himself (in his letter of December 11, 1817) by describing it as a "genuine picture of my own mind" (IX, 266). It is a radically different picture from that in the notes on *Queen Mab*. Unlike the earlier poem, *The Revolt of Islam* is the product of a poet dedicated, resolute, compelled. Nevertheless, as a poem it is a failure, and the nature of that failure must now be explored.

The poet who knows himself, as Shelley did, to be on the "pinnacle of the ages" knows also that, in some sense, he is above that pinnacle looking down at it. To view all life as symbolically congealed upon the Hindu Zodiac or to view all poetry as a single, cyclic work is to stand outside the ages, beyond rather than within the circumference of life-in-time. Newton did not convert Shelley, the man, to Hinduism; rather he converted the poet to an archetypal mode of perception preserved in the Hindu Zodiac, but applicable to all religions and to all poetry. The Zodiac, therefore, enters Shelley's poetry not as Hinduism, but as pattern. While the content of religions may "change and pass," the single pattern "remains." And he who has grasped the pattern need no longer commit himself to a mutable content. Content belongs to men in the realm of Becoming; pattern belongs to God in the realm of Being. "There is this difference between a story and a poem," Shelley writes in *A Defence of Poetry* (VII, 115), "that a story is a catalogue of detached facts, which have no other bond of connexion than time, place, circumstance, cause and effect; the other is the creation of actions according to the unchangeable forms of human nature, as existing in the mind of the creator, which is itself the image of all other minds." This distinction ultimately led Shelley to identify ideal poetry with pure pattern—a vision of man as divinity with all the human content removed.

What it did not lead to, of course, was an ability to write narrative poetry. Mary Shelley did her best to persuade him to put aside his single-minded preoccupation with the "metaphysical anatomy of human passion" and get down to the human passion itself. She pleaded with him to write a "mere human" story, partly, as she points out in her note on *The Witch of Atlas*, to "obtain a greater mastery over his own powers" and partly to "increase his popularity by adopting subjects that would more suit the popular taste." Shelley's response was perfectly in character, and may be described by quoting his lines to Mary attached to the same poem (1–4):

> How, my dear Mary,—are you critic-bitten
>   (For vipers kill, though dead) by some review,
> That you condemn these verses I have written,
>   Because they tell no story, false or true?

"But my persuasions were in vain," she concludes in her note on *The Witch of Atlas*, "the mind could not be bent from its natural inclination. Shelley shrunk instinctively from portraying human passion, with its mixture of good and evil, of disappointment and disquiet."[7]

Her statement, however, is not quite accurate. In his Preface to *The Revolt of Islam* (p. 32) Shelley writes: "I have chosen a story of human passion in its most universal character, diversified with moving and romantic adventures, and appealing, in contempt of all artificial opinions or institutions, to the common sympathies of every human breast." This is partly, but not completely, what Mary had in mind. She would have preferred him to drop the "universal character" and "the contempt of all artificial opinions or institutions." Indeed she would have preferred him to drop the mythical framework. And here again Shelley partly succumbed. In his letter of October 13, 1817, to his prospective publisher (IX, 251), he says that "the first canto is indeed in some measure a distinct poem." He goes on to admit that if the whole poem were mythological his audience would be extremely limited. Nevertheless, he argues, the myth is "very necessary to the wholeness of the work."

On the basis of this evidence, it would appear that Shelley was attempting both to please himself and please the public in the composition of *The Revolt of Islam*. Had Mary not been on the side of the public, it is likely that he would simply have ignored it and written what he obviously wanted to write: a mythological poem in the tradition of Dante, Spenser and Milton, conceived "with an utter disregard of anonymous censure." There is something rather pathetic about Shelley's effort in his Preface (p. 36) simultaneously to appeal to the "Public," condemn the popular taste, and point out that he

[7]Mrs. Shelley's Preface to 1839 edition of Shelley's poems (*Poetical Works*, p. x); Shelley's letter of Oct. 13, 1817, to a publisher (IX, 250); Mrs. Shelley's note on *The Witch of Atlas* (pp. 388, 389).

must be judged by "the tribunal from which Milton received his crown of immortality."

Shelley's divided state of mind is revealed in the poem. He fails to bring together in a sustained way the myth and the narrative. The myth presumably sets the poem, as it was intended to do, within a supernatural framework, the rehabilitation of Lucifer serving as the type of the creative activity of Laon and Cythna. That creative activity, in turn, is meant to embody Shelley's notion of an ideal revolution providing a visionary corrective to the excesses of the French Revolution. In other words, Shelley originally had in mind an allegorical poem functioning, like Spenser's *Fairie Queene*, on various different, though interdependent, levels: as a "genuine picture of my own mind," a personal allegory; as a vision of an ideal revolution, a political allegory; as a vision of the struggle between good and evil, a moral allegory; as a vision of the rehabilitation of Lucifer, an anagogical allegory. Shelley's attempt to please Mary and an audience he despised made him settle for something like a "mere human" story set within a myth that was "in some measure a distinct poem." The weakness of the narrative portion of the poem can best be explained by imagining what Spenser's *Fairie Queene* would be like if its action were stripped of its allegorical significance. Professor Baker accurately remarks: "we have in [Shelley's] poem as it stands only the shreds and patches of what might have been a closely woven allegorical fabric."[8]

For all its deficiencies, *The Revolt of Islam* shows a great improvement over *Queen Mab*. For one thing, Shelley has partially substituted myth for "methodical and systematic argument." For another, he has brought his vision of the universe ruled by "consentaneous love" (*Q.M.*, viii, 108) into a more human perspective, so that man, viewed in terms of the psyche-epipsyche relation, becomes the centre of the drama. Finally, the poem shows an inner consistency, not of technique, but of vision. Shelley here emerges as a Promethean poet dedicated to the renovation of the world through the redeeming power of love. It is, as it were, the vision of *Queen Mab* translated into a human drama in which the marring effects of D'Holbach's materialism are supplanted by Plato's Eros seen in the esoteric form which Shelley derived from Newton.

[8]Carlos Baker, *Shelley's Major Poetry: The Fabric of a Vision* (Princeton: Princeton University Press, 1948), p. 83.

7

PROMETHEUS
UNBOUND:
Psyche

Many of the contradictions in *Queen Mab* stem from a conflict within Shelley between two modes of mental action, the rational and the imaginative. By December of 1812 he had surrounded himself with a new set of friends and from them received an ideal education in mythopoeic classical literature. He had, of course, been introduced to this literature at Eton and Oxford, but, because he considered the method of instruction tyrannical, he rejected it, preferring what he calls in the Preface to *The Revolt of Islam* (p. 34) his "accidental education" to the formal education of a public school and a university. As is evident in the previous two chapters, the kind of "accidental education" he received under the influence of such men as Darwin, Newton and Peacock was of a highly imaginative, rather than purely rational, kind. The two modes of mental action which conflict within *Queen Mab*, therefore, show the influence of Godwin and D'Holbach, on the one hand, and the influence of Newton and Darwin, on the other.

Shelley's attitude to the doctrine of Necessity illustrates one form of the conflict. The doctrine as he originally received it from Godwin and the *philosophes* was simply a statement of the immutable law of cause and effect which governs both the material and the mental universe. In Newton this immutable law is conceived in mythological terms; it is simply the four phases of the Hindu Zodiac viewed as the cosmic cycle of creation, preservation, destruction and renovation. It is the full circle of the wheel of life viewed from without in terms of its total revolution. This is the sense in which Peacock presents it in the opening stanzas of the first version of *Ahrimanes*:

> Parent of being, mistress of the spheres,
> Supreme Necessity o'er all doth reign.
> She guides the course of the revolving years,
> With power no prayers can change, nor force restrain:
> Binding all nature in her golden chain,
> Whose infinite connection links afar
> The smallest atom of the sandy plain,
> And the last ray of heaven's remotest star,
> That round the verge of space wheels its refulgent car.
>
> Her sovereign laws four rival gods fulfil:
> Each holds in turn her delegated sway:
> Unnumbered genii, creatures of their will,
> Gird their respective thrones in proud array,
> Speed at their beck, and their behests obey.

When Necessity is viewed in mythological terms, the passive acquiescence to the "eternal chain of causes" is transformed into an active, erotic participation in the restoration of the golden age. Thus Peacock writes in his prose outline to the first version of *Ahrimanes*: "But some of [Oromazes'] genii come forth from time to time to mingle with mankind, knowing that through their ministry must the reign of the restorer be brought on. . . . Few indeed are the favored mortals that can know and feel their influence: but to them is given an impulse and a power of mind which rises triumphant over all the tyranny of Ahrimanes."[1]

In *Queen Mab*, Ianthe is one of "the favored mortals that can know and feel" the influence of the genii manifest in the Fairy Queen. But Shelley attempts to explain what she sees outside of the mythical frame of reference which alone can justify her imaginative existence. Only a sustained myth could give the poem an organic unity.

[1]*The Works of Thomas Love Peacock*, ed. H. F. B. Brett-Smith and C. E. Jones (10 vols., London: Constable, 1931), VII, 428.

In *The Revolt of Islam*, a sustained myth is again lacking, and again its absence provides an explanation of the poet's failure. Although Shelley described his poem as "a mere human story without the smallest intermixture of supernatural interference," believing that to be better than "methodical and systematic argument," he still stopped short of what his imagination demanded. He was still writing in fetters, failing to show his "utter disregard of anonymous censure." By 1817, he had given up trying to please Godwin. What was still left to do, however, was to give up trying to please Mary and the "public" for which she stood. He had to be answerable to Milton's "tribunal." He had to write a purely mythological poem. In other words, he had to write *Prometheus Unbound*.[2]

When Shelley wrote to Godwin (Dec. 11, 1817) that *The Revolt of Islam* was "a genuine picture of [his] own mind" (IX, 266), he was thinking of the dedication stanzas to Mary in which he offers a brief spiritual autobiography that reaches its climax in his identification not with Godwin, but with Godwin's daughter. The narrative itself is the "objective correlative" of those stanzas. Repeating, in part, the story of *Alastor* (which, significantly, he describes as "allegorical"), Shelley presents the education of Laon. He has been nurtured "beside the echoing sea" (676), felt within himself the impulses of "this vital world" (712), communed with "deathless minds" (838), soared on "fancy wings" (844), found his "second self" (875), and gone out to conquer the hearts of men. Yet, in the poem, Laon remains a shadowy figure, a reflection of Cythna whose character and action dominate the narrative. Laon remains somehow dependent, as if Shelley could not yet create and sustain an image of him adequate to his role of epic hero. He is, at best, a feeble reflection of the Lucifer archetype in the image of which Shelley conceived him. Once again Shelley's failure to follow his own imaginative bent is evident. In *The Revolt of Islam*, Shelley's curious dependence upon Mary is indirectly expressed. Not the resurrected Lucifer, but the wounded serpent who falls into the sea and is nurtured by the beautiful maiden, is the image of Shelley's "ideal prototype"[3] that emerges. The Promethean poet is not yet "unbound." It is the evident contrast between

---

[2]Letter to a publisher, Oct. 13, 1817, IX, 250–1; Preface to *The Revolt of Islam*, pp. 32, 36.
[3]*On Love*, VI, 202.

the Laon of *The Revolt of Islam* and the Prometheus of his lyrical drama that at once defines Shelley's realization of himself as a poet. For this reason, the apocalyptic vision in *Prometheus Unbound* is the fullest, though still imperfect, expression of Shelley's creative imagination viewed as a renovating power.

Next to *Adonais*, *Prometheus Unbound* is Shelley's most successful apocalyptic poem not because of *what* he attempts to present (which is in no way radically different from *Queen Mab* and *The Revolt of Islam*), but because of the *way* in which he presents it. The key to an understanding of the inner structure of the poem lies in the nature of the imagery. Shelley discusses it in his Preface to the poem. "The imagery which I have employed," he writes (p. 205),

> will be found, in many instances, to have been drawn from the operations of the human mind, or from those external actions by which they are expressed. This is unusual in modern poetry, although Dante and Shakespeare are full of instances of the same kind: Dante indeed more than any other poet, and with greater success. But the Greek poets, as writers to whom no resource of awakening the sympathy of their contemporaries was unknown, were in the habitual use of this power; and it is the study of their works (since a higher merit would probably be denied me) to which I am willing that my readers should impute this singularity.

Professor Rogers in *Shelley at Work* quotes a footnote to Shelley's draft Preface for *The Cenci* (quoted in part by Mrs. Shelley in her note on *Prometheus Unbound*) which further clarifies the significance of Shelley's imagery in *Prometheus Unbound*:

> . . . in the Greek Shakespeare Sophocles we find this image,
>
> Πολλὰς δ' ὁδοὺς ἐλθόντα φροντίδος πλάνοις
>
> a line of almost unfathomable depth of poetry; yet how simple are the images in which it is arrayed!
>
> "Coming to many ways in the wanderings of careful thought."
>
> . . . What a picture does this line suggest of the mind as a wilderness of intricate paths, wide as the universe, which is here made its symbol; a world within a world which he who seeks some knowledge with respect to what he ought to do searches throughout, as he would search the external universe for some valued thing which was hidden from him upon its surface. Such is the dim ghost of an imagination which is now dead for want of breathing the native air in which it was conceived and born.[4]

[4]Neville Rogers, *Shelley at Work: A Critical Inquiry* (Oxford: Clarendon Press, 1956), p. 15.

In this commentary on a line from Sophocles, Shelley is asserting the reality of the mental universe viewed as a "world within a world." The complex activity of the human psyche is in no sense less real than the activity of external Nature. Life within the psyche follows its own paths and discovers its own wildernesses. These paths and these wildernesses are not metaphors based upon an observation of the outer world of Nature; they are "absolute" pictures of the mind itself, providing an immediate, rather than borrowed, image of its "operations."[5] They are direct projections of the mind providing a mirror in which it can observe (and therefore discover) its own activity.

But Shelley does not stop here. He goes on to suggest that Sophocles uses the external actions of the universe as symbols of the internal actions of the mind. The images of Nature's activity are metaphors of mental action. And the mental action itself is viewed as "the dim ghost of an imagination" which has lost its way in the mental labyrinth because it cannot remain in touch with the "native air" in which the original idea of the imagination "was conceived and born."

Shelley returns to both of these points in his *Defence of Poetry*.[6] In his discussion of language, he argues that "language is arbitrarily produced by the imagination, and has relation to thoughts alone." Language is thus "a mirror which reflects" that "imperial faculty, whose throne is curtained within the invisible nature of man." Because it is "a mirror which reflects," it cannot ultimately penetrate beyond the curtain which surrounds the throne of man's invisible nature. Struggling to express in prose what can only be suggested in poetry, Shelley continues: "Poetry . . . arrests the vanishing apparitions which haunt the interlunations of life, and veiling them, or in language or in form, sends them forth among mankind, bearing sweet news of kindred joy to those with whom their sisters abide— abide, because there is no portal of expression from the caverns of the spirit which they inhabit into the universe of things." The absence of any "portal of expression" from man's invisible nature to the external world necessarily limits the verbal imagination and sets up a dichotomy between the poet's power and its verbal medium. Thus Shelley concludes that words come between the poet and his original

[5]Mrs. Shelley's note on *Prometheus Unbound*, p. 273.
[6]VII, 113, 137, 135.

inspiration: "when composition begins, inspiration is already on the decline, and the most glorious poetry that has ever been communicated to the world is probably a feeble shadow of the original conception of the Poet." In other words, the poem itself is "the dim ghost of an imagination" because it cannot remain in the "native air in which it was conceived and born." "The wingèd words," he says near the end of *Epipsychidion*, "are chains of lead around [the spirit's] flight of fire" (588, 590).

The following interpretation of *Prometheus Unbound* focuses upon a conception of the hero as the archetypal image of the imagination creating out of its original conception of man's divinity a "feeble reflection" which Demogorgon in his peroration in the last act (568–9) describes as "spells by which to reassume / An empire o'er the disentangled doom." Demogorgon, who stands ultimately outside the mental action of the drama, serves to recall the reader to the limitations of man's creative activity by reminding him, as he reminds Asia, that "the deep truth is imageless" (II, iv, 116). While the *Defence* was written after the completion of *Prometheus Unbound*, it will nevertheless be used in part to interpret the action of Shelley's lyrical drama. The justification for using the *Defence* lies in the belief that Shelley in writing it was drawing upon his own experience as a poet and interpreting the works of other poets (Milton, for example) in the light of that experience. *A Defence of Poetry*, in other words, provides a better understanding of *Prometheus Unbound* than of Milton's *Paradise Lost*.

Prometheus Unbound, following the classical method, begins *in medias res*. While Shelley uses this structural device to engage at the outset the audience's interest in and sympathy for the suffering hero, he has at the same time another, more significant, purpose in mind. The bound Prometheus is suffering from an arrested perception of himself. Not only has he forgotten the words of his curse uttered some three thousand years before, but also he has forgotten the nature of his own psychic power which alone can bring about his release. In Prometheus' initial outburst, Shelley presents an image of unregenerate man bound by the "eternal chain of causes" which makes him the passive victim of Necessity. D'Holbach's doctrine, which Shelley had examined at some length in *Queen Mab*, governs the spirit of Prometheus' lament. Moving back and forth in his mind, like a caged animal, between self-pity and defiant endurance, he attempts to console himself in the passive knowledge that time, the "wingless, crawling hours" (48), shall eventually release him. The power, which Shelley will later identify with Demogorgon, does not reside within him.

Not until Asia enters the cave of Demogorgon in the second act and actually confronts this power is the drama of Prometheus' regeneration placed in its proper perspective. In her account of the cosmological myth embracing the four ages of man, Asia reveals Prometheus' total form, the divinity within him. His struggle with Jupiter then falls into place as one phase in the gradual victory of the mind over all those obstacles that impede its creative power. For this reason, the hour of Prometheus' release arrives in the cave of Demogorgon. Through Asia's penetration to the source of all life, in itself "neither limb, / Nor form, nor outline" (II, iv, 5–6), she is able in her cosmological myth to reconstruct its imaginative form, which is the Promethean archetype of man. Thus the process of Prometheus' regeneration is not complete until the mythological vision of the universe and man comes into focus in the second act. The point may be illustrated with reference to Shelley's defence of myth-making in *Mont Blanc*. "The secret Strength of things / Which governs thought," Shelley argues in *Mont Blanc* (139–40), remains meaningless and remote so long as "to the human mind's imaginings" its "silence and solitude" are "vacancy" (143–4). When, however, the human mind brings to that strength "its tribute . . . with a sound but half its own" (5–6), it becomes "a voice . . . to repeal / Large codes of fraud and woe" (80–1) which "the wise, the great, and good / Interpret, or make felt, or deeply feel" (83–4). Through Asia, Prometheus ("the human mind's imaginings") unites with Demogorgon ("the secret Strength of things") to become the human image of that power. The movement of the drama resides in the process whereby Prometheus dissociates himself from Jupiter and identifies himself, through Asia, with Demogorgon. It is that identification that gives him the power "to repeal / Large codes of fraud and woe."

The drama, then, can be read as a psychic process whereby Prometheus revives the divinity within himself through a series of shifting and complex relations with Jupiter, Asia, Earth, and Demogorgon. These relations must now be explored within the drama itself and interpreted first in terms of what Shelley has to say about the creative process in his *Defence of Poetry* and then in terms of Asia's cosmological myth viewed as the "objective correlative" of that process.[7]

In his analysis of the first act of *Prometheus Unbound*, Professor Wilson argues that Shelley, by having Prometheus recall his curse upon Jupiter, allows the reader to see the character of the unregenerate Prometheus. In the Phantasm of Jupiter, he writes, "Prometheus, like Zoroaster, has 'met his own image'—but an image of what he was, not is."[8] The point is well taken and is worth a detailed consideration for it reveals the complex relation between Jupiter and Prometheus. "Neither the eye nor the mind can see itself, unless reflected upon that which it resembles," Shelley writes in his *Defence* (VII, 121). The Phantasm of Jupiter is the resemblance of the bound Prometheus and not until Prometheus has directly confronted the Phantasm is he thoroughly aware of what his hatred has done to him.

It is therefore wrong to argue, as Professor Wilson does, that the conversion of Prometheus takes place in line 53 of the first act when Prometheus declares that he pities, rather than hates, Jupiter. The statement by Prometheus finds no sanction from within until he actually recalls the words of his curse and is able to place them within the larger perspective of his own divinity. Thus, when the initial declaration of pity is examined in its immediate context it becomes evident that Prometheus' pity is more closely related to a lingering desire for revenge than to an active desire to forgive. Prometheus in soliloquy is consoling himself in the knowledge that the "wingless, crawling hours" are moving of necessity towards the hour of his release. He then describes his release in terms not of forgiveness but of revenge (I, 48–52):

> The wingless, crawling hours, one among whom
> —As some dark Priest hales the reluctant victim
> Shall drag thee, cruel King, to kiss the blood
> From these pale feet, which then might trample thee
> If they disdained not such a prostrate slave.

As if suddenly aware of the implications of his own simile, which is the expression of his unregenerate desire, Prometheus rapidly shifts

---

[7]The latter interpretation is discussed in chap. 8.

[8]Milton Wilson, *Shelley's Later Poetry* (New York: Columbia University Press, 1959), p. 64.

his position. "Disdain! Ah no! I pity thee," he cries. He is psychically unable, however, to sustain this shift of attitude. Thus he continues (53–6):

> What ruin
> Will hunt thee undefended through wide Heaven!
> How will thy soul, cloven to its depth with terror,
> Gape like a hell within!

And then again he attempts to curb his malignity (56–8):

> I speak in grief,
> Not exultation, for I hate no more,
> As then ere misery made me wise.

The wisdom of Prometheus, however, is impotent, because it is, as yet, unsupported by love. At the end of the first act (807–11), he declares:

> and yet I feel
> Most vain all hope but love; and thou art far,
> Asia! who, when my being overflowed,
> Wert like a golden chalice to bright wine
> Which else had sunk into the thirsty dust.

Prometheus, then, has not yet found the way to release himself from the vicious circle in which good and evil merge in a legalistic morality. Shelley brilliantly emphasizes the plight of his unregenerate hero by making Prometheus and Jupiter mirror images of each other. The Phantasm, repeating Prometheus' words, declares (ɪ, 272–9):

> Ay, do thy worst. Thou art omnipotent.
>   O'er all things but thyself I gave thee power,
> And my own will. Be thy swift mischiefs sent
>   To blast mankind, from yon ethereal tower.
> Let thy malignant spirit move
> In darkness over those I love:
> On me and mine I imprecate
> The utmost torture of thy hate.

And Jupiter, from his "ethereal tower," makes his reply (ɪɪɪ, i, 3–10):

> Rejoice! henceforth I am omnipotent.
> All else had been subdued to me; alone
> The soul of man, like unextinguished fire,
> Yet burns towards heaven with fierce reproach, and doubt,

And lamentation, and reluctant prayer,
Hurling up insurrection, which might make
Our antique empire insecure, though built
On eldest faith, and hell's coeval, fear.

Jupiter is convinced that his "antique empire" is about to be rendered secure because, like Prometheus, he awaits the "destined hour" (III, i, 20) which will bear "from Demogorgon's vacant Throne / The dreadful might of ever-living limbs" (21–2). He awaits, that is, the offspring of his love-union with Thetis much as Prometheus awaits the recreated universe which is the offspring of his union with Asia. Jupiter thus engages for the moment in his own vision of the apocalypse which anticipates rather exactly Prometheus' own rejoicing after his release (III, i, 25–33):

Pour forth heaven's wine, Idaean Ganymede,
And let it fill the Daedal cups like fire,
And from the flower-inwoven soil divine
Ye all-triumphant harmonies arise,
As dew from earth under the twilight stars:
Drink! be the nectar circling through your veins
The soul of joy, ye ever-living Gods,
Till exultation burst in one wide voice
Like music from Elysian winds.

Shelley preserves the parallelism between Prometheus and Jupiter until the climax of the drama in the first scene of the third act. He is not, of course, attempting by this means to sustain suspense. The reader is never in doubt about the outcome of the struggle. Why, then, does Shelley do it? The answer lies, in part, in his distinction between the analytical power of reason and the creative power of imagination. In his *Defence*[9] he argues that reason, in the analytical sense, depends upon the intuitive power of the imagination for its materials. "The human mind," he writes, "could never, except by the intervention of these excitements [imaginative activity], have been awakened to the invention of the grosser sciences, and that application of analytical reasoning to the aberrations of society, which it is now attempted to exalt over the direct expression of the inventive and creative faculty itself." Jupiter embodies the power of analytical reasoning which depends upon the creative faculty symbolized by Prometheus. Thus, Prometheus declares that he gave power to Jupi-

[9]VII, 134, 109, 134.

ter on condition that man be left free, that is, he gave the power of reason to man on condition that man not become its slave. To be the slave of reason is to reject the creative faculty in favour of its shadow, reason being to the imagination "as the body to the spirit, as the shadow to the substance." The result of this rejection of creative power is that "the cultivation of those sciences which have enlarged the empire of man over the external world, has, for want of the poetical faculty, proportionally circumscribed those of the internal world; and man, having enslaved the elements, remains himself a slave." Man, in other words, worships Jupiter and, as such, remains a bound Prometheus. In the bound Prometheus (and the apparent victory of Jupiter) Shelley presents the Promethean conquest of Nature through science which is but the shadow of the larger apocalyptic conquest of man's selfhood, the proper subject of Shelley's drama.

Shelley, then, by sustaining the parallelism between Prometheus and Jupiter, is simultaneously presenting two approaches to the apocalypse. Through Jupiter and Thetis he dramatizes the secular apocalypse of the *philosophes* which he was already in process of rejecting during the composition of *Queen Mab*. Through Prometheus and Asia, he dramatizes the pagan apocalypse of the Orphic poets which, with his growing faith in the creative imagination, came to replace his earlier mechanistic philosophy.

Within a philosophical framework, therefore, Jupiter is the personification of D'Holbach's Necessity, and the bound Prometheus suggests Shelley's earlier acceptance of it. As an allegory of Shelley's own mental growth, the conflict between Jupiter and Prometheus is the image of Shelley's earlier conflict between D'Holbach's Necessity and Godwin's immaterialism. Shelley is dramatizing in the release of Prometheus his re-creation of both D'Holbach and Godwin into a Neo-Platonic vision of the universe ruled by love, a universe which Shelley believed was the product of the creative imagination imaging forth its objects.

Viewed in this allegorical context, it is possible to gain further insight into the limited nature of Prometheus' repentance in the first act. In his first letters to Godwin, Shelley expressed his hatred of the tyranny to which as a youth he was forced to submit. He wrote to Godwin on January 10, 1812: "Passive obedience was inculcated and enforced in my childhood. I was required to love . . . coercion obviated its own intention" (VIII, 239). Partly under the influence of Godwin's *Political Justice*, Shelley attempted to replace this negative state with a more positive outlook which he found in Godwin's doctrine of disinterested benevolence. He therefore wrote to Godwin (VIII, 233) that, although he had been the victim of human persecution, he had managed to remain sufficiently detached not to "alter [his] wishes for their renovation." Consequently, he was still "ardent in the cause of philanthropy and truth." By line 305 of the first act, Prometheus has recapitulated this earlier development of Shelley. When he hears the actual words of his curse, Prometheus replies:

> It doth repent me: words are quick and vain;
> Grief for awhile is blind, and so was mine.
> I wish no living thing to suffer pain.

Prometheus has attained to a state of disinterested benevolence.

By 1817, however, Shelley had rejected what he considered the Stoical resignation demanded by Godwin in favour of the more active, more creative conception of love found in Plato's *Symposium*. Prometheus' rather passive "pity" (Shelley does not use the word love), with its undercurrent of lingering hostility, therefore, was essentially too negative, too closely identified with self-love, to bring about the release of his imagination. Not pity, but active love, is the recreative power in man. Before Prometheus can be unbound, he must undergo a further psychic growth; his power to love must inwardly expand until it embraces the entire universe. This growth is not accomplished until the end of the third act. Only then does love in the "wise heart" of Prometheus fold "over the world its healing wings" (IV, 561).

In *Prometheus Unbound*, Godwin's doctrine of a gradual growth of consciousness has been replaced by Plato's doctrine of the gradual enlargement of the capacity to love as the true vision of ascending man. A dialectical process based upon discursive reason has been replaced by a dialectical process based upon spiritual passion. The action does not end when Prometheus consciously repents and grows benevolent; on the contrary, only then does it properly begin to scale the Platonic ladder of love leading to the "intense inane" (III, iv, 204).

The limited vision of the first act, therefore, is governed by the notion of an impersonal will, of which time is the agent, moving irresistibly towards the millennium. Seen within the time continuum, which is the restricted consciousness of man, this will manifests itself in the dialectical struggle between good and evil embodied in the struggle between Prometheus and Jupiter. Good and evil, however, are merely relative terms, the one dependent upon the other. So long as life is viewed through these rigid moral categories mankind cannot advance.

Prometheus himself comes to realize the limitations of a purely moral framework during his temptations by the Furies. The Fury speaks to him (1, 483–91):

> Thou think'st we will live through thee, one by one,
> Like animal life, and though we can obscure not
> The soul which burns within, that we will dwell
> Beside it, like a vain loud multitude
> Vexing the self-content of wisest men:
> That we will be dread thought beneath thy brain,
> And foul desire round thine astonished heart,
> And blood within thy labyrinthine veins
> Crawling like agony?

And Prometheus replies (1, 491–5):

> Why, ye are thus now;
> Yet am I king over myself, and rule
> The torturing and conflicting throngs within,
> As Jove rules you when Hell grows mutinous.

Prometheus admits that the evil within him must be controlled in the same way as Jove controls the Furies. Within a moral perspective, isolated from the redeeming power of imagination, Prometheus rules his own evil inclinations as Jupiter rules his mutinous slaves. In this limited moral framework Prometheus and Jupiter merge through their dependence upon each other: so long as man is actively engaged in combating evil he must, like Jupiter, assume the role of king, ruling his rebellious subjects.

Perhaps for this reason Shelley in his *Defence* (VII, 118) argues that the creations of the imagination are not directly concerned with the poet's conception of right and wrong. "The great instrument of moral good is the imagination," writes Shelley, "and poetry administers to the effect by acting upon the cause." The poet must concern himself with the cause rather than the effect. If he attempts to "embody his own conceptions of right and wrong" in his art he must assume the "inferior office" of a moral reformer and "resign the glory in a participation in the cause." Poets like Euripides and Spenser, for example, "have frequently affected a moral aim," with the result that "the effect of their poetry is diminished in exact proportion to the degree in which they compel us to advert to this purpose." This argument, when applied to the first act of Shelley's drama, reveals the moral rock to which Prometheus is bound. Prometheus has assumed the "inferior office" of exploring the moral effects of the imagination upon himself and resigned the "glory" of "a participation in the cause." His imaginative power is, as a result, "diminished."

The complexity of the relation between Jupiter and Prometheus may therefore be summarized in the following manner: so long as Prometheus defines himself in relation to his opposition to Jupiter he functions within the shadow world of the analytical reason, sacrificing his creative faculty to an analysis of its effects. As a result, he is unable actively to participate in the "cause" of his own release; he resigns himself to an impersonal will operating in time through the "eternal chain of causes" which he believes must eventually bring about his release. Prometheus in the first act remains, therefore, suspended in time between hope and despair, unable to image the object of his hope and unwilling to submit to the object of his despair. He is, like Matthew Arnold's Victorian, wandering between two worlds, the one dead, the other as yet powerless to be born. Thus, in his concluding speech in the first act (812–18), Prometheus laments:

> alas! how heavily
> This quiet morning weighs upon my heart;
> Though I should dream I could even sleep with grief
> If slumber were denied not. I would fain
> Be what it is my destiny to be,
> The saviour and the strength of suffering man,
> Or sink into the original gulf of things.

Prometheus has arrived at the crisis of vision; he must either rise to the level of his own divinity or sink with Jupiter into the "original gulf." The crisis that confronts Prometheus at the end of the first act may perhaps be better understood by examining it in the context of the similar crisis that confronts Beatrice in *The Cenci*. Shelley turned to the composition of *The Cenci* after completing the third act of *Prometheus Unbound*. Possibly with his divine comedy in mind, he makes in the Preface to *The Cenci* the following comment upon Beatrice's decision to seek revenge (p. 276): "Undoubtedly, no person can be truly dishonoured by the act of another; and the fit return to make to the most enormous injuries is kindness and forbearance, and a resolution to convert the injurer from his dark passions by peace and love. If Beatrice had thought in this manner she would have been wiser and better; but she would never have been a tragic character."

Beatrice fails to make a "fit return" to the injury done to her because, unlike Prometheus, she fails to invoke the "immortal God'" of imagination which alone could redeem her "mortal passion." Instead, she invokes the God of Roman Catholicism and acts according to the dictates of a religion which, for the Italian Catholic at least, is, in Shelley's view, "a passion, a persuasion, an excuse, a refuge; never a check" (p. 277). For Shelley, the Roman Church is, in the final analysis, on the side of Count Cenci because his behaviour to Beatrice reflects the behaviour of the Catholic God whom Shelley in his notes on *Queen Mab* describes as a "hypocritical Daemon" announcing Himself "as the God of compassion and peace, even whilst He stretches forth His blood-red hand with the sword of discord to waste the earth" (p. 820). Beatrice, in other words, fails to ascend in imagination beyond the limits of Jupiter; in both her act of revenge and the judgment passed upon it she is the victim of Prometheus' adversary.

What, then, distinguishes the fate of Prometheus in *Prometheus Unbound* from the fate of Beatrice in *The Cenci* is the descent in Asia of the "immortal God" of imagination through which Prometheus' "mortal passion" is redeemed. Without Asia, incarnate in the second act, Prometheus, like Beatrice, would "sink into the eternal gulf of things" (I, 818).

By exorcising the images of hatred and terror in his resistance to the Furies, Prometheus, unlike Beatrice, is able to find comfort in a series of shadowy images of various degrees of love, none of which entirely takes up residence in his mind. What Professor Wilson interprets as a

regeneration of the will is more properly a regeneration of the power
to love to which the will is tied.[10] When the chorus of comforting
spirits departs towards the conclusion of the first act, Ianthe asks
Panthea where they are gone. Panthea replies (802–6):

> Only a sense
> Remains of them, like the omnipotence
> Of music, when the inspired voice and lute
> Languish, ere yet the responses are mute,
> Which through the deep and labyrinthine soul,
> Like echoes through long caverns, wind and roll.

In the "deep and labyrinthine soul" of Prometheus, echoes of a song,
now almost mute, can be heard. His power of release depends upon
his ability to revive that music within himself, even as Coleridge's
power to build his pleasure dome depends upon reviving the "symphony and song" of the damsel that he once heard in a vision.
Prometheus' "damsel" is Asia, and as the first act draws to a close,
his mind, gradually awakening to love, begins to focus upon her.
Having experienced the reviving influence of the "airborn shapes"
(i, 807), he realizes that hope, if not in vain, must be rooted in love.
But Asia is still in exile, the Asia to whom his being must overflow or
else sink "into the thirsty dust" (i, 811).

Had the memory of Asia been entirely obliterated during the cen-
turies of his captivity, the divinity in man symbolized by Prometheus
would have been completely annihilated. Prometheus would have
sunk "into the original gulf of things." Shelley, therefore, is careful
to suggest Asia's continuing influence throughout the first act. In
order properly to grasp the nature of that influence, however, it is
necessary to examine Asia's role in the drama, especially at this point
her relation to the Earth, who, as Prometheus' mother, is continuously
present throughout the first act.

The ambiguity of Shelley's Earth, viewed as a *dramatis persona*,
is evident in the various metamorphoses which this androgynous
figure undergoes as the drama unfolds. In the first act (153–8) she
is Mother Earth

> within whose stony veins,
> To the last fibre of the loftiest tree
> Whose thin leaves trembled in the frozen air,

---

[10]*Shelley's Later Poetry*, pp. 63ff. Professor Wilson argues (p. 154) that Shelley
is "only tentatively" concerned with the imagination in *Prometheus Unbound*.

> Joy ran, as blood within a living frame,
> When [Prometheus] didst from her bosom, like a cloud
> Of glory, arise, a spirit of keen joy!

After the binding of Prometheus, her "wan breast was dry / With grief" (176–7) with the result that plague and famine fell upon man, beast and worm. The whole of Nature (177–9)

> was stained
> With the contagion of a mother's hate
> Breathed on her child's destroyer.

At the same time, however, Prometheus' curse preserves "a treasured spell" upon which the elements "meditate / In secret joy and hope" (184–5). And it is from this "treasured spell" that the Earth sends forth (658–61)

> those subtle and fair spirits,
> Whose homes are the dim caves of human thought,
> And who inhabit, as birds wing the wind,
> Its world-surrounding aether.

These spirits (661–3)

> behold
> Beyond that twilight realm, as in a glass,
> The future.

Mother Earth, therefore, serves as a custodian of the racial memory. The Chorus of Spirits which she bids ascend are "from unremembered ages" the "gentle guides and guardians . . . / Of heaven-oppressed mortality" (672–4). For this reason, Prometheus, after receiving comfort from them, declares: "Earth can console, Heaven can torment no more" (820).

The consolation of the Earth reveals the shrouded presence of Asia. In the second act, the Chorus of Spirits sent by the Earth merge with Asia, who in the cave of Demogorgon has witnessed the arrival of the destined hour. Asia, following her experience in the cave, is restored to her original form in which love, "like the atmosphere / Of the sun's fire filling the living world" (II, v, 26–7), burst from her and (28–30)

> illumined earth and heaven
> And the deep ocean and the sunless caves
> And all that dwells within them.

The grief which had eclipsed her power has been lifted. She has become the "Life of Life" (ii, v, 48) whose smiles "make the cold air fire" (51), the "Child of Light" (54) whose burning limbs are "as the radiant lines of morning" (56), the "Lamp of Earth" (66) that apparels Earth's "dim shapes" with "brightness" (67).

As a result of the transformation of Asia, the Earth responds to her celestial power released through her reunion with Prometheus. Thus, she declares to Prometheus (iii, iii, 84–90):

> I hear, I feel;
> Thy lips are on me, and their touch runs down
> Even to the adamantine central gloom
> Along these marble nerves; 'tis life, 'tis joy,
> And through my withered, old, and icy frame
> The warmth of an immortal youth shoots down
> Circling.

This "immortal youth" whose warmth circles through Earth's "withered, old, and icy frame" is the power of perpetual renewal in Nature, the source of which is Asia. Thus, the Spirit of the Earth addresses Asia as "mother, dearest mother" (iii, iv, 24). Accepting Shelley's usual confusion of the sexes, one may conclude that the "immortal youth" is the product of Asia casting her shadow on the earth to become its "Lamp."

The complex relation between Mother Earth, the Spirit of the Earth, Prometheus and Asia may be further clarified with reference to *Adonais*. In his elegy, Shelley speaks of the power "which wields the world with never-wearied love, / Sustains it from beneath, and kindles it above" (377–8). The Spirit of the Earth is the power which "sustains" the Earth from beneath, while Asia is the power which "kindles it above." In the first act, Prometheus identifies himself with the power which sustains him from beneath; by turning to Asia in the second act, he identifies himself with the power which "kindles" his divinity from above. Shelley, in his *Defence* (VII, 136), argues that the release of the creative faculty from the curse which binds it to the world of surrounding impressions blunted by reiteration is the result of an "interpenetration of a diviner nature through our own." Asia is that "diviner nature" interpenetrating the soul of Prometheus to release his creative power. There is, therefore, a line of direct ascent within Prometheus from his relation to Mother Earth, to the Chorus of Spirits (which reflect the Spirit of Nature), to Asia herself. And it is this line of ascent which reveals the continuing influence of Asia throughout the first act and the gradual release of psychic power which culminates in apocalypse.

The apocalypse itself, however, is the "intense inane" existing beyond the veil of life. It is the "white radiance" which in *Adonais* Keats presumably enters when, through death, he awakens from the dream of life. The "deep truth" of this ultimate and Platonic reality must, by its very nature, remain "imageless." Prometheus' union with Asia, therefore, is something which cannot be seen, though, of course, its effects can be felt, and what can be felt can presumably be imaged. From this point of view, Shelley has constructed in his presentation of Prometheus' psychic growth leading to his union with Asia an extended simile of the reality of apocalypse. He has attempted to communicate the timeless in time, Plato's "movable image of eternity" in the *Timaeus* (p. 490).

When the Prometheus-Asia relation is contrasted with the Prometheus-Jupiter relation it becomes evident that Shelley in his lyrical drama was attempting to bring together two impulses: a desire to transform the world and a desire to transcend it. After *Prometheus Unbound*, Shelley found it increasingly difficult to relate them; his desire to transcend the world led him in *Epipsychidion, Adonais* and *The Triumph of Life* to abandon the Promethean, revolutionary impulse in favour of the erotic impulse which, as in Plato's *Symposium*, conducts to a realm of pure Being. While the recreative impulse is common to both, the former stops short of the "one annihilation" (*Epipsychidion*, 587). In his *Defence*, he argues that the poetry of Dante served "as the bridge thrown over the stream of time, which unites the modern and antient World" (VII, 129). That bridge is the doctrine of Eros. Milton, he believed, presented in the creation of Satan its revolutionary aspect, while Dante stripped Eros of its Promethean implications and concerned himself exclusively "with the secret things of love" (VII, 128). In *Prometheus Unbound*, Shelley, as in *The Revolt of Islam*, is still following Milton; after *Prometheus Unbound* he tends on the whole to follow Dante.

Shelley, therefore, will not allow his Prometheus to take up his abode in the "intense inane." Prometheus' Heaven, in this sense, remains "unascended" (III, iv, 203) because he must fulfil his earthly destiny as "the saviour and the strength of suffering man" (I, 817). "Imagination is as the immortal God which should assume flesh for the redemption of mortal passion," writes Shelley in his Preface to *The Cenci* (p. 277). As an "immortal God," Prometheus must "veil" his power to become a revelation of the "divinity in Man."[11] Within the curtain of flesh, man is not exempt "from chance, and death, and mutability" (*P.U.* III, iv, 201); they are the "clogs" that stand between him and that "loftiest star of unascended Heaven." Nevertheless, the divinity within him can rule these "clogs" like slaves so that man is "the king / Over himself" (III, iv, 196–7). He need not tremble before his own limitations as man or create out of his fear an image of omnipotent power before which he bows and sues for grace "with suppliant knee." He need not, that is, worship Jupiter, "the tyrant of the world" (III, iv, 183).

In his Preface to *Prometheus Unbound*[12] Shelley argues that the "moral interest of the fable" is "powerfully sustained by the sufferings and endurance of Prometheus." Shelley, however, is not primarily concerned with the "moral interest" ("didactic poetry is my abhorrence"). For this reason Prometheus' suffering is in some sense vicarious. By giving power to Jupiter, he deliberately assumes the condition of men, as Christ had done, that men might, through him, find the way to their release. And when his mission has been accomplished he retires into the caverns of his own spirit, without at the same time becoming inaccessible. Henceforth, he tells Asia, "we will not part" (III, iii, 10). Instead they will dwell together in their enchanted cave (III, iii, 23–4),

> Where we will sit and talk of time and change,
> As the world ebbs and flows, ourselves unchanged.

They will talk about the human condition ("What can hide man from mutability?"—25) from which they are themselves exempt. They will receive "the echoes of the human world" (44) and through their intercourse with man cast upon the "lovely apparitions" (49) of his mind the "gathered rays which are reality" (53). Thus, man's "pro-

---

[11]*Defence*, VII, 137.
[12]Pp. 205, 207.

geny immortal / Of Painting, Sculpture, and rapt Poesy" (54–5) shall be (58–60)

> the mediators
> Of that best worship, love, by him and us
> Given and returned.

By thus focusing his erotic vision upon the love of man (as distinct from the love of the One), Shelley is able to present Prometheus as the mediator between man's earthly condition and the divinity within him. The Prometheus-Jupiter conflict (man's condition within the order of Nature) is resolved by the Prometheus-Asia relation (man's condition beyond the limits of that order, which, if Shelley were a Christian, he might describe as the order of Grace). The latter condition interpenetrates the former with the result that the lyrical drama is a revelation of a state of tension within man between his mortality and his divinity. Love in *Prometheus Unbound* does not, as in the *Epipsychidion*, explode into the "one annihilation" of apocalypse; rather, it leaves "its awful throne of patient power," binds itself to the "slippery, steep, / And narrow verge of crag-like agony," and then springs, not back into the source of its own power, but "over the world" with "healing wings" (IV, 557–61).

Another way of describing the vision in *Prometheus Unbound* is to say that Shelley in his drama is concerned with Demogorgon as a *dramatis persona*, as a power which is felt rather than a power inaccessible to feeling. Demogorgon is presented in the second act (IV, 1–7) as a "veilèd form" sitting on an "ebon throne," or more specifically in this case as a "mighty darkness / Filling the seat of power" which is "Ungazed upon and shapeless; neither limb, / Nor form, nor outline." "Yet we feel," says Panthea, "it is / A living Spirit." There is, therefore, some similarity between love on its "awful throne of patient power," which Demogorgon describes in the peroration of the final act, and Demogorgon himself upon his "ebon throne." When Demogorgon confronts Jupiter in the third act, however, he calls himself not love but eternity and warns Jupiter not to demand a "direr name" (III, i, 51). The "direr name" may perhaps be "retributive Justice," which seals the doom of Jupiter. Prometheus, entangled in his struggle with Jupiter in the first act, awaits the triumph of "Justice" (404) which he describes as the "retributive

hour" (406). The "retributive hour," however, with its con-
notations of revenge, is a limited perception which Prometheus is
struggling to overcome. For this reason, he looks beyond the "retributive hour" and declares that (I, 403–5):

> . . . Justice, when triumphant, will weep down
> Pity, not punishment, on her own wrongs,
> Too much avenged by those who err.

Prometheus is aware that "evil minds / Change good to their own
nature" (I, 380–1), that justice, which in itself is virtue, is changed
"by those who err" into a justification for revenge. The wrongs done in
the name of justice must, therefore, ultimately be forgiven. But
only when justice is triumphant.

The triumph of justice is achieved when Demogorgon hurls Jupiter into the abyss. Prometheus himself, who pities Jupiter and wishes
"no living thing to suffer pain" (I, 305), recognizes the necessity
of the event while, at the same time, dissociating himself from it.
And Jupiter, in a moment of profound insight, realizes that Prometheus' pity might have saved him had he not rejected it in favour
of his own "detested prodigy," which he had believed would secure
his throne. Thus he cries out to Demogorgon (III, i, 64–9):

> Mercy! mercy!
> No pity, no release, no respite! Oh,
> That thou wouldst make mine enemy my judge,
> Even where he hangs, seared by my long revenge,
> On Caucasus! he would not doom me thus.
> Gentle, and just, and dreadless, is he not
> The monarch of the world? What then art thou?

"What then art thou?": Jupiter asks the question that critics have
been asking ever since. Like the "deep truth" itself Demogorgon is
"imageless." And it is precisely because he is "imageless" that he is
capable of assuming an infinite variety of masks. These masks, however, reveal not Demogorgon himself, but the forms which man
creates to interpret his power. In himself, he is the source of all life,
the "white radiance of Eternity" which men can only view through
"a dome of many-coloured glass." Without that "dome," which fuses
the "unapprehended" inspiration described in the Defence (VII, 116)
with the phenomena of sense, this "white radiance" is a "mighty darkness" (II, iv, 3). Filtered through the dome, it is like "light from the

meridian sun" (ii, iv, 4). Within the poem, therefore, Demogorgon is the blinding darkness of the "white radiance" which the veils (or rays) of the imagination render visible. And in this form, he is both the image of justice that governs the Jupiter-Prometheus struggle and the image of love that governs the Asia-Prometheus relation. Demogorgon, in other words, is the presiding spirit of the drama, the "divinity in Man" rendered visible through the release of creative power.

But, of course, he is more than that. Demogorgon functions both within and without the drama. In the cave, he functions specifically as a *dramatis persona*, guiding in the manner of Socrates the direction of Asia's thought. He then ascends in his chariot to dethrone Jupiter. Finally, at the conclusion of the drama, he reappears, both from within and without. Panthea senses him bursting from the earth, the air and sky, but when he speaks, his vantage point is that of eternity viewing as in a mirror its own image. What he sees is a moving likeness of himself which, because it is a likeness, is tied to mutability. He is able to distinguish between the apocalyptic world of eternity and its shadowy form as the "Mother of many acts and hours" (iv, 566). In this temporal form eternity has an "infirm hand" and may, as a result, disentangle the doom from which the Titan has released man.

The purpose of Asia's journey into the cave of Demogorgon is to return to the source of all life, both within man and the universe, in order that life may be recreated from that source. Panthea and Asia have journeyed (ii, iii, 54–62)

> To the deep, to the deep,
>   Down, down!
> Through the shade of sleep,
> Through the cloudy strife
> Of Death and of Life;
> Through the veil and the bar
> Of things which seem and are
> Even to the steps of the remotest throne,
>   Down, down!

And when Asia leaves the cave, she describes her experience in the presence of Demogorgon in the following manner (ii, v, 98–103):

> We have passed Age's icy caves,
> And Manhood's dark and tossing waves,
> And Youth's smooth ocean, smiling to betray:
> Beyond the glassy gulfs we flee

> Of shadow-peopled Infancy,
> Through Death and Birth, to a diviner day.

In other words, Asia in the cave of Demogorgon has passed in reverse through the entire cycle of life and come out on the other side, which is the "diviner day" ruled by love. In her intercourse with Demogorgon she has gained that apocalyptic perspective of which the recreated universe of the concluding act is the moving image. She has seen Prometheus as in himself he really is: an immortal god. By virtue of this perception, Prometheus is not only unbound, but free to create anew the universe in his own image.

"All things exist as they are perceived; at least in relation to the percipient," writes Shelley in his *Defence* (VII, 137). " 'The mind is its own place, and of itself can make a Heaven of Hell, a Hell of Heaven.' " Prometheus, by giving power to Jupiter and then perpetuating that power through his curse, has made "a Hell of Heaven." By repenting his curse, he declares that Jupiter's Heaven, which is the Promethean Hell, can "torment no more" (I, 820), and by uniting with Asia, as a result of her descent into Demogorgon's cave, he is able to recreate Jupiter's Heaven into the true Heaven of the creative mind. That is, he is able to make "a Heaven of Hell."

This pattern of the way in which the mind functions to create its own worlds is similar in many respects to the pattern described by Blake in *The Marriage of Heaven and Hell*. Blake distinguishes between conventional morality based upon rigid codification of the moral law and true morality based upon the imagination. Conventional morality conceives of good as "the passive that obeys Reason" and of evil as "the active springing from Energy." True or apocalyptic morality, however, is the exact opposite of this: good is "the active springing from Energy" and evil is "the passive that obeys Reason."[13]

Much in the manner of Shelley, Blake goes on to structure the "Mental Fight" within man between the "Contraries" that are necessary to "progression." In one of his dialogues between angels (the morally good) and devils (the really good), Blake's Isaiah declares "that the voice of honest indignation is the voice of God." The release of man's power, therefore, begins when he actively opposes the angels who would restrain his desire and place his imagination "in fetters." Rintrah, who "roars and shakes his fires," is Blake's "voice of honest indignation," and as "the voice of God" is one of the trumpets that

[13]*Poetry and Prose of William Blake*, ed. Keynes, p. 181.

announce the apocalypse. The wrath of Prometheus, therefore, finds its analogue in Blake's Rintrah.[14]

The danger of making an absolute identification between Rintrah and God is that indignation, if perpetuated indefinitely, becomes a mere echo of itself. Desire under restraint, argues Blake, can "by degrees become passive, till it is only the shadow of desire."[15] Prometheus in the first act realizes that this is precisely what has happened to his wrath. His indignation has by degrees become so passive that he cannot even remember the words of his curse, let alone the honest indignation from which they sprang. Thus, when the Chorus of Spirits, embodying the spirit as distinct from the letter of his rage, disappear at the end of the first act, Panthea declares (I, 802–6):

> Only a sense
> Remains of them, like the omnipotence
> Of music, when the inspired voice and lute
> Languish, ere yet the responses are mute,
> Which through the deep and labyrinthine soul,
> Like echoes through long caverns, wind and roll.

The second stage of progression through "Contraries" lies for Blake in the separation of man from the state to which indignation, if perpetuated beyond the limits of its creative function, leads. "Sooner murder an infant in its cradle than nurse unacted desires," writes Blake in one of his "Proverbs of Hell."[16] Throughout most of the first act Prometheus has been murdering his infant imagination and he realizes in recalling the curse that the time has come to put an end to it. According to Blake the only way to put an end to it lies in a change of perception.[17] In one "Memorable Fancy," Ezekiel instructs Blake that the "Poetic Genius" is the first principle of human perception and "all the others merely derivative." In another "Memorable Fancy," Blake puts this principle to the test. He invites an angel to show him what the angel considers to be his "eternal lot." They go off together, winding their tedious way through a boundless void until they finally encounter Leviathan, the image of chaos. At this point the angel leaves Blake, with the result that the entire appearance of the Inferno changes. Blake finds himself sitting on a pleasant moonlit bank listening to a bard who sings, accompanied by his harp. His theme is: " 'The man who never alters his opinion is like standing

---

[14]*Ibid.*, pp. 181, 186, 182, 181. [15]*Ibid.*, p. 182.
[16]*Ibid.*, p. 185. [17]*Ibid.*, pp. 186, 189.

water, & breeds reptiles of the mind.'" What, then, Blake has witnessed are the "reptiles" in the passive mind of the angel, which disappear as soon as the latter leaves. When Blake goes to find his angel, the angel is astonished to see him and asks him how he escaped. Blake answers: "All that I saw was owing to your metaphysics."

The Hell that Prometheus saw was also, as already pointed out, owing to his metaphysics. When he repents his curse, therefore, he is in fact rejecting an entire philosophical system rooted in Shelley's earlier acceptance of D'Holbach's Necessity. And having recanted, Prometheus must now either recover his lapsed creative power or "sink into the original gulf of things." This "original gulf" is Blake's Leviathan, the image of chaos which the mind perceives at the nadir of passivity. Blake describes it as "the infinite Abyss, fiery as the smoke of a burning city" beneath which, at an immense distance, can be seen the sun "black but shining."[18] His description reveals a certain similarity to Shelley's description of Demogorgon as "a mighty darkness" around which dart "rays of gloom" like "rays from the meridian sun." And the journey to Demogorgon's seat of power is described (II, iii, 72–80) as a journey

> Through the gray, void abysm,
>   Down, down!
> Where the air is no prism,
> And the moon and stars are not,
> And the cavern-crags wear not
>   The radiance of Heaven,
>   Nor the gloom to Earth given,
> Where there is One pervading, One alone,
>   Down, down!

But, as already noted, there is another way to view the cave of Demogorgon and the journey to it. It all depends upon whether it is viewed through the eyes of Blake's devil or the eyes of Blake's angel which is to say, through the eyes of the imagination or the eyes of the passive intellect. In *Prometheus Unbound*, it all depends upon whether it is viewed through the eyes of Jupiter or the eyes of Asia. To Jupiter, the journey into the realm of Demogorgon is a journey into "the abyss" (III, i, 53) where he must dwell with Demogorgon "henceforth

[18]*Ibid.*, p. 188.

in darkness" (56). To Asia, who knows that within the abyss "a spell is treasured" (II, iii, 88) for Prometheus alone, the journey is one through the veils of illusion to the discovery of a "diviner day" (II, v, 103). What Shelley records is the journey of Asia into the Hell of Prometheus' own creation in order that he may rise again from the dead and fulfil his creative mission.

The final phase for Blake is the release of man's imagination. Blake presents this final phase in his last "Memorable Fancy." Once again there is a dialogue between a devil and an angel. The devil attempts to persuade the angel that God dwells in other men and that the worship of God lies in "loving the greatest men best." The angel, who views this as idolatry, argues the orthodox view that God is visible only in Jesus Christ, who gave "his sanction to the law of ten commandments." Other than Christ, all men are "fools, sinners, & nothings." In that case, the devil replies, you ought to worship Christ "in the greatest degree." He then proceeds to show the angel that Christ broke all the commandments and to conclude that "Jesus was all virtue, and acted from impulse, not from rules." When the angel hears this "infernal or diabolical" interpretation, he stretches out his arms, embraces the flame of fire in which the devil exists, is consumed, and rises again as Elijah. "This Angel, who is now become a Devil," Blake concludes, " is my particular friend."[19]

Shelley does not go as far as Blake. From Blake's point of view, Shelley is a "fool" who fails to "persist in his folly"[20] sufficiently to become wise. And he fails to become wise because of the limitations which he imposes upon the creative imagination. For Shelley, reality exists beyond the reach of the imagination; for Blake, reality is the imagination. Thus, viewed within Blake's mode of perception, the weakness of *Prometheus Unbound* lies in the figure of Demogorgon as a "mighty darkness" which can never be completely transformed by man's creative fire into the image of man's divinity. Had Demogorgon not remained outside and beyond the reach of man's imagination, then, of course, he would have become Prometheus' own divinity (as he does in part, though only in part, become). Jupiter, like Blake's angel, would then have been consumed and reborn. And Jupiter recognizes this fact when he laments not having made Prometheus his judge.

[19]*Ibid.*, p. 191.   [20]*Ibid.*, p. 183.

Thus both Shelley and Blake agree that "all things exist as they are perceived." Unlike Blake, however, Shelley (in his *Defence*) adds this qualification: "at least in relation to the percipient" (VII, 137). Once this limitation is recognized, it is possible to grasp the nature of the restriction which Shelley imposes upon the apocalyptic vision in *Prometheus Unbound* and to view more accurately the nature of his achievement. In the unbinding of Prometheus and its consequences, Shelley has presented the creative process whereby man taps and releases the divinity in him in order to reconstruct the universe into an image of his own "ideal prototype." *Prometheus Unbound*, like the ideal poem described in *A Defence of Poetry* (VII, 137), "creates anew the universe, after it has been annihilated in our minds by the recurrence of impressions blunted by reiteration." It releases man from the passive and habitual mode of perception symbolized by Jupiter's reign. The basis of this creative act lies in what Shelley describes in his *Defence* (VII, 135) as "the interpenetration of a diviner nature through our own" of which the conscious mind is "unprophetic." This act of interpenetration is dramatized in Asia's descent into the cave of Demogorgon where she stands in the presence of that ultimate power or energy mirrored within Prometheus himself as well as in the universe external to him. She has penetrated to the "ideal prototype" within man which Shelley in his essay *On Love* (VII, 202) describes as a "mirror whose surface reflects only the forms of purity and brightness."

Shelley, however, asserts in his *Defence* that this act of interpretation which arises "unforeseen" also departs "unbidden," with the result that what the Promethean poet can create out of his inspiration is a "feeble shadow" of his own divinity (VII, 136). And Demogorgon, as the imageless power (the God outside His creation), is that ultimate divinity within and without Prometheus existing in its own right, casting neither its shadow nor its reflection.

Because of the limitations of the apocalyptic imagination, Shelley, in his *Defence*, falls back upon other and lesser expressions of its power to justify its existence. He argues in the first instance that the moments of apocalyptic power "may produce in the mind an habit of order and harmony" (VII, 139) correlative with those moments which are the emblems of eternity. This habit of mind constitutes man's moral sensibility, kept alive by the moral imagination which teaches him to avoid self-inflicted pain and to seek the highest pleasure. Thus, at the end of *Prometheus Unbound* (IV, 562–73), Demogorgon, warning that the poet's apocalyptic power must wane, points out that it leaves behind a moral model of "Gentleness, Virtue, Wisdom, and Endurance." Men, through Prometheus, the archetype of the apocalyptic imagination, will have learned "to suffer woes which Hope thinks infinite," "to forgive wrongs," "to defy Power," "to love, and bear."

Closely related to the moral imagination is the sympathetic imagination. Morality without sympathy is dead because, as Shelley states in his *Defence* (VII, 118), "the great secret of morals is love; or a going out of our own nature, and an identification of ourselves with the beautiful which exists in thought, action, or person, not our own." Through the sympathetic imagination, "the pains and pleasures of his species must become his own." Thus, in his long interval of apocalyptic power, Prometheus relies upon his sympathetic imagination through which he is able to continue to identify himself with suffering man. What, in fact, takes place in the process of his regeneration is the gradual linking of his moral and sympathetic imagination to his apocalyptic power. The "effects" of that power which he sought to interpret in the first act are gradually, through Asia's interpenetration, restored to their source.

To sum up, it may be argued that the effect that Shelley wished to produce in his lyrical drama is clearly described in his own account of Greek tragedy in his *Defence* (VII, 121):

The tragedies of the Athenian poets are as mirrors in which the spectator beholds himself, under a thin disguise of circumstance, stript of all but that ideal perfection and energy which every one feels to be the internal type of all that he loves, admires, and would become. The imagination is enlarged by a sympathy with pains and passions so mighty, that they distend in their conception the capacity of that by which they are conceived; and the good affections are strengthened by pity, indignation, terror and sorrow; and an exalted calm is prolonged from the satiety of this high exercise of them into the tumult of familiar life: even crime is disarmed of half its horror and all its contagion by being represented as the fatal consequence of the unfathomable agencies of nature; error is thus divested of its wilfulness; men can no longer cherish it as the creation of their choice. In a drama of the highest order there is little food for censure or hatred; it teaches rather self-knowledge and self-respect.

8

PROMETHEUS
UNBOUND:
Myth

In one of the most suggestive passages of *A Defence of Poetry*, Shelley writes: "The drama, so long as it continues to express poetry, is as a prismatic and many-sided mirror, which collects the brightest rays of human nature and divides and reproduces them from the simplicity of these elemental forms, and touches them with majesty and beauty, and multiplies all that it reflects, and endows it with the power of propagating its like wherever it may fall" (VII, 121). The reference to the prism derives from Sir Isaac Newton's account in his *Optics* of the way in which particles of light when refracted through a prism divide to form distinct colours. Shelley's application of Newton's discovery to an exploration of the nature of drama is characteristic of the way in which Sir William Drummond relates the same experiment to an exploration of certain epistemological problems in his *Academical Questions* and of the way in which Berkeley makes use of it in *Siris*. Drummond, influenced by Berkeley, argues that it is impossible for the mind to perceive a world external to the mind itself. What in fact we perceive, he suggests, is our own sensations resulting from the operation of "animal spirits" which deliver to the soul the object created in the act of perception. When these "animal spirits," possibly acting through the medium of waves of light, strike the retina of the eye they are refracted into a "painted field of . . . vision" and it is this "painted field" which we actually perceive.[1]

While Drummond adds little or nothing to Berkeley's theory of vision, *esse est percipi*, he does draw from it a very different conclusion from that of Berkeley. Drummond uses Berkeley to reinforce a Humian scepticism about the nature of reality; Berkeley, on the other hand, assumes the reality of God as the omniscient and omnipresent perceiver. Thus, he argues in his *Siris*:

Blue, red, yellow, and other colours have been discovered by Sir Isaac Newton to depend on the parted rays of particles of light. And, in like manner, a particular odour or flavour seemeth to depend on peculiar particles of light or fire: as appears from heats being necessary to all vegetation whatsoever and from the extreme minuteness of volatility of those vegetable souls or forms, flying off from the subjects without any sensible diminution of their weight. These particles, blended in one common ocean, should seem to conceal the distinct forms, but, parted and attracted by proper subjects, disclose or produce them. As the particles of light, which, when separated, form distinct colours, being blended are lost in one uniform appearance.

While they are lost to human perception, however, they are not lost to the perception of God. "This Divine Love and Intellect," Berkeley writes, "are not themselves obvious to our view, or otherwise discerned than in their effects. Intellect enlightens, Love connects, and the Sovereign Good attracts all things." The "Sovereign Good," in other words, blends all particles "in one common ocean," while man refracts them that they might be perceived. Man perceives "the many"; God perceives "the One."

In his pioneer essay, "Shelley's Relation to Berkeley and Drummond," Professor Brett suggests (pp. 176–7) that the real value of Berkeley's theory of perception for Shelley lay in a new conception of persons. "The material philosophy," he writes,

hampered him because it gave him only a world of bodies and made him look on all persons as individuals rigidly separate and mechanically

[1]As quoted in G. S. Brett, "Shelley's Relation to Berkeley and Drummond" in *Studies in English by Members of University College, Toronto*, ed. Malcolm M. Wallace (Toronto: University of Toronto Press, 1931), p. 198. The following quotations from Drummond and Berkeley are from the same source, pp. 181, 182.

impenetrable. With the discovery of the immaterial philosophy this terrible separateness of persons vanished: there was no more any necessity to think of persons as primarily flesh and blood; on the contrary the form, the voice, the look are our own experiences, the sense-material through which the other person is revealed; and that other person in its inner self is what we are, a living experience. If, then, two persons have the same thoughts, the same feelings, are they not truly one? In the language of mechanical philosophy, with its time and space and matter, they cannot be: but that world is now transcended: it is not the only reality: it has no more ultimate value than the ink and paper which similarly embody the meaning of a poem.

While there is solid ground for this conclusion, Professor Brett has ignored the fact that the immaterial philosophy could and did lead Shelley at times to an even greater awareness of the "terrible separateness of persons" than had the mechanical philosophy. Alastor, "the spirit of solitude," haunted Shelley until the end of his life. But what Professor Brett really ignores is the fact that for Shelley the discovery that the "other person in its inner self is what we are" depends upon the sympathetic, moral and, above all, apocalyptic imagination. The many are one only when man transcends the limits of human perception through the release of the divinity within him.

When these important qualifications are made, however, Professor Brett's conclusion stands. His solid ground is to be found where in fact he did find it: in Shelley's essay *On Life*. "The view of life presented by the most refined deductions of the intellectual philosophy," writes Shelley in his essay,

is that of unity. Nothing exists but as it is perceived. The difference is merely nominal between those two classes of thought, which are vulgarly distinguished by the names of ideas and of external objects. Pursuing the same thread of reasoning, the existence of distinct individual minds, similar to that which is employed in now questioning its own nature, is likewise found to be a delusion. The words *I*, *you*, *they*, are not signs of an actual difference subsisting between the assemblage of thoughts thus indicated, but are merely marks employed to denote the different modifications of the one mind. [VI, 196]

In his comment upon the nature of drama, Shelley has in mind the application of the "intellectual philosophy" to Newton's prism. Drama is like a prism which collects "the brightest rays" of the "one mind" and then divides and reproduces them into a multiplicity of forms or images emanating from their common source. Thus the prism, being a "many-sided mirror" does more than merely refract; it touches the images "with majesty and beauty" and has the power "of propagating its like wherever it may fall." What Shelley has attempted in *Prometheus Unbound* is to present, in the manner of "a prismatic and many-sided mirror," the "different modifications of the one mind." Following Berkeley, he realizes that the "one mind" itself is "imageless" so long as the act of perception remains an act of refraction through a prism. The life we perceive is, in Drummond's phrase, "the painted field of . . . vision."

Like Berkeley, however, Shelley sought to transcend the limitations of this "painted field." While Berkeley relies upon his Christian faith in a God of love, Shelley affirms the creative power of the imagination which allows man to rise above the limitations of his senses and communicate with the "one mind." When, however, the poet seeks to express his mystical insight, he must make use of the prismatic verbal imagination which refracts his pure vision into a series of images which stain its "white radiance." Nevertheless, since these images are closer to what Shelley calls in *Adonais* (339) the "burning fountain" of reality, they tear aside "the painted veil" which in *Prometheus Unbound* mimics "as with colours idly spread / All men believed or hoped" (iii, iv, 190–2). Thus, in *Prometheus Unbound*, Shelley distinguishes between the "painted veil" of the familiar world of passive perception and the imaginative veil of the apocalyptic world of creative perception.

Drummond argued to his own satisfaction that the world we perceive with the eye is not the real world because the visible images of things painted on the retina are always inverted. And Shelley accepted this, at least in the symbolic sense. The world as perceived without the imagination is a complete inversion of the real world: good is accepted as evil and evil is accepted as good; visionaries are put to death and tyrants are deified. By exploring the psychic structure of the two worlds, Shelley sought through his creative power to invert what is perceived, to turn "the curse" which binds man to "the accident of surrounding impressions," as he says in the *Defence* (VII, 137), into a vision of the ideal world perceived by the "one mind."

"It is difficult," writes Shelley in his essay *On Life* (VI, 196) "to find terms adequate to express so subtle a conception as that to which the Intellectual Philosophy has conducted us. We are on that verge where words abandon us, and what wonder if we grow dizzy to look down the dark abyss of how little we know." Asia looks down into this "dark abyss" when she enters the realm of Demogorgon. And Demogorgon tells her that she cannot know the primal cause of all things (II, iv, 114–16):

> If the abysm
> Could vomit forth its secrets.... But a voice
> Is wanting, the deep truth is imageless.

Shelley, lacking Berkeley's faith in the Christian conception of God, remains in doubt. "But cause," he writes in his essay *On Life* (VI, 197),

is only a word expressing a certain state of the human mind with regard to the manner in which two thoughts are apprehended to be related to each other. If any one desires to know how unsatisfactorily the popular philosophy employs itself upon this great question, they need only impartially reflect upon the manner in which thoughts develop themselves in their minds. It is infinitely improbable that the cause of mind, that is, of existence, is similar to mind.

Standing before the "mighty portal" leading to Demogorgon's realm, Panthea compares it (II, iii, 3–10) to

> a volcano's meteor-breathing chasm,
> Whence the oracular vapour is hurled up
> Which lonely men drink wandering in their youth,
> And call truth, virtue, love, genius, or joy,
> That maddening wine of life, whose dregs they drain
> To deep intoxication; and uplift,
> Like Maenads who cry aloud, Evoe! Evoe!
> The voice which is contagion to the world.

The tone, here is sceptical; the "oracular vapour" is called by a series of names, none of which can provide an actual account of the cause of life. Nevertheless, the "deep intoxication" which the vapour creates "is contagion to the world," by which Shelley presumably means the world as habitually and passively perceived. As such, the "deep intoxication" has a renovating power.

In another sense, however, Shelley recognizes that the "deep intoxication" of the Dionysian world is a contagion within the imagination itself. When the poet affirms as ultimate reality the verbal universe created by his imagination then he fails to distinguish between what he constructs with his limited materials and the original conception that inspired it. What is required of the poet is a "willing suspension of disbelief" in his own creative act, a "poetic faith" capable of sustaining him in the act of composition. He must for the moment believe in his own magic and, when the time comes, abjure it like Prospero in *The Tempest*. In other words, he must realize, when his imagistic structure is complete, that the "deep truth" still remains "imageless." Through Demogorgon, Shelley returns more than once to this realization in *Prometheus Unbound*. It is, however, kept at bay. In *Adonais* and *The Triumph of Life*, on the other hand, the imageless truth lies at the very core of the poems, propelling the poet towards a transcendence of his art, which demands the annihilation of his entire imagistic structure.

What then is presented in the cosmological myth in the cave of Demogorgon is the "oracular" truth of the imagination, which the poet affirms in a "willing suspension of disbelief." Asia, in this sense, is "like Maenads who cry aloud, Evoe! Evoe!" She drains "the maddening wine of life" to "deep intoxication." As a result, the earth declares in the final Dionysian jubilation (IV, 319–24):

> The joy, the triumph, the delight, the madness!
> The boundless, overflowing, bursting gladness,
> The vaporous exultation not to be confined!
> Ha! Ha! the animation of delight
> Which wraps me, like an atmosphere of light,
> And bears me as a cloud is borne by its own wind.

The moon, rendered fertile by the beams of love issuing from the earth, gives birth to living shapes. Her movement about the earth and the earth's movement about the sun become an inspired Bacchanalia (IV, 457–75):

> Thou art speeding round the sun
> Brightest world of many a one;
> Green and azure sphere which shinest
> With a light which is divinest
> Among all the lamps of Heaven
> To whom life and light is given;
> I, thy crystal paramour
> Borne beside thee by a power
> Like the polar Paradise,
> Magnet-like of lovers' eyes;

I, a most enamoured maiden
Whose weak brain is overladen
With the pleasure of her love,
Maniac-like around thee move
Gazing, an insatiate bride,
On thy form from every side
Like a Maenad, round the cup
Which Agave lifted up
In the weird Cadmaean forest.

When, however, the "new Earth and new Heaven," which Coleridge in "Dejection: An Ode" (68–9) says that "wedding Nature
to us gives in dower," is complete, Demogorgon steps forth to remind
man that the apocalyptic vision is the product of "oracular vapour."
Again to quote Coleridge (64–5), it is the vision of joy "that ne'er
was given, / Save to the pure, and in their purest hour." And because
it is the product of the "purest hour" (the "hour" of Prometheus'
release), the doom, as Coleridge knew to his sorrow, may be "disentangled" (*P.U.*, IV, 569). Nevertheless, Demogorgon consoles, mankind by virtue of Prometheus' vision now knows what are the "spells"
by which to "reassume / An empire" (IV, 568–9).

Asia's cosmological myth reveals the continuing influence of John
Frank Newton's Zodiacal account of the four ages of man which he
describes as creation, preservation, destruction and renovation. It is
therefore necessary to return at this point to Newton's myth, explored
at some length in the examination of *The Revolt of Islam,* and observe
the way in which Shelley has further refined it in *Prometheus
Unbound.* Peacock, it will be recalled, in summarizing Newton's
myth, states that Newton, following the pattern of the Hindu Zodiac,
divides the cosmos into an upper and lower hemisphere. The upper
hemisphere is governed by Uranus or Brahma, the Creator, and by
Saturn or Vishnu, the Preserver. The lower hemisphere is governed
by Jupiter or Siva, the Destroyer, and by Apollo or Krishna, the
Restorer. Creation is the result of "eternal light" penetrating "celestial
matter" which had slept "under the all-covering water, on which
Brahma floated in a lotus-flower for millions of ages." Out of their
union emerges in the reign of Saturn, "Primogenial Love . . . who
produced the pure and perfect nature of things . . . and the equality
of man's happy existence." When Jupiter assumes power, however,
celestial matter is changed into terrestrial matter. Man becomes a

hunter and kills wild beasts. Prometheus, the agent of Jupiter, gives man fire with which to cook animal flesh, thereby bringing disease and death to mankind. Finally, in the last compartment of the Zodiac, Aquarius arises from the sea "with a jug of pure water and a bunch of fruit" and restores the golden age.[2]

Shelley's account of the creation of "Primogenial Love" in *Prometheus Unbound* follows Newton's pattern. The "celestial matter" sleeping under the "all-covering water, on which Brahma floated in a lotus-flower" finds its parallel in Asia's "veinèd shell, which floated on / Over the calm floor of the crystal sea" (II, v, 23–4). Asia stands within the shell and bursts forth as love, which Shelley compares to the "atmosphere / Of the sun's fire filling the living world" (II, v, 26–7). In *The Witch of Atlas*, the parallel is even more explicit. The witch, who is Asia more playfully constructed, is, like Asia, one of the Atlantides. She is conceived as a "dewy splendour" within a cave around which the billows, "bidden ... to indent / The sea-deserted land" (74–8), come and go. Through the heat of the sun the cave grew warm so that the splendour "took shape and motion" and emerged as a "lovely lady garmented in light / From her own beauty" (79–82).

The first order of creation, then, finds its centre in Asia who, in her original union with Prometheus ("the sun of this rejoicing world"), symbolizes the original reign of "Light and Love" (II, iv, 33) which, as the drama opens, is about to be restored. Thus, to announce the glad tidings of the "diviner day" (II, v, 103), Prometheus asks the Spirit of the Hour to take the curved shell which Proteus created for Asia and discharge over the surface of the earth the message of its mighty music. The earth shall be restored to its original form, alive in the presence of Asia, reflecting her "awful Loveliness." Accordingly, in the final act (370–5), the Earth describes the movement of love's atmosphere through its mass:

> It interpenetrates my granite mass,
> Through tangled roots and trodden clay doth pass
> Into the utmost leaves and delicatest flowers;
> Upon the winds, among the clouds 'tis spread,
> It wakes a life in the forgotten dead,
> They breathe a spirit up from their obscurest bowers.

[2]Thomas Love Peacock, *Memoirs of Shelley* (London: Henry Frowde, 1909), pp. 30ff.

Shelley's desire to restore the universe to its apocalyptic form, to view reality in as unrefracted a form as possible, is communicated when the Earth declares that "Thought's stagnant chaos" (iv, 380) has been vanquished by light leaving "this true fair world of things, a sea reflecting love" (iv, 384). What Shelley has in mind is, among other things, Newton's distinction between celestial matter and terrestrial matter. Celestial matter sleeps "under the all-covering water" until awakened by "eternal light" to become, like Spenser's Garden of Adonis, the eternal substance, "the first seminarie / Of all things" (iii, vi, 30). Terrestrial matter, on the other hand, is the Earth's "granite mass," "tangled roots" and "trodden clay," Spenser's borrowed matter by which the eternal substance "doth then inuade / The state of life, out of the griesly shade" (iii, vi, 37). The reconversion of fallen terrestrial matter into celestial matter in Newton's Zodiacal myth takes place when Aquarius arises from the sea to make the earth "a sea reflecting love." Shelley presents the same idea when he declares after the re-union of Asia and Prometheus that man "who was a many-sided mirror, / Which could distort to many a shape of error" is now "as the sun's heaven / Gliding o'er ocean, smooth, serene, and even" (iv, 382–6).

Shelley, it would appear, has here substituted the "heaven-reflecting sea" (iii, ii, 18) for the "many-sided mirror" of Sir Isaac Newton's prism. Asia, whose dwelling place is with "the Nereids under the green sea" (iii, ii, 44) has replaced the "painted veil" (iii, iv, 190) of terrestrial matter with the "heaven reflecting sea" of celestial matter.

Thus, after the release of Prometheus, the universe is pictured as floating in a serene and vast ocean of air. The "light-laden moon" is a "floating bark"; the "white star" of morning is "its sightless pilot's crest"; together, they are "borne down the rapid sunset's ebbing sea" (iii, ii, 26–8). The Spirit of Earth, which "guides the earth through heaven," describes itself hiding in a fountain where it lay "like the reflex of the moon," watching the shapes of evil pass "floating through the air." And when they fade into the wind that scatters them, the Spirit rejoices to watch lovely forms "in the deep . . . imaged as in a sky" (iii, iv, 61–83). "Before Jove reigned," Panthea tells Ione (iii, iv, 15–18):

> It loved our sister Asia, and it came
> Each leisure hour to drink the liquid light
> Out of her eyes.

And Asia herself is an "enchanted boat" floating "upon the silver waves of [the air's] sweet singing," until "like one in slumber bound" she floats "into a sea profound, of ever-spreading sound" (II, v, 72–84). Finally, Shelley describes the temple of Prometheus not in terms of the temple itself, but in terms of its water-reflected image (III, iii, 159–61):

> Beside the windless and crystalline pool,
> Where ever lies, on unerasing waves,
> The image of a temple.

What, then, Shelley is presenting in his vision of the recreated universe (which may be influenced by Coleridge's *Kubla Khan*) is the fusion of all life into "one common ocean" which is the *sensorium* of love. It is therefore singularly appropriate that the sound of the echoing sea contained in Asia's curved shell is the music of apocalypse, breathing as it does "a voice to be accomplished" (III, iii, 67).

The functional similarity between Asia's curved shell and the cave of the witch of Atlas has already been pointed out. By returning to Shelley's account of the contents of that cave, the message contained in Asia's shell may be more fully appreciated. In *The Witch of Atlas* (186–92) Shelley describes the witch's cave as stored with

> The works of some Saturnian Archimage,
> Which taught the expiations at whose price
> Men from the Gods might win that happy age
> Too lightly lost, redeeming native vice;
> And which might quench the Earth-consuming rage
> Of gold and blood—till men should live and move
> Harmonious as the sacred stars above.

The witch's cave, like most of Shelley's caves, is a seat of oracular power which offers man a vision of the Saturnian world, the blissful abode of the gods that nourishes the human imagination. If the "voice" which it contains is "to be accomplished" then man must pierce the "painted veil" of terrestrial matter and allow the power of that "diviner nature" to interpenetrate his own.

And this is precisely what happens after the release of Prometheus. When Asia and Prometheus retire to their enchanted cave (III, iii, 40–4):

> hither come, sped on the charmèd winds,
> Which meet from all the points of heaven, as bees
> From every flower aëreal Enna feeds,

> At their known island-homes in Himera,
> The echoes of the human world.

These "echoes" are at first dim, but then (III, iii, 49–53) grow radiant

> as the mind, arising bright
> From the embrace of beauty (whence the forms
> Of which these are the phantoms) casts on them
> The gathered rays which are reality.

The "progeny immortal" which arise from the "embrace of beauty" are the Promethean arts of civilized life, the "mediators / Of that best worship, love" (III, iii, 57–8), given and returned in the intercourse between man and his diviner nature embodied in the love-union of Asia and Prometheus. "Such virtue has the cave and place around," concludes Prometheus (III, iii, 63).

Viewed from within the psyche, the Promethean cave is the fertile womb of creativity which, following Wordsworth, Shelley associates with the pre-existent world of "celestial light" that briefly surrounds the infant and apparels his world in the glory of his dreamlike existence. Thus, Prometheus describes his activity with Asia in the cave as similar to "human babes in their brief infancy" (III, iii, 33). This dreamlike existence is further amplified in the *Epipsychidion* (446–56) when the poet describes to Emily their life on a "far Eden" (417) arrived at by following "a path on the sea's azure floor" (410):

> The light clear element which the isle wears
> Is heavy with the scent of lemon-flowers,
> Which floats like mist laden with unseen showers,
> And falls upon the eyelids like faint sleep;
> And from the moss violets and jonquils peep,
> And dart their arrowy odour through the brain
> Till you might faint with that delicious pain.
> And every motion, odour, beam, and tone,
> With that deep music is in unison:
> Which is a soul within the soul—they seem
> Like echoes of an antenatal dream.

Thus, it may be concluded that Shelley's vision of the Saturnian age is a vision of that oceanic state before birth which man seeks to recreate as the object of his desire. It is not surprising, therefore, that Shelley's vision of the terrestrial world recreated into Newton's celestial matter is a vision of the "adamantine mass" of rock to which

Prometheus is bound, penetrated by love to assume the transparency of sea.

Shelley, therefore, does not visualize his Atlantis rising again out of the sea after being overwhelmed by the flood. On the contrary, he visualizes Atlantis remaining under the ocean where, as a "heaven-reflecting sea" it properly belongs. Blake, following the Biblical symbolism, conceives of the ocean as chaos and the drying up of the ocean as apocalypse, the reason being that, unlike Shelley, he never thought of the perceived forms of this world as the shadows or reflections of the ideal. Shelley's Atlantis is not an actual world, but a Platonic mirror image of the ideal. Shelley was enough of a Newtonian (Sir Isaac, whom Blake placed in Ulro) to accept the notion that what man perceives is a refracted light and that the best that man can do is to purify the medium of refraction. It was not without a reason that the witch of Atlas wove her veil of three threads of mist, three long lines of light and as many star beams. Asia, the "life of Life" (II, v, 48) must veil herself in a similar manner to become the "Lamp of Earth" (II, v, 66). "Beyond our atmosphere," Shelley writes in his notes on *Queen Mab* (p. 800), "the sun would appear a rayless orb of fire in the midst of a black concave. The equal diffusion of its light on earth is owing to the refraction of the rays by the atmosphere, and their reflection from other bodies. Light consists either of vibrations propagated through a subtle medium, or of numerous minute particles repelled in all directions from the luminous body." Shelley's vision of celestial matter as described by Ocean after the overthrow of Jupiter is a vision of the heavens reflected in a bottomless sea.

Shelley's vision of the recreated universe, however, is the product of the apocalyptic hour that comes through the release of the psychic potential within the "enchanted cave" of man's own being, which Shelley in his essay *On Love* (VI, 202) describes first as "a mirror whose surface reflects only the forms of purity and brightness" and then as "a soul within our soul that describes a circle around its proper paradise, which pain, and sorrow, and evil dare not overleap." In the original reign of Saturn, this psychic potential remains dormant in the sense that man's "proper paradise," while present to him, is not perceived. Man's state is passive like a "mirror which reflects"; he has not yet awakened from his "antenatal dream" to create in his own image the living forms of his desire. Thus Shelley states of the reign of Saturn that "earth's primal spirits beneath his sway" exist "as the calm joy of flowers and living leaves / Before the wind or sun has withered them." As such, their vegetative bliss is little better than that of "semivital worms." Shelley then enlarges upon this radical limitation of their existence (II, iv, 38–43):

> but he refused
> The birthright of their being, knowledge, power,
> The skill which wields the elements, the thought
> Which pierces this dim universe like light,
> Self-empire, and the majesty of love;
> For thirst of which they fainted.

And he returns to the same point when in his "Ode to Liberty" he says that "this divinest universe" remained "a chaos and a curse" (21–2) until man was granted freedom.

Shelley's age of Saturn, therefore, is similar to Blake's lower Paradise, Beulah, which man must leave in order to create the true Eden. Instead of submitting to the elements, he must wield them; instead of reposing within "this dim universe," he must pierce it; instead of vegetating within Saturn's empire, he must create an empire of his own. Man's task is that of Bacon described by Shelley in _The Triumph of Life_ (269–73): Bacon's "'eagle spirit'" lept "'like lightning out of darkness'" and

> "compelled
> The Proteus shape of Nature, as it slept
>
> To wake, and lead him to the caves that held
> The treasure of the secrets of its reign."

In _The Book of Thel_, Blake describes a virgin who fails to make the passover, who fails to awaken from the "antenatal dream" and recreate it into a living reality. Terrified by the "little curtain of flesh on the bed of [her] desire," she flies back into her own unborn world, which Blake describes as the "vales of Har." She refuses, that is, to become a body with which to "inuade / The state of life," which Blake describes as Generation and, like Spenser, associates with time. Blake's world of Generation is similar to Newton's "terrestrial matter" and Shelley, following the Newtonian pattern, conceives, in the manner of both Spenser and Blake, of man's descent into "terrestrial matter" as a descent into time, the "envious shadow" of eternity. As a companion piece to *The Book of Thel*, Blake wrote *Tiriel*, which explores the consequences of Thel's failure to act on the basis of her dreamlike desire. The world of innocence has become a spectral form. The loving Father who walked in his garden in the cool of the evening is now embodied in Tiriel, "blind as the orbless skull among the stones." His idiot children, Har and Heva (a parody of Adam and Eve), who spend their time playing with flowers and running after birds, bless his "poor bald pate" and his "hollow winking eyes" when they realize that he is harmless. Thus, by attempting to preserve the security of a negative innocence, Thel has turned the world into a vast graveyard of repressed desire which assumes, in the spectral Tiriel, the shape of an angry, though impotent, god destroying his own creatures in a futile attempt to rejuvenate himself.[3]

The failure of man to carry over into the terrestrial world the latent energy of Saturn's reign produces in *Prometheus Unbound* the rule of Jupiter. Like Blake's Tiriel, Jupiter embodies "those foul shapes, abhorred by god and man," "Strange, savage, ghastly, dark and execrable" (III, iv, 180, 182). And, again like Blake's Tiriel, Jupiter realizes too late that the laws which he upholds and his own perverted wisdom "end together in a curse."[4] Tiriel dies, like Jupiter, the victim of his own law.

Asia, turning from the reign of Saturn to that of Jupiter, makes it clear that Prometheus "gave wisdom, which is strength, to Jupiter" (II, iv, 44). What he did not give, however, is the law embodied in that strength. Asia thus adds: "And with this law alone, 'Let man be free,' / Clothed him with the dominion of wide Heaven."

The law of liberty is of a radically different nature from D'Holbach's law of Necessity which Jupiter's wisdom upholds. In his *Ode to Liberty*, published in 1820 with *Prometheus Unbound*, Shelley identifies liberty with the creative imagination flung forth prophetically in "dim melody" from "enchanted caves" (49–50). Liberty, he suggests, has its source in "man's thought dark in the infant's brain" (55) and in "Art's deathless dreams" (57). Its voice can be heard in the murmur of verse, "a speechless child" (58), and vaguely perceived when "Philosophy did strain / Her lidless eyes" (59–60). Shelley goes on to record the history of liberty as it manifests itself

---

[3]*Poetry and Prose of William Blake*, ed. Keynes, pp. 165, 150, 152.
[4]*Ibid.*, p. 160.

in the waxing and waning of the creative faculty in man and then
ends his ode as his own imagination suddenly withdraws into the
abyss:

> My song, its pinions disarrayed of might,
>   Drooped; o'er it closed the echoes far away
> Of the great voice which did its flight sustain,
>   As waves which lately paved his watery way
> Hiss round a drowner's head in their tempestuous play.

The conflict, then, between Prometheus and Jupiter dramatizes
the psychic struggle in man between a perverse desire to realize a
false security through adjusting to the curse which binds him to the
familiar and terrestrial world and a desire to transcend it through his
imagination. Science itself binds man to terrestrial life if it seeks to
place in fetters the creative imagination. It is therefore significant
that during the age of Jupiter science dominates man's life. Crucial to
the outcome of this struggle is man's attitude to the "antenatal dream,"
which is the Saturnian age. Either he can refuse to wake up, in which
case his passive dreaming will turn to nightmare, or he can in fact
awaken and build a Promethean world, which is the living form of
desire. Prometheus' task during the reign of Jupiter is to awaken the
dreamer. While Jupiter sent "fierce wants" into the "desert hearts"
of men, and "mad disquietudes, and shadows idle / Of unreal good,"
Prometheus "waked the legioned hopes / Which sleep within folded
Elysian flowers," with the result that "the harmonious mind / Poured
itself forth in all-prophetic song" (II, iv, 59–76).

Shelley's most radical break with John Frank Newton in his exploration of the reign of Jupiter is the role which he assigns to Prometheus. In his notes on *Queen Mab* (pp. 826–7) Shelley follows
Newton in making Prometheus a cohort of Jupiter:

Prometheus (who represents the human race) effected some great change
in the condition of his nature, and applied fire to culinary purposes; thus
inventing an expedient for screening from his disgust the horrors of the
shambles. From this moment his vitals were devoured by the vulture of
disease. It consumed his being in every shape of its loathsome and infinite
variety, inducing the soul-quelling sinkings of premature and violent
death. All vice rose from the ruin of healthful innocence.

Shelley's rejection of Prometheus in 1812 was rooted in his view
that man must coalesce with Nature to undertake the work of re-

generation. Prometheus was the enemy of man because he broke with Nature, thereby undertaking the work of degeneration. By 1817, however, Shelley's view of Nature had radically, though not entirely, changed. Nature, he now believed (or partly believed), assumes the form of the mind which perceives it. Man's duty, then, lies not in coalescing with Nature but in coalescing with his psychic power which creates the Nature he perceives. Prometheus did not break with Nature; rather he released in man the power to recreate it into an image of his own divinity. Newton, on the other hand, did not properly understand that his Hindu Zodiac was a psychic vision of reality. Like Bacon and Darwin, he saw in myth simply an imaginative way of interpreting scientific facts. And for him, the scientific facts were his astrological charts recording the cyclic movement of the universe and man which myth dresses out in a parabolical manner.

Shelley, for whom in 1817 Prometheus remained like Satan a "magnificent fiction," as he says in his Preface to the poem (p. 205), never entirely rejected this approach to myth. While too much has been made of the influence of science upon Shelley (he was more a magician than a scientist), he was sufficiently the product of Godwin and the *philosophes* not to doubt, in spite of his *Defence*, the metaphysical validity of man's creative faculty. Professor Frye is therefore quite correct when he writes: "*Prometheus Unbound* comes a little way along Blake's path, but Shelley's imagination plunges upward to burst into a shower of lyrical sparks, hiding the stars an instant with a strange illumination of its own, then fading quickly and leaving us with what Blake calls 'the black incessant sky' once more."[5] What, to be more specific, Shelley leaves with us is Demogorgon's "imageless" truth and his talk of "spells" by which to "reassume / An empire o'er the disentangled doom" (IV, 568–9).

Nevertheless, as his *Ode to Liberty* eloquently testifies, Shelley believed that the sole hope for man lay in the free expression of his creative faculty. In his Preface to *The Revolt of Islam*, he condemns those reactionary literary critics who sought to put that power in fetters. At the same time, however, he realized (in *The Hymn to Intellectual Beauty*, for example) that the creative power which is the basis of "Love, Hope, and Self-esteem" departs and comes like clouds

[5]Northrop Frye, *Fearful Symmetry: A Study of William Blake* (Princeton: Princeton University Press, 1947), p. 305.

"for some uncertain moments lent." Shelley's visionary world built by spasmodic creative power is, as Professor Milton Wilson has amply demonstrated, "pavilioned upon chaos."[6] It must always be remembered for a proper understanding of Shelley, that his Prometheus gave power to Jupiter, and that the universe groaned for three thousand years under the influence of the Promethean curse that followed.

It would appear, therefore, that the transformation of the Prometheus of 1812 to the Prometheus of 1819 is not quite the apocalyptic reversal of roles that one might at first imagine. Shelley implies rather than states that Prometheus imposed upon man a creative responsibility which he cannot altogether assume. Prometheus' brother, Atlas, fought an unsuccessful war against the Olympian gods and was condemned by Zeus to support the heavens on his shoulders for all eternity. Such are the limitations of the creative faculty that mankind, like the poet, cannot for long support the burden of his vision. The "heaven-reflecting sea" in the intervals of inspiration becomes once again the distant, remote and oppressive sky pinnacled in the "envious shadow" (II, iv, 34) of space and time. Atlas, it is worth noting, was once the ruler of Atlantis.

In Asia's account of the reign of Jupiter, she ignores the fact that for three thousand years of his reign Prometheus has remained unregenerate. She ignores, that is, the fact that Jupiter reigns by virtue of Prometheus' curse. Thus she attributes the "famine," "toil," "disease," "strife, wounds, and ghastly death unseen before" to Jove, whereas the Earth in the first act (178–9) attributes these horrors to "the contagion of a mother's hate / Breathed on her child's destroyer." As Professor Wilson points out, Shelley is concerned in the first act with the process of regenerating his hero. Implicit at least in this process is his earlier view of Prometheus who, in his effort to forgive Jupiter, is in fact attempting to forgive himself by freeing his mind of the "awful thoughts" which sweep "obscurely through [his] brain, like shadows dim" (I, 146–7).

In his account of the bound and unregenerate Prometheus, Shelley has in mind Milton's Satan, and in the process of Prometheus' regeneration, he is attempting to create "a more poetical character" than Milton's hero. "Prometheus," he writes in his Preface to *Pro-*

[6]*Shelley's Later Poetry* (New York: Columbia University Press, 1959), pp. 171–206.

metheus Unbound (p. 205), "is, in my judgement, a more poetical character than Satan, because, in addition to courage, and majesty, and firm and patient opposition to omnipotent force, he is susceptible of being described as exempt from the taints of ambition, envy, revenge, and a desire for personal aggrandisement, which, in the Hero of *Paradise Lost*, interfere with the interest."

In the mythological framework of *The Revolt of Islam*, Shelley was also attempting to redeem Satan by describing the fall and resurrection of Lucifer, which, like his Prometheus, serves as a model for man's aspiring nature. Lucifer, it will be recalled, is crowned in the Temple of the Spirit to which Laon and Cythna ascend after meeting a martyr's death. Shelley therefore suggests that so long as man remains on earth the release of his own divine nature is never complete. Man can never fully rid himself of the "contagion of the world's slow stain" (*Adonais*, 356) which binds him as by a curse to the familiar world of tyrants and slaves. Man in *Prometheus Unbound* is in the same predicament. He cannot reach "the loftiest star of unascended heaven, / Pinnacled dim in the intense inane" (III, iv, 202–4). Prometheus, on the other hand, can, like Lucifer, make the ascent to the unfallen form of his own divinity (Lucifer is "the loftiest star").

Prometheus is what man becomes through death, and death itself is the awakening from the dream of life. In this sense, Prometheus is the psychic potential of the dreaming divinity in man. Ultimately to awaken is to die. In *Adonais* the Promethean fire "for which all thirst" finally consumes "the last clouds of cold mortality." The "massy earth and sphered skies are riven" and the poet is "borne darkly, fearfully, afar," beaconed by Lucifer burning "through the inmost veil of Heaven" (486–95).

Concerned as he is with man's earthly redemption, Shelley in *Prometheus Unbound* must stop short of this ultimate form of apocalypse. Here on earth man can become no more than "the mirrors of / The fire for which all thirst" (*Adonais*, 484–5); he must accept a "heaven-reflecting sea" pavilioned as it is on chaos. The recreated universe of the Promethean imagination is a world which mediates between man's mortality and man's divinity. And when the high noon of the imagination is reached ("the sun will rise not until noon") Prometheus is able to rest from his labours ("We shall rest from long labours at noon"—II, iv, 172). He returns, like Lucifer in *The Revolt of Islam*, to the temple of his immortal spirit, leaving behind him a model of ascent and the assurance of continuous intervention on man's behalf.

Like *The Revolt of Islam*, though in a far more complex manner, *Prometheus Unbound* uses the Prometheus-Lucifer myth of man's divinity as a framework within which the mortal struggle is placed. The weakness of Shelley's epic, as he himself recognized, lies in the fact that the mythological framework is in some sense a separate poem. In *Prometheus Unbound*, however, framework and narrative fuse. Because of this fusion, the lyrical drama emerges as Shelley's most successful realization in poetry of the way in which man's diviner nature interpenetrates his mortal being to create out of the flux of time an image of eternity.

This image of eternity is the vision of the last act. It takes place before the cave of Prometheus and Asia where the "echoes of the human world," mingling with the diviner nature of Prometheus and Asia, receive "the gathered rays which are reality." Asia, it will be recalled, has optimistically foretold that "Prometheus shall arise / Henceforth the sun of this rejoicing world" (II, iv, 126–7). In New-ton's Zodiacal myth, the resurrection of fallen man is viewed in terms of Aquarius, the Waterman, arising from the sea with a jug of pure water and a bunch of fruit. Newton is describing the re-emergence of Atlantis from the abyss of ocean which signifies the recovery of the Saturnian world. Shelley (III, iii) is describing man's "lovely apparitions" (49) of Atlantis in the "gathered rays" (53) of love, "dim at first / Then radiant" (49–50) from the "embrace of beauty" (51). The "embrace of beauty" is the reality which, through the imagination, creates its "phantoms" as the "ideal prototype" described in the essay *On Love* creates its "antitype." At the con-clusion of his address to Asia, Prometheus describes these "lovely apparitions" as the shadows "Of all that man becomes, the mediators / Of that best worship, love" (58–9). They are (60–2) the

> swift shapes and sounds, which grow
> More fair and soft as man grows wise and kind,
> And, veil by veil, evil and error fall.

The development of the last act is presented in a series of falling veils. First the "Spectres" of the "dead Hours" pass confusedly by, bearing "Time to his tomb in eternity" (14) as Demogorgon bore Jupiter into the abyss. Then the "Spirits of Air and Earth" draw back "the figured curtain of sleep" (58) where the diviner day, the hour of Prometheus' release, has lain concealed. Finally, "the Spirits of the human mind" (81) whose "eyes are as love which is veilèd not" (92) emerge from the mind "which was late so dusk, and obscene, and blind" (95) and transform it into some bad poetry (96–8):

> an ocean
> Of clear emotion,
> A heaven of serene and mighty motion.

As a result (111–13) "Man's ear and eye" become temples "roofed over sculpture and Poesy." The chorus of the "Spirits of the human mind" thus join the hours of the Promethean day to "weave the web of the mystic measure" (129) which is "as the waves of a thousand streams" rushing "to an ocean of splendour and harmony" (133–4).

The kind of mystical perception which Shelley is here straining to describe is discussed in his notes on *Queen Mab* (p. 825):

Time is our consciousnes of the succession of ideas in our mind. Vivid sensation, of either pain or pleasure, makes the time seem long, as the common phrase is, because it renders us more acutely conscious of our ideas. If a mind be conscious of an hundred ideas during one minute, by the clock, and of two hundred during another, the latter of these spaces would actually occupy so much greater extent in the mind as two exceed one in quantity. If, therefore, the human mind, by any future improvement of its sensibility, should become conscious of an infinite number of ideas in a minute, that minute would be eternity. I do not hence infer that the actual space between the birth and death of a man will ever be prolonged; but that his sensibility is perfectible, and that the number of ideas which his mind is capable of receiving is indefinite.... Perhaps the perishing ephemeron enjoys a longer life than the tortoise.

Shelley's apocalyptic fourth act celebrates the perfection of man's sensibility. Such perfection means "that he is conscious of an infinite number of ideas in a minute" with the result that the minute of perfected consciousness is eternity. Even if this eternal minute is a "perishing ephemeron" (and Shelley clearly states in his *Defence* that it is) the man who has experienced it has enjoyed "a longer life than the tortoise." Shelley returns to this idea of the "perishing ephemeron" in his *Defence*,[7] when he describes the eternity ex-

[7]VII, 136, 137.

perienced by the poet as "the record of the best and happiest moments of the happiest and best minds. . . . always arising unforeseen and departing unbidden, but elevating and delightful beyond all expression." He goes on to say that poetry "arrests the vanishing apparitions which haunt the interlunations of life" by "veiling them, or in language or in form" in order that they may be sent forth among mankind. In themselves, he adds, these "vanishing apparitions" dwell in "the caverns of the spirit" and must therefore be veiled because "there is no portal of expression from the caverns . . . into the universe of things."

These two radical limitations—eternity can be experienced only for a moment and in itself cannot be expressed—manifest themselves in the three movements of the last act which mount, explode, collapse, only to mount again. Finally, as it were, Demogorgon comes to the rescue and calls a halt. He addresses the Earth as the "calm empire of a happy soul," and the Earth replies: "I am as a drop of dew that dies" (523). He addresses the Moon as "beauty, love, calm, harmony" to all living creatures, and the Moon replies: "I am a leaf shaken by thee" (528). He addresses the "happy Dead, whom beams of brightest verse / Are clouds to hide, not colours to portray," and "a Voice from beneath" replies: "we change and pass away" (538). He addresses the "elemental Genii" whose homes are both in man's mind and in the "sullen lead," and "a confused Voice" replies: "thy words waken Oblivion" (543). Finally, he addresses man, warns him of the "disentangled doom," encourages him with "spells" of virtue, but man does not reply. The "deep truth is imageless" and the rest is silence.

Demogorgon thus emerges at the end of the drama either as the voice of Shelley's own scepticism or (as is more likely) the expression of Shelley's acceptance of the limitations of the creative imagination. To say that the "deep truth is imageless" is not to deny the "deep truth"; on the contrary, it is to affirm the Neo-Platonic One. At the same time, however, this affirmation, as will be evident in the examination of *Adonais*, demands the rejection of art. Shelley was finally forced by the dialectic of his own spiritual passion to exile himself from his own republic of art, even as Plato had done. The irony of Plato's *Republic* (and herein lies perhaps the ultimate significance of Socratic irony) is that it rejected the creative mind that produced it.

In the discussion of Plato in the first part of this study of Shelley's apocalyptic vision it was pointed out that Plato affirms the notion that the poet, under the influence of a supernatural possession, achieves a direct perception of ultimate reality. What he rejects is the Dionysian presentation of that reality as the reality itself. Shelley affirms the same idea (though in a different way) when in his *Defence* (VII, 135) he says that when composition begins, "inspiration is already on the decline, and the most glorious poetry that has ever been communicated to the world is probably a feeble shadow of the original conception of the Poet." Shelley was certainly aware of the fact that by the conclusion of the third act of *Prometheus Unbound* all that remained of his original conception was a "feeble shadow." He presumably felt the need, as he says in the *Defence* (VII, 135), to ascend once again "to bring light and fire from those eternal regions where the owl-winged faculty of calculation dare not ever soar."

"There is this difference between a story and a poem," writes Shelley in his *Defence* (VII, 115) "that a story is a catalogue of detached facts, which have no other bond of connexion than time, place, circumstance, cause and effect; the other is the creation of actions according to the unchangeable forms of human nature, as existing in the mind of the Creator, which is itself the image of all other minds." In the third act of *Prometheus Unbound* especially, Shelley was confronted with a "catalogue of detached facts" carried over from the Promethean story, and these facts had to be dealt with in terms of "time, place, circumstance, cause and effect." That he was impatient with the whole business is perhaps evident in the manner in which he removes Jupiter from Heaven and Prometheus from the rock. Demogorgon is brought on to do the former and Hercules to do the latter (though only in a "stage note" to scene iii: "Hercules *unbinds* Prometheus, *who descends*"). What is worse, of course, is that the action is taken out of Prometheus' hands. The Promethean "story" forced the action of the play at its climax to divert radically from the spirit with which Shelley had invested it. Nowhere is this more evident than in Jupiter's lament as he sinks with Demogorgon into the abyss (III, i, 63–9):

> Mercy! mercy!
> No pity, no release, no respite! Oh,
> That thou wouldst make mine enemy my judge,
> Even where he hangs, seared by my long revenge,
> On Caucasus! he would not doom me thus.
> Gentle, and just, and dreadless, is he not
> The monarch of the world?

Much of the action in the first act is concerned with Prometheus' repentance of his curse upon Jupiter. In terms of what actually happens to Jupiter the repentance is meaningless. Shelley, at least in his treatment of Jupiter, falls into the same trap as Milton in *Paradise Lost*. Shelley condemns Milton's idealization of Christian distortions in his presentation of God as an angry and vengeful Jehovah who destroys Satan. But, having rehabilitated Milton's Satan in Prometheus, Shelley then turns around and metes out the same vengeful treatment on Satan's adversary. There is, of course, a dramatic justification for sending Jupiter to Hell even as Jehovah sent Satan to Hell. Demogorgon's wisdom is inscrutable and presumably the manner in which he hurls Jupiter into the abyss is part of the great mystery. Demogorgon's chief function in the play, it would here appear, is to place in fetters Shelley's creative imagination.

Earlier in this chapter another dramatic justification was offered for the manner in which Jupiter is hurled from Heaven: he is the victim of his own wisdom upholding as it does the law of Necessity. In this respect, it was shown that he is like Blake's Tiriel. But the tragedy of Tiriel is that he is never confronted by the positive innocence which could in fact redeem him; he never escapes his own spectre. Blake is writing a scathing parody in the manner of Swift. Shelley's *Prometheus Unbound*, however, belongs in quite a different category. His hero regains the positive innocence of Blake's devils in *The Marriage of Heaven and Hell* and these devils, as is evident in the radical transformation of the angel, have redemptive power. Unlike Blake, Shelley is driven by his Platonic angel to limit the redemptive power of the creative imagination. As a poet, he fights a losing battle with him, especially in the third act. And perhaps for this reason he decided, six months later, to try again.

The second movement of the final act is introduced by Panthea and Ione. The Chorus of Hours and Spirits "break the dance, and scatter the song" (175) and in the pause that follows, Panthea compares their dissolution to a soft cloud vanishing in rain "to the unpavilioned sky" (183). Immediately, however, "new notes arise" which Panthea describes (186–8) as

> the deep music of the rolling world
> Kindling within the strings of the waved air
> Aeolian modulations.

Shelley is now reaching from the mind of man, awakened in the apocalyptic hour, to the "unpavilioned sky" into which all things dissolve as the colours of the spectrum dissolve into the "white radiance of Eternity."

Ione sees a chariot with wheels of "solid clouds, azure and gold" (214) propelled by their own inward power. Within the chariot sits a "wingèd infant" (219) which is of a transcendent whiteness. Its two eyes (IV, 225–30)

> are heavens
> Of liquid darkness, which the Deity
> Within seems pouring, as a storm is poured
> From jaggèd clouds, out of their arrowy lashes,
> Tempering the cold and radiant air around,
> With fire that is not brightness.

In this vision of the moon, which Professor Bloom accurately compares to Ezekiel's vision of the enthroned man,[8] Shelley is attempting to envision the "unpavilioned" world of divinity existing beyond the many-coloured dome of the earth's atmosphere. "Beyond our atmosphere the sun would appear a rayless orb of fire in the midst of a black concave" Shelley writes in his notes on *Queen Mab* (p. 800). Beyond the "cold and radiant air" (229) dwells a "fire that is not brightness" (230). The deity within the chariot of the moon is a "white radiance" which appears as "liquid darkness" (226). In *Adonais* this "white radiance" is the "fire for which all thirst" (485), the Promethean fire that burns "through the inmost veil of Heaven" (493) and guides Keats to "the abode where the Eternal are" (494–5). Shelley's vision of the moon is a beacon fire that propels man towards eternity. He is not, however, concerned to smash the dome of life in his lyrical drama. He is writing an epithalamion celebrating the marriage of Heaven and Earth.

For this reason, in *Prometheus Unbound* Shelley presents a second and complementary vision of Earth which again is influenced by Ezekiel's vision and Newton's prism (IV, 238–43):

> A sphere, which is as many thousand spheres,
> Solid as crystal, yet through all its mass
> Flow, as through empty space, music and light:

[8]Harold Bloom, *Shelley's Mythmaking* (New Haven: Yale University Press, 1959), pp. 231–6.

> Ten thousand orbs involving and involved,
> Purple and azure, white, and green, and golden,
> Sphere within sphere.

Within this sphere the Spirit of the Earth is laid asleep. Panthea says that its lips are moving "like one who talks of what he loves in dream." And Ione replies: " 'Tis only mocking the orb's harmony" (268–9). What the Spirit of the Earth loves in dream is Asia, the "Lamp of Earth." This love, however, mocks the reality of "the orb's harmony" because it waxes and wanes like the cycle of the seasons. The Spirit of the Earth cannot love Asia as Prometheus does. Asia, who in the third act tells the Spirit that he is not yet old enough to love her in the manner of Prometheus, nevertheless makes a promise (III, iv, 86–90):

> And never will we part, till thy chaste sister
> Who guides the frozen and inconstant moon
> Will look on thy more warm and equal light
> Till her heart thaw like flakes of April snow
> And love thee.

The word "till" would seem to suggest that Asia is telling the Spirit of the Earth that his dependence upon her will disappear when he is old enough to marry his sister. The universe in its apocalyptic form will contain within itself the divinity which propels it. In order to bring about this marriage, of course, it was necessary for Shelley to change the Earth from a female to a male. This radical metamorphosis, by way of apology, is Shelley's method of symbolizing the rebirth of the Earth in the last act.

Thus the two complementary visions describe the preparations of the Earth and Moon for their mystical marriage which brings to its climax the second movement. When the wedding nuptials have been erotically celebrated, Panthea declares that once again "the stream of sound has ebbed away" (506).

However, "an universal sound like words" (518) soon replaces it to introduce the third and final movement of the last act. The "mighty Power, which is as darkness" (510), emerges for the third and final time. He rises from the elements and bursts "like eclipse which had been gathered up / Into the pores of sunlight" (513–14). Here, if anywhere, the dome might be smashed; instead, Demogorgon reaffirms the dome in his strident recapitulation of the action. Man must continue to weave the spells of his imagination. This side of the grave the glory of the Titan can be imaged in no other way. Beyond the grave the image will be revealed for what it is: "clouds to hide, not colours to portray" (535). As such, they will "change and pass" (538) like everything else in the phenomenal world. Thus Demogorgon is at once the affirmation and the denial of life on earth. And it is his double-edged perspective that explains the tension that preserves *Prometheus Unbound* from dissolving either into the "original gulf of things" (I, 818) or into the "intense inane" (III, iv, 204).

9

ADONAIS

As an Orphic poet, Shelley could never come to rest in the epic vision of art with its conception of the poet as the unacknowledged legislator of the world. The Orphic apocalypse is intended to free man from the relentless revolutions of the wheel of life by releasing the buried divinity within him. The anagogical vision in the concluding stanzas of *Adonais* presents this final transcendence and, as such, brings to completion Shelley's apocalyptic career. After *Adonais*, Shelley filled out his "sad duration" as "the unwilling sport / Of circumstance and passion" (*Q.M.*, I, 151–2) by attempting to write occasional verse. As a man, he remained in some sense attracted to life, but as an Orphic poet, he was repelled. Shelley committed psychic suicide in *Adonais*, with the result that "what still is dear / Attracts to crush, repels to make [him] wither" (473–4). In his last poem, *The Triumph of Life*, he sees life as a vast graveyard in which he is still forced to "keep / With phantoms an unprofitable strife." Those who live are "like corpses in a charnel," preyed upon by "cold hopes" which "swam like worms within our living clay" (*Adonais* 345–51).

The anagogical dimension of *Adonais* provides the focus of the entire poem. It is the energizing principle which compels the poet to press on towards the object of knowledge as distinct from the mythical account which defines the limits of his art. Shelley's goal is the "deep truth" which is "imageless." The dialectic of sacred passion drives the poet, as it drives Dante in the *Paradiso*, beyond imagery to its primal source.

If Plato's *Symposium* provides the model for Shelley's ascent in *Adonais*, then Dante's *Convivio* provides the commentary of ascent in terms of which Shelley was able to structure his vision into what he himself described as a "highly wrought *piece of art*."[1] Specifically, in his description of his elegy, Shelley had in mind Dante's discussion of the four levels of meaning in the second tractate of the *Convivio*, which he studied in 1821, translating the last *canzone* of the fourth tractate and including it in his Advertisement to *Epipsychidion*. It is with reference to Dante's discussion of the four levels that *Adonais* will be examined.

Dante in the *Convivio* distinguishes between the literal, allegorical, moral, and anagogical levels of his own vision. His discussion is neatly summarized in his letter to Can Grande Della Scala, and for this reason it is worth quoting. "For the clarity of what is to be said," he writes,

one must realize that the meaning of this work [*The Divine Comedy*] is not simple, but rather is to be called polysemous, that is, having many meanings. The first meaning is the one obtained through the letter; the second is the one obtained through the thing signified by the letter. The first is called literal, the second allegorical or moral or anagogical. In order that this manner of treatment may appear more clearly, it may be applied to the following verses: "When Israel went out of Egypt, the house of Jacob from a people of strange language, Judah was his sanctuary and Israel his dominion." For if we look to the letter alone, the departure of the children of Israel from Egypt in the time of Moses is indicated to us; if to the allegory, our redemption accomplished by Christ is indicated to us; if to the moral sense, the conversion of the soul from the woe and misery of sin to a state of grace is indicated to us; if to the anagogical sense, the departure of the consecrated soul from the slavery of this corruption to the liberty of eternal glory is indicated. And though these mystic senses may be called by various names, they can generally be spoken of as allegorical, since they are diverse from the literal or the historical.[2]

On the literal or historical level, *Adonais* concerns the death of John Keats as a result of the vicious attack made upon his *Endymion*

---

[1] X, 270 (letter to John and Maria Gisborne, June 5, 1821).
[2] As quoted in Allan H. Gilbert, *Literary Criticism: Plato to Dryden* (New York: American Book Co., 1940), pp. 202–3.

in the *Quarterly Review*; on the allegorical level, the poem concerns the plight of the visionary in a society controlled by tyrannical forces; on the moral level, it concerns the release of the soul from the corruptions of earthly existence; on the anagogical level, it concerns, to use Dante's words, "the departure of the consecrated soul from the slavery of this corruption to the liberty of eternal glory." The first two levels, the literal and allegorical, are presented within the framework of the myth of the dying and rising vegetation god, Adonis; the last two levels, the moral and anagogical, move beyond the myth of Adonis and find their archetype in Adonai, the Hebrew Lord revealed in, though transcending, His creation. Professor Wasserman has pointed out the significance of the amalgamation of the two words in the title of the poem, and Professor Foakes has noted the dropping of the Adonis myth in the last section of the elegy (stanzas 38–55).[3]

Unlike Dante, Shelley in *Adonais* radically opposes the literal and allegorical to the moral and anagogical dimensions of his poem. Following the characteristic late mediaeval Aristotelian approach to Christianity, Dante places great emphasis upon the literal meaning of his own art. He argues that the literal level is "that sense in the expression of which the others are all included, and without which it would be impossible and irrational to give attention to the other meanings, and most of all to the allegorical."[4] Drawing an analogy from Aristotle's *Physics*, he argues that the literal level may be considered as the matter, while the other levels may be considered as the form. Unless the matter is properly set forth, it will be impossible either to impose a form upon it or to interpret its meaning. Dante, in other words, does not oppose matter and form; rather he sees form arising out of matter, rendering explicit the potential inherent in it. At the end of the *Paradiso*, therefore, he is not left suspended in an "intense inane"; on the contrary, he is able to return to this world, his sense purified and sanctified, and see in earthly love the emblem of God's Grace.

As an Orphic poet, Shelley in *Adonais* opposes flesh to spirit by

³Earl R. Wasserman, "Adonais" in *The Subtler Language* (Baltimore: The Johns Hopkins University Press, 1959), pp. 311–13; R. A. Foakes, *The Romantic Assertion: A Study of the Language of Nineteenth Century Poetry* (London: Methuen & Co., 1958), p. 102.

⁴Dante Alighieri, *Convivio*, trans. W. W. Jackson (Oxford: Clarendon Press, 1909), p. 74.

asserting that the annihilation of flesh is necessary to the release of spirit. Viewed within the framework of spirit, man on earth confronts "invulnerable nothings" (348). The literal level of *Adonais*, therefore, is a vision of the death of Keats seen as the cessation of matter in a state of motion. The literal level finds its source in D'Holbach's materialism, which Shelley with his anagogical focus in mind rejects as sensory delusion.

On the literal level, therefore, Shelley presents a picture similar in many respects to the daemonic vision of *Alastor*. In that poem he relates his own fear of sudden extinction to what he considers the slow and withering decay of Wordsworth's powers. Confronted with the dismal spectacle of Wordsworth's ruin as he sees it revealed in *The Excursion*, Shelley is partially consoled: sudden death is preferable to the fate of those who, as he says in his Preface (p. 15) "prepare for their old age a miserable grave." This same consolation is offered to Keats in *Adonais* (356–60), and in images that echo the earlier *Alastor*:

> From the contagion of the world's slow stain
> He is secure, and now can never mourn
> A heart grown cold, a head grown gray in vain;
> Nor, when the spirit's self has ceased to burn,
> With sparkless ashes load an unlamented urn.

In *Alastor*, the entire daemonic vision comes to a climax in the poet's passive submission to that "colossal Skeleton" that rules "this frail world" with "devastating omnipotence" (611–14). And this same imagistic focus defines the literal level of *Adonais*. Keats has been led to "that high Capital, where kingly Death / Keeps his pale court in beauty and decay" (55–6). He is the victim of that "invisible Corruption" (67) drawn over the curtain of flesh. Shelley describes him as he describes the dead poet in *Alastor*: the "silent, cold, and motionless" (661) form of one "yet safe from the worm's outrage" (702).

Within the materialistic framework of the first seventeen stanzas of *Adonais*, Shelley accepts the fact that there is nothing to mourn in the death of Keats. He is the victim of "the law / Of change" (71–2); "Death feeds on his mute voice, and laughs at our despair" (27). And here again, his fate is similar to that of the poet in *Alastor* over whose death "no lorn bard / Breathed ... one melodious sigh"

(58–9). Yet Keats, unlike the poet in *Alastor*, has "moulded into thought" (118) his own desires and aspirations. They have, therefore, a legitimate cause for grief; cut off from their source in the physical activity of the brain, they must perish like sheep deserted by the shepherd. And Nature also can mourn the passing of that beauty with which Keats has invested her. Unlike Keats's "Desires and Adorations" (108), however, Nature can survive his passing. Thus Shelley, in the opening stanzas of the second section of his elegy (stanzas 18–37) ironically sets the rebirth of Nature over against the death of Keats. Nature's lament becomes a mock despair. Shelley suggests this by comparing Keats's "fading melodies" to "flowers that mock the corse beneath" (16–17).

When Shelley turns from his contemplation of Keats's annihilation to his attack upon the critics whom he considered responsible, he is forced by the logic of his first hypothesis to recognize that they acted according to the law of Necessity. To condemn them for their murderous action in the *Quarterly Review* is futile. Shelley can no more condemn the critics who murdered Keats than mourn his death. Although their "wings rain contagion" (248), the poison is not something alien to life; rather it is the "contagion of the world's slow stain" (356) to which all men, including critics, must succumb. In the final section of the poem, the critics become an emblem of life itself, a symbol of the human condition to which all men are bound as by a curse.

On the literal level Shelley recreates in *Adonais* his own earlier materialism derived primarily from D'Holbach. From this literal level, he moves on to the allegorical in which he makes use of the myth of a dying and rising god. While the allegorical dimension allows him to view Keats less as a mortal and more as a poet, Shelley is still bound by the very character of his myth to the eternal cycle of Nature. The second movement of the elegy focuses on rebirth, just as the first movement focuses upon death. Both death and rebirth, however, belong within the fallen order of Nature, within the framework of Necessity. For this reason, the second movement is set within the pattern of the first and provides no real advance; there is as yet no principle of transcendence in operation. The first two movements of *Adonais*, which partially recreate the vision of *Alastor*, simply serve to purge "from our inward sight the film of familiarity which obscures from us the wonder of our being."[5] The third movement reveals that wonder, which is the "divinity in Man" released from the law of Necessity.

On the allegorical level Keats is identified with Adonis, the dying and rising vegetation god of Greek mythology. In the Greek myth, Adonis is a comely youth beloved by Aphrodite. In his infancy, Aphrodite hides him from Ares, his jealous rival, in a chest which she entrusts to Proserpine, Queen of Hades. When Proserpine opens the chest and gazes upon the infant, she is so enamoured of his beauty that she refuses to return him to Aphrodite. The dispute between the two goddesses over who should possess the child is finally decided by Zeus, who decrees that he will dwell with Proserpine for one part of the year and with Aphrodite for the other part.

The joint possession of Adonis by Proserpine and Aphrodite is dramatized in the myth by presenting Adonis as a youthful and eager hunter. Aphrodite, fearing that he will be killed, attempts to persuade him to give up hunting. One day, however, when Aphrodite is absent, presiding over ceremonies in her honour, Adonis returns to the hunt and is mortally wounded by his jealous rival, Ares, who has disguised himself as a wild boar. When Aphrodite is informed of what has happened, she hastens to his side in a futile effort to revive him. Her tears mix with his blood and from that mixture the rich profusion of vegetable life emerges. Thus, the return of Adonis to Proserpine contains in the rebirth of Nature the promise of his resurrection and reunion with Aphrodite.

In Bion's *Lament for Adonis*,[6] which was Shelley's immediate source, all the elements of the myth are present. At the death of Adonis, Aphrodite laments that he must return to Proserpine (or Persephone): "Take thou my husband, Persephone, for thou art mightier far than I, and all that is fair comes down to thee; while I am hapless utterly, a prey to sorrow unassuaged, and weep for my Adonis who is dead, and I fear thee" (52–6). From her tears mixed with Adonis' blood flowers come forth: "As fast from the Paphian flow tears as from Adonis blood, and both on the ground are turned to flowers; of the blood are roses born, and of the tears anemones"

---

[5]*A Defence of Poetry*, VII, 137.
[6]The quotations that follow are taken from *The Greek Bucolic Poets*, trans., with notes, by A. S. P. Gow (Cambridge: Cambridge University Press, 1933).

(63–5). Finally, the cyclic recurrence of death and resurrection is implied in the last lines: "Cease thy laments to-day, Cytherea; stay thy dirges. Again must thou lament, again must thou weep another year" (97–8).

On the allegorical level, Shelley makes use of Bion's poem. After calling upon Urania (Bion's Aphrodite) to leave her Paradise and weep for Adonais who is dead, he then tells her to quench her "fiery tears" (22). Adonais has returned to Proserpine ("the amorous Deep") "where all things wise and fair / Descend" (24–5). Nevertheless, Urania leaves her "secret Paradise" and laments over the corpse of Adonais (235–43):

> "O gentle child, beautiful as thou wert,
> Why didst thou leave the trodden paths of men
> Too soon, and with weak hands though mighty heart
> Dare the unpastured dragon in his den?
> Defenceless as thou wert, oh, where was then
> Wisdom the mirrowed shield, or scorn the spear?
> Or hadst thou waited the full cycle, when
> Thy spirit should have filled its crescent sphere,
> The monsters of life's waste had fled from thee like deer."

At this point, however, the allegory breaks off. Shelley does not go on to describe the resurrection of Adonais in terms of his reunion with Urania. And the reason is evident in Urania's lament (232–4):

> "I would give
> All that I am to be as thou now art!
> But I am chained to Time, and cannot thence depart!"

Bion's Adonis has become Shelley's Adonais, the "divinity in Man" released from the cyclic pattern of Nature.

Within the allegorical framework of the Adonis myth, Shelley describes the fate of the visionary in a hostile society. In the lament of Urania, he argues that had Keats been strong enough to survive the review in the *Quarterly Review*, he might have completed his cycle and filled his "crescent sphere" (242). The cyclic imagery, however, contains within it the suggestion of futility. Shelley argues that Keats's survival depended upon his ability to arm himself with the shield of wisdom and the spear of scorn and join forces with the enemies of tyranny. He would have to "dare the unpastured dragon in his den." Implicit in this battle is the fear that the poet who fights back, as Prometheus fought back, may himself become the victim of his own wrath. This was Prometheus' fate in the first act of *Prometheus Unbound*, and Shelley was unable adequately to resolve it in the third. The central incongruity in the drama lies in Shelley's vision of love, on the one hand, and the awful judgment upon Jupiter, on the other. Jupiter in *Prometheus Unbound* is not redeemed, and, to that extent at least, Prometheus' recreative power is limited. The most obvious evidence of that limitation is the fact that Prometheus' imaginative achievement belongs within the cycle of Nature. Necessity must reassert itself. Eternity, "Mother of many acts and hours," has an "infirm hand" (IV, 565–6); Jupiter must inevitably rise again.

In Urania's dubious hope that Adonais, had he lived, might have armed himself to deal with society, Shelley had Byron in mind. Byron is the "Pythian of the age" (250) from whom the critics fled when he loosed in *English Bards and Scotch Reviewers* one spear of scorn upon them. Shelley wrote to Byron after receiving the news of Keats's death telling him of the devastating effect of the criticism of *Endymion* upon Keats's mind. On April 26, 1821, Byron replied:

I am very sorry to hear what you say of Keats—is it *actually* true? I did not think criticism had been so killing. Though I differ from you essentially in your estimate of his performances, I so much abhor all unnecessary pain, that I would rather he had been seated on the highest peak of Parnassus than have perished in such a manner. . . . I read the review of "Endymion" in the *Quarterly*. It was severe,—but surely not so severe as many reviews in that and other journals upon others.

I recollect the effect upon me of the *Edinburgh* on my first poem; it was rage, and resistance, and redress—but not despondency nor despair. I grant that those are not amiable feelings; but, in this world of bustle and broil, and especially in the career of writing, a man should calculate his powers of *resistance* before he goes into the arena.[7]

Shelley could not whole-heartedly accept this attitude. While it allowed Byron the strength to deal with a corrupt society, he had paid severely for it in the sacrifice of his own idealism. In his conversational poem, *Julian and Maddalo*, Shelley, under a thin disguise of fiction, vividly describes the nature of his quarrel with Byron. Byron, in the guise of Maddalo, argues that man's destiny is the grave, which mocks all of his immortal longings. Shelley, in the guise of Julian, argues

[7]As quoted in X, 254n.

that the divine and eternal aspirations of the human mind are not a delusion. Man can only be chained to Necessity by the permission of his will. Should the will be strengthened, then man could be in deed what he is in desire. Maddalo answers that Julian talks Utopia and to prove it invites him to visit a madman locked in an asylum. They visit him the next day and Julian is submitted to the incoherent mumblings of the pathetic creature who has been driven mad by his unfaithful mistress. Julian, however, is not convinced; on the contrary, he sees in the ravings of the maniac the chaos of high poetry which, could he find some entrance into "the caverns of his mind" (573) might be reassembled into a genuine poetic vision. His ravings are the daemonic parody of apocalypse.

Shelley's optimism concerning the potential inherent in the incoherent monologue of the emotionally diseased figure finds its counterpart in his hopes for Keats's future. In November, 1820 (X, 218), several months after the event, he described Keats's reception of the criticism of *Endymion* in a letter to the Editor of the *Quarterly Review*: "The first effects are described to me to have resembled insanity, and it was by assiduous watching that he was restrained from effecting purposes of suicide. The agony of his sufferings at length produced the rupture of a blood-vessel in the lungs, and the usual process of consumption appears to have begun." At the time this news reached Shelley, he believed that if he could see Keats he would be able to help him. He had himself been driven close to insanity in 1814 and during the crisis over Mary Godwin had been driven to attempt suicide. More than that, in 1815 he had been told by his physician that he had not long to live. Out of that despair had emerged *Alastor*, in which the wretched wanderings of the poet parallel in a very real sense the wanderings of Keats's poet in *Endymion*. Moved by the memory of these experiences, Shelley wrote to Keats on July 27, 1820, asking him to come and stay near him in Pisa. After issuing his invitation, he continued:

I have lately read your "Endymion" again and ever with a new sense of the treasures of poetry it contains, though treasures poured forth with indistinct profusion. This, people in general will not endure, and that is the cause of the comparatively few copies which have been sold. I feel persuaded that you are capable of the greatest things, so you but will. I always tell Ollier to send you copies of my books.—"Prometheus Unbound" I imagine you will receive nearly at the same time with this letter. [X, 194]

But the death of Keats defeated Shelley's hopes, and in that defeat the words which he had attributed to Byron in *Julian and Maddalo* (120–30) must have come home to him with peculiar impact. Maddalo is moralizing upon the vesper bells ringing from the tower of an asylum:

> "And such,"—he cried, "is our mortality,
> And this must be the emblem and the sign
> Of what should be eternal and divine!—
> And like that black and dreary bell, the soul,
> Hung in a heaven-illumined tower, must toll
> Our thoughts and our desires to meet below
> Round the rent heart and pray—as madmen do
> For what? they know not,—till the night of death
> As sunset that strange vision, severeth
> Our memory from itself, and us from all
> We sought, and yet were baffled."

The impact of Keats's death upon Shelley is explained by his close identification with Keats as a poet. He believed that only Keats and himself among all the Romantics had remained faithful to the pursuit of the ideal. In sending Keats copies of his own poems and in inviting him to Pisa, he hoped that they might support each other in their arduous task. Shelley had attempted to follow in the path of Byron, but he found it temperamentally impossible to develop within himself a defensive satirical scorn for society. He remained, in some sense, as vulnerable as he believed Keats to be. Thus, in his self-portrait in *Adonais*, there is no evidence of the Promethean poet. Instead, there is a vision of the poet "who in another's fate now wept his own" (300). Shelley describes Keats as "a pale flower" (48), its "petals nipped before they blew" (52), and he uses the same image to describe himself: "the withering flower" on which "the killing sun smiles brightly" (286–7). His "power," like Keats's, is "girt round with weakness" (281–2). Instead of the spear of scorn, he carries, again like Keats, " a light spear topped with a cypress cone" (291). As an Orphic poet, he carries the Dionysian thyrsus, thus finding his archetype in the peace-loving Orpheus whose music had the power to tame the wildest beasts. Nevertheless, Shelley remains, as Keats had remained, the victim of "the herded wolves" and "the obscene ravens" (244–5). He believes that his Promethean power has failed him.

And for this reason, Shelley returns (274–9) to that early daemonic
image of himself which he presented in *Alastor*:

> he, as I guess,
> Had gazed on Nature's naked loveliness,
> Actaeon-like, and now he fled astray
> With feeble steps o'er the world's wilderness,
> And his own thoughts, along that rugged way,
> Pursued, like raging hounds, their father and their prey.

Shelley's refusal to contain his vision within the myth of a dying
and rising god, the myth either implicit or explicit in his Promethean
poetry, only partly derives from the gnawing sense of his own failure
as an apocalyptic poet. Ultimately, it derives from his growing awareness of the limitations of all art. Four months before composing
Adonais, he wrote his impassioned *Defence of Poetry* in which he
describes that single cyclic poem built up since the beginning of the
world. The poet, he argues, is inspired by "the interpenetration of a
diviner nature" through his own, and as such participates in the
"eternal, the infinite, and the one" (VII, 112). The poet, released
from the bondage of time, dwells in eternity, offering to men the vision
upon which all civilization rests. The *Defence* is a justification of
Promethean art in which the poets emerge as "the unacknowledged
legislators of the world" (VII, 140). Shelley planned to continue his
Defence by applying his principles to the actual achievement of
contemporary poets. This second part, however, was never written.
Instead he turned to the composition of *Adonais*, which provides an
explanation for the abandonment of his earlier plan.

At first glance it appears impossible that the Urania of *Adonais*
who is "chained to Time" (234) is Shelley's "mistress Urania" in
whose honour he told Peacock he wrote *A Defence of Poetry*.[8] Professor Wasserman in his analysis of the elegy argues that she is not.
Carefully distinguishing between the "quickening life" which springs
out of matter (stanza 19) and the "plastic stress" of the one Spirit
which descends into matter (stanza 43), Wasserman goes on to separate
Urania and the poet by identifying Urania with the former and the
poet with the latter.[9] This distinction is reinforced when Shelley in
the third section of his elegy describes Keats as having returned to

[8]In a letter dated Feb. 15, 1821, X, 234.
[9]*The Subtler Language*, p. 331.

that power "which wields the world with never-wearied love, / Sustains it from beneath, and kindles it above" (377–8). Keats has returned to the power which kindles life "above"; Urania remains sustaining it "from beneath." Urania, in other words, is the poet's shaping spirit of imagination which, like the "quickening life," must spring out of the world of the senses and shape it into an image of the "divinity in Man." Urania creates the vision of apocalypse, but not the apocalypse itself. She is the myth-making power in the poet which constructs the "probable account" of the poet's object. Shelley, therefore, accurately identifies her with Bion's Aphrodite who must share her beloved Adonis with Proserpine, the goddess of Hades. To pursue Urania is to be half in love with death, as Keats recognizes in his *Ode to a Nightingale.*

Because Shelley is preoccupied with the Promethean vision of art in his *Defence of Poetry*, he does not bring into focus the anagogical dimension of his vision. He describes the poet in terms of Urania, which is to say, in terms of his earthly mission as a recreator of the universe. At the same time, however, he clearly anticipates the anagogic when he draws a careful distinction between the poet's "original conceptions" and his actual productions. "But when composition begins," he writes, "inspiration is already on the decline, and the most glorious poetry that has ever been communicated to the world is probably a feeble shadow of the original conception of the Poet" (VII, 135). Urania is not the poet's conception; she is the poet's fading creativity which, out of that conception, constructs a "feeble shadow." She is, in other words, the "awful shadow of some unseen power" which waxes and wanes in accordance with Nature's mutability. She exists only within the myth of Adonis, and when Shelley abandons the myth, Urania disappears.

One possible reason, therefore, for Shelley's failure to compose the second part of his *Defence* is that he had watched in his own lifetime the waning of creative power among his favourite living poets. He could not, as a result, put to the test his faith in the apocalyptic power of his contemporaries. The best he could do, when confronted by the actual texts, was to recreate the vision of *Alastor* to include not only Wordsworth, but Coleridge and Southey as well. And this, of course, is precisely what Shelley does do in the first two sections of *Adonais*. Urania is deserted; in Keats, her "youngest, dearest one, has perished" (46), and there is no one left to invoke her. All that is left to her is to curse those who robbed her of her prize.

It may therefore be concluded that the Urania of *A Defence of Poetry* is the same Urania who laments the death of Keats in *Adonais*. The change is not in Urania; it is in Shelley, who, in *Adonais*, views her within an anagogical perspective. Shelley, it may be said, abandoned Urania for Proserpine believing that in and through her the object of his quest was to be ·found. To move from the vision of apocalypse to the apocalypse itself, it is necessary to descend first to the daemonic. The path which Shelley follows in *Adonais* is the path of Dante in *The Divine Comedy*; he descends into the Hell of material annihilation that he may truly rise into the "white radiance of Eternity" (463). Those who remain with Urania, playing with lovely images, ultimately delude themselves.

The moral dimension of Shelley's elegy, therefore, concerns itself with the release of the soul from the "contagion of the world's slow stain" (356). Shelley has anticipated this moral level from the outset. His allusions to Urania have all been ironic. In calling upon her to weep for Adonais, he points out the futility of her tears. In calling upon her to weep again as she had earlier wept for Milton, he points out that Milton "went, unterrified, / Into the gulf of death" (34–5). As for those who yet live, they tread "the thorny road" of "toil and hate" (44–5), even as Urania treads it. At the same time, however, those poets who, like Milton, are willing to follow this path find their reward in "Fame's serene abode" (45). Urania, on the other hand, within her "secret Paradise" (208) sits with "veilèd eyes" rekindling "fading melodies" surrounded by "listening Echoes" (12–15). Like a mistress grown old with time, her only consolation is the memory of her former glory (226–30): ·

> "Stay yet awhile! speak to me once again;
> Kiss me, so long but as a kiss may live;
> And in my heartless breast and burning brain
> That word, that kiss, shall all thoughts else survive,
> With food of saddest memory kept alive."

The real crisis, which defines the transition from the allegorical to the moral dimension of the elegy, comes when Shelley in his self-portrait exposes his branded brow which, he says, is "like Cain's or Christ's" (306). The radical ambiguity evident in placing Christ and Cain side by side as prototypes of himself as poet reveals Shelley's increasing misgivings about the nature of his own poetic power. These misgivings may have been further clarified by his reading of Byron's *Cain, A Mystery*, conceived partly under Shelley's influence,[10] and executed during the summer shortly after Shelley completed *Adonais*. Shelley considered the poem "a revelation not before communicated to man";[11] it is therefore worth examining for the possible light which it casts upon Shelley's somewhat Byronic identification with Cain in *Adonais*.

In Byron's vision, Cain, like Shelley's Prometheus, rebels against the Jehovah-Jupiter conception of God. Guided by Lucifer (Shelley's archetypal hero) he journeys into a pre-Adamite underworld and into an empyrean beyond the sun and moon. As the journey unfolds, Lucifer suggests to Cain that death may hold the key to the deepest mysteries which perplex man in his earthly state. Instead, however, of leading Cain to smash the "dome of many-coloured glass" to find the "white radiance of Eternity," Lucifer's suggestion leads him to return to the world and murder his brother, Abel. The murder of Abel vividly (and ironically) dramatizes the rejection of the familiar world in favour of an ideal world beyond the limits of man's mortality.

[10]In a letter to Horace Smith (April 11, 1822) Shelley writes (X, 377–8): "Amongst other things, however, Moore, after giving Lord B. much good advice about public opinion, etc., seems to deprecate MY influence on his mind, on the subject of religion, and to attribute the tone assumed in 'Cain' to my suggestions. Moore cautions him against my influence on this particular, with the most friendly zeal; and it is plain that his motive springs from a desire of benefiting Lord B., without degrading me. I think you know Moore. Pray assure him that I have not the smallest influence over Lord Byron, in this particular, and if I had, I certainly should employ it to eradicate from his great mind the delusions of Christianity, which, in spite of his reason, seem perpetually to recur, and to lay in ambush for the hours of sickness and distress. 'Cain' was *conceived* many years ago, and begun before I saw him last year at Ravenna. How happy should I not be to attribute to myself, however indirectly, any participation in that immortal work!"
In spite of Shelley's assertion that he had no influence upon Byron, it is evident that it is Shelley's view of Christianity that governs many of the speeches of Byron's Cain. Shelley admits to a knowledge of the conception of the poem "many years ago" and, in admitting that he would be happy *not* to be in any sense identified with it, he may be referring to the daemonic light which Byron's poem casts upon his own Promethean vision. Such an interpretation of the last sentence in the above passage would certainly help to explain the significance of the extraordinary juxta-position of Christ and Cain as prototypes of himself as a Dionysian poet in *Adonais*.
[11]In a letter to John Gisborne, Jan. 26, 1822, X, 354.

While Shelley in his letter to Gisborne did not define the precise nature of the "revelation" which the poem offered (beyond describing it as "apocalyptic"), he probably recognized, as indeed Byron likely intended that he should, some mark of identity with Cain and gained from it a richer insight into the daemonic aspect of his own apocalyptic vision which was destined to bear fruit in *The Triumph of Life*. The release of Prometheus required the destruction of Jupiter, even as Cain's vision in Byron's poem required the murder of Abel. The underside of Shelley's apocalyptic vision was the complete destruction of human society in its present form as exemplified in the passive submission of Byron's Abel to the vengeful Jehovah. Byron, unwilling, for example, to expose his natural child to the influence of the Shelley household, was keenly aware of the danger of Shelley's "atheism," especially when it was lost to sight in the clouds of his soaring idealism. In *Adonais* Shelley questions whether he bears the wounds of the suffering Christ or the mark of the accursed Cain. By rounding his first two movements with the curse of Cain which leads him directly to the question, Shelley, consciously or unconsciously, arrives at the impasse which he faced with Prometheus in the third act of his drama. In *Prometheus Unbound* he was unable to resolve it; he allowed Prometheus both to repent his curse and see it fulfilled.

In *Adonais*, however, Shelley is concerned neither to repent the curse on society as embodied in Urania and the critics nor to enjoy the imaginative benefits of seeing it fulfilled. So far as any earthly redemption is concerned he seems to have succumbed to Prometheus' tempter and affirmed that good and the means to good are incompatible. He turns what in Byron's vision amounts to a metaphysical explanation of murder into a metaphysical defence of self-murder. The moral dimension of the elegy resides in a metaphysical defence of suicide (415–23):

> Oh, come forth,
> Fond wretch! and know thyself and him aright.
> Clasp with thy panting soul the pendulous Earth;
> As from a centre, dart thy spirit's light
> Beyond all worlds, until its spacious might
> Satiate the void circumference: then shrink
> Even to a point within our day and night;
> And keep thy heart light lest it make thee sink
> When hope has kindled hope, and lured thee to the brink.

In *Adonais*, Shelley has been lured "to the brink" first by his rejection of materialism, which conducts to annihilation, and then by his rejection of mutability, which traps the poet within the limits of Nature. Beyond both is the "void circumference," which is the realm of pure mind revolving in its own divinity. It is the poet's "ideal prototype" partially discovered in the creation of its "antitype." The "antitype," however, is nothing more than an image shaped by the imagination out of the sensory data offered to the mind. It is the distorting mirror in which the "divinity in Man" first recognizes itself; it cannot, however, truly know itself by gazing upon its own mirror image. Thus, in the stanza quoted above, the divinity within Shelley calls upon the poet to "come forth" from the mirror world of images and know himself "aright." He must dart his spirit beyond the range of his own shaping power, which is the range of Urania, until "its spacious might / Satiate the void circumference." Confronted by this vast abyss, which to the physical eye is nothingness, the heart, so long dependent upon the senses to guide its promptings, must remain detached, lest it sink back into that "pendulous earth" which it is now called upon to abandon. Shelley is describing the suicidal moment seen, not as defeat, but as victory. Death is the awakening to life, to that ultimate self-knowledge which is the goal of Eros and the purpose of the Orphic purification rites. In his own moral defence, Shelley could argue that in his apocalyptic vision he reveals his own "metaphysical anatomy."[12] Within the womb of Urania, which is the womb of time, it takes shape. He is now ready to leave the womb of his "melancholy Mother" (20), sever the umbilical cord that attaches him to the mythological vision of Necessity, and find his proper abode in the kingdom of pure mind. Viewed from within the womb of Urania, the reality of death, which is the awakening to life, cannot be perceived. So long as Shelley functions within that illusory world, his theme in *Adonais* is despair. Once, however, he rids himself of that illusion, he is able completely to reverse his perspective and see not only himself but the universe aright (343–8).

> Peace, peace! he is not dead, he doth not sleep—
> He hath awakened from the dream of life—
> 'Tis we, who lost in stormy visions, keep

---

[12]Mrs. Shelley's Preface to 1839 edition of Shelley's poems (*Poetical Works*, p. x).

> With phantoms an unprofitable strife,
> And in mad trance, strike with our spirit's knife
> Invulnerable nothings.

It is the absence of this apocalyptic awakening from "the dream of life" that largely limits the earlier vision of *Alastor* to the first two movements of *Adonais*. *Alastor* presents, however ambiguously, the triumph of Necessity; *Adonais* presents, however ambiguously, the triumph over Necessity. Viewed within the anagogical perspective of *Adonais*, the poet's vision of the ideal in *Alastor* is indeed a "mad trance" in which the poet struggles with what D'Holbach himself declared to be mere "phantoms," mere "invulnerable nothings." Shelley, striving in *Alastor* to break free of the rational grip of the mechanistic philosophy by exploring the realm of his imagination, presents an image of the poet whose vision, like Rousseau's vision of Iris in *The Triumph of Life*, has turned into a nightmare. Thus, the passion quickened by the poet's vision of the "veilèd maid" (151) is "like the fierce fiend of a distempered dream" (225). The passion burns in his breast like the poison of a "green serpent" (228). It is to this image of the poet that Shelley returns at the end of his career. Indeed, Shelley's portrayal of himself in *Adonais* as one crushed and repelled by that which attracts him is precisely the image which he constructs of the poet in *Alastor*. With this difference, however: Shelley in *Adonais* views the poet in *Alastor* with the ironic detachment of one who has worked out an affirmative answer to the question that obsesses the poet who found an "untimely tomb" (50):

> Does the dark gate of death
> Conduct to thy mysterious paradise,
> Oh sleep? Does the bright arch of rainbow clouds,
> And pendent mountains seen in the calm lake,
> Lead only to a black and watery depth,
> While death's blue vault, with loathiest vapours hung,
> Where every shade which the foul grave exhales
> Hides its dead eye from the detested day,
> Conducts, O Sleep, to thy delightful realms?[13]

Attached to the power which "kindles from above" (378), Shelley

---

[13]*Alastor* (211–19). Shelley in this elegaic poem reveals a dissatisfaction with a mechanistic philosophy for which he had not as yet found a substitute. The poem is perhaps best understood when read in the light of *Adonais*, the first two movements of which recreate its vision.

is able in the last section of *Adonais* to view with new understanding its modification in that which "sustains it from beneath." So long as "the many" which "change and pass" can be viewed in the anagogical focus of "the One" which "remains" (460), Shelley can rejoice in the evidence of his own and Keats's spirit in the infinite variety of Nature's music. Both poets have for a time coalesced with Nature's' "plastic stress" (381), though neither poet when thus immersed can properly grasp the divine reality, the "ideal prototype," behind what was being shaped.

In his *Defence of Poetry* (VII, 136), Shelley writes: "This instinct and intuition of the poetical faculty is still more observable in the plastic and pictorial arts; a great statue or picture grows under the power of the artist as a child in the mother's womb; and the very mind which directs the hands in formation is incapable of accounting to itself for the origin, the graduations, or the media of the process." What is being shaped by the artist is the image of his own divinity, of which, until he confronts that image, he remains unaware. But once he is aware, the image as such no longer attracts him, for he has awakened to the reality within him that it both conceals and reveals. For this reason, Shelley suggests, the poet leaves his image behind where it may dwell with and in Nature. The divinity in the poet, like God in the great creation myths, creates out of matter His own image and then withdraws into Himself, leaving behind His own visionary form which is the reality both of Nature and of art. In this sense, Keats "is made one with Nature," and his voice is heard "in all her music" (370–1). Beyond that, however, like the God without creation alone in the omnipotence of His own mind, the divinity within Keats resides. This ultimate dimension of Shelley's vision is the anagogic.

From the outset of his early training in the occult, Shelley instinctively sought for some hidden meaning in whatever he read. On the surface, often expressing the poet's conscious intention, he saw "a thin disguise of circumstance" behind which the poet's real intention lay buried. Those who could penetrate below that surface and discover what lay hidden were the elect, whom Shelley defines as "the more select classes of poetical readers."[14] Like so many aristocrats who reject the social hierarchy on the grounds that it is unjust, Shelley found an outlet for his inherited sense of class in the occult, where he was

[14] *A Defence of Poetry*, VII, 121; Preface to *Prometheus Unbound*, p. 207.

able to recreate on the inner levels of consciousness what he had rejected on the outer. Shelley was perfectly at home in the psychic hierarchy of the occult in which all men were judged not according to the accidents of family or school or economic position, but according to the more fundamental criterion of psychic penetration. While, in theory, Shelley was committed to universal love and brotherhood, in fact he lived and wrote by a rigid code in terms of which men were accepted or rejected according to their degree of spiritual sensibility. Thus Shelley was actively repelled by the gross insensitivity of the familiar world; so acute, in fact, was his repulsion that he spent most of his life as a poet attempting to destroy that world. Of course, like most prophets functioning outside the established order, Shelley hoped that, if he annihilated the world of custom and habit, all men would find their way into his own kingdom of the elect. He was subject to the Romantic illusion that all men were potentially poets, prophets and visionaries. It is not surprising, therefore, that in Shelley's Heaven only the poets are to be found. Shelley's Heaven is an exclusive club to which belong only the aristocrats of the imagination.

Boris Pasternak has vividly described this peculiar character of the Romantic genius, which is at the same time the Romantic failure. "In the poet who imagines himself the measure of life and pays for this with his life," he writes,

the Romantic conception manifests itself brilliantly and irrefutably in his symbolism, that is in everything which touches upon Orphism and Christianity imaginatively. . . . But outside the legend, the Romantic scheme is false. The poet who is its foundation is inconceivable without the non-poets who must bring him into relief. . . . Romanticism always needs philistinism and with the disappearance of the petty bourgeosie loses half its poetical content.[15]

So long as Shelley stands in need of the familiar world as something both to oppose and recreate, he has a background in terms of which his dialectic of vision can be seen. He has his materials. When, however, as in the closing stanzas of *Adonais*, his background dissolves and he is left with the "intense inane" (*P.U.*, III, iv, 204), he moves, as he himself realizes, beyond the reach of art. And it is precisely in

---

[15]Boris Pasternak, "The Safe Conduct" in *The Collected Prose Works* (London: Lindsay Drummond, 1945), pp. 115–16. Boris Pasternak is discussing Mayakovsky's art in the passage quoted.

this anagogical sphere that the contrast between Dante and Shelley comes into sharp relief. While Dante can be blinded by the radiance of his empyrean, he lived in the midst of a tradition which seeks at every turn to reveal the invisible world to the outward sense. For this reason, he can argue that the literal level contains the anagogical. His art is supported by his belief in a God who incarnated Himself in flesh without at the same time losing His divinity. For all his overwhelming sense of mystery and wonder as he scales with Beatrice the circles of Heaven, Dante also knows that he is moving over familiar theological ground at every point open to the intellect. His ascent to the tenth Heaven is a training in revealed theology under the direction of Beatrice issuing ultimately in the intellectual love of God. Shelley, in contrast, is forced to abandon all his sensible and rational supports, and find his sole support in that divine madness which Plato ironically describes in the *Ion*. Writing within an esoteric tradition both alien and isolated from the European traditions of thought which surrounded him, he is forced ultimately to look into himself and find his divinity there. He has somehow to make his poetic faith, which in the end he recognizes as a "willing suspension of disbelief," a matter of religious faith, which is to say, a matter of absolute truth. While, on one level of anagogy, Shelley can declare that Keats has been absorbed into the "white radiance of Eternity," on another level he can see himself, in setting out to join Keats, "borne darkly, fearfully, afar" (492). There is some slight, lingering suggestion of the daemonic in this closing stanza of *Adonais*. Again, as in *Alastor*, he makes use of the image of the little boat hurled upon the tempest to describe his own spirit setting out on its final journey (488–91):

> my spirit's bark is driven,
> Far from the shore, far from the trembling throng
> Whose sails were never to the tempest given;
> The massy earth and spherèd skies are riven!

What emerges in Shelley's vision of death in the closing section of *Adonais* is a revelation of the poet's effort to drive his will towards an anagogical focus. By 1821, the realm of mythopoeic literature had become Shelley's familiar world; in his *Defence of Poetry* he had demonstrated to himself his mastery of it. But now he is forced to admit, as Plato admits in his seventh Epistle, that he has not composed, nor ever can compose, a work which deals with the actual object of his quest. "Acquaintance with it," Plato writes, "must come rather after a long period of attendance or instruction in the subject itself and of close acquaintance when suddenly like a blaze kindled by a leaping spark, it is generated in the soul and at once becomes self-sustaining" (341D). In the concluding stanzas of *Adonais*, Shelley must rely entirely upon that self-sustaining fire within his own soul which had gradually been generated through his period of instruction in the occult. "The fire for which all thirst," he writes, "now beams on me, / Consuming the last clouds of cold mortality" (485–6).

It is, however, those "last clouds" that in some sense hold him back. Thus, he struggles to persuade himself (469–77):

> Why linger, why turn back, why shrink, my Heart?
> Thy hopes are gone before: from all things here
> They have departed; thou shouldst now depart!
> A light is passed from the revolving year,
> And man, and woman; and what still is dear
> Attracts to crush, repels to make thee wither.
> The soft sky smiles,—the low wind whispers near:
> 'Tis Adonais calls! oh, hasten thither,
> No more let Life divide what Death can join together.

And yet he does linger. His spirit moves restlessly, like some caged animal, from Nature where he catches the echoes of Adonais beckoning him, to a vision of Keats assuming his position on the vacant throne among the immortals, to the ruins of Rome and Keats's grave where he seeks "shelter in the shadow of the tomb" (458). Finally, however, he moves beyond all these images of death; the breath of Adonais, suggested in the "low wind," descends upon him. The "soul of Adonais" burns "through the inmost veil of Heaven" (493–4) and, as in the closing lines of *Epipsychidion*, Shelley feels himself consumed in that fire. Setting forth, he sees "Earth's shadows fly" (461) as the "massy earth and spherèd skies are riven" (491). He has smashed the "dome of many-coloured glass." Before him is spread "the white radiance of Eternity" which, in a combination of dread and ecstasy, he images (one final support) as the beacon star of Adonais.

Commenting upon Dante's vision in his *Defence of Poetry* (VII, 131), Shelley says that "veil after veil may be undrawn, and the inmost naked beauty of the meaning never exposed." In *Adonais*, he believed he had pierced the "inmost veil" of Dante's Heaven, but, as in Dante, what lay beyond it could never be revealed. "The names of Demon, Ghost, and Heaven," he writes in his *Hymn to Intellectual Beauty*, remain the record of the poet's "vain endeavour" to describe what by its very nature cannot be rendered articulate. In some sense, the poet, like Wordsworth's "Mighty Prophet," remains "deaf and silent" before the "eternal Deep."

10

THE TRIUMPH OF LIFE

Looking back over Shelley's career from the vantage point of *Adonais*, one can see that for Shelley the problem of evil remained insoluble. He was forced, as a result, ultimately to reject life by arguing that man is liberated from the world's contagion only when he awakens from the dream of life, which, viewed in terms of that awakening, is a nightmare. Shelley's most concerted effort to resolve the problem is to be found in *Prometheus Unbound*. In the figure of Prometheus he offers man a vision of his divinity which the familiar world, symbolized by Jupiter, seeks to annihilate. This vision, however, does not release man from the limits of his morality, with its mixture of good and evil. What it does is to allow the moral will to rule the Furies which plague him as Jove rules his slaves when Hell threatens mutiny. Jupiter is not redeemed; at best, he is kept under control. The vision of man's divinity is, therefore, "pavilioned upon chaos" (*Hellas*, 772).

In this sense, the imagination is not a redemptive power. Shelley asserts in his Preface to the drama that the moral interest of the Promethean fable resides in the suffering and endurance of the hero. He is able to endure his suffering because he knows that it must come to an end, that the hour of his release must inevitably arrive. Destiny is on his side. Destiny, however, is not on the side of man so long as he remains man. Unlike Prometheus, who is a god, man remains in some sense bound. His will must continue to subdue the unruly

slaves within and the unruly universe without. Suffering and endurance are the lot of man; they are not the lot of Prometheus. The
image of divinity which man constructs with his imagination does
not release him from the bonds of his mortal nature.

Shelley returns to this in his *Defence of Poetry* (VII, 135) when
he speaks of the necessity of the poet ascending, Promethean-like, to
the eternal regions to bring light and fire to man. This Promethean
fire, however, is experienced within the poet as a "fading coal"
awakened by some invisible influence to a "transitory brightness."
What, therefore, he is capable of creating with his imagination is
merely a feeble reflection of that for which his being longs. When,
however, this feeble reflection is viewed in terms of what man's earthly
condition would be without it, its renovating virtue becomes self-
evident. Only when viewed in terms of the One do its limitations
stand out in sharp relief.

In *Adonais*, Shelley focuses upon the realization that the imagination is to the One as the familiar world is to the imagination. The
horror with which he views man enslaved by Jupiter in *Prometheus
Unbound* is briefly extended to a vision of the poet caught in his
"mad trance" and striking with his spirit's knife "invulnerable nothings" (*Adonais*, 347–8). Urania, like Jupiter, is chained to time. In
The Triumph of Life, this realization is further developed. The poem
focuses upon the extension of Jupiter's domain into the world of the
imagination so that Caesar and Plato are both perceived as chained
to the wheel of life. Art in the final analysis imitates Nature; the
former is simply an imaginative re-creation of the cyclic round of the
latter.

With the completion of *Adonais*, Shelley had explored the apocalyptic limits of art. For this reason, he found it increasingly difficult
after *Adonais* to drag Prometheus from his enchanted cave vicariously
to take upon himself the plight of suffering humanity. His last major
effort to do so was *Hellas*, a poem which he described as "a mere
improvise," written "without much care, in one of those few moments
of enthusiasm which now seldom visit me, and which make me pay
dear for their visits."[1] Unlike *Prometheus Unbound*, *Hellas* is a
lyrical drama without a hero. In the place of Prometheus, Shelley
resurrects Ahasuerus from *Queen Mab*, who in that poem distinctly

[1]Preface to *Hellas*, p. 446; Letter to John Gisborne, April 10, 1822, X, 370.

prefigures Shelley's Prometheus. While the majority of mankind are deceived into accepting Jehovah's Son as their saviour, Ahasuerus, in words which anticipate the early speeches of Shelley's Prometheus, refuses to submit because he knows that in the end the truth of his insight into the tyrannical nature of God will be revealed to man (*Q.M.*, vii, 254–66):

> "Thus have I stood,—through a wild waste of years
> Struggling with whirlwinds of mad agony,
> Yet peaceful, and serene, and self-enshrined,
> Mocking my powerless Tyrant's horrible curse
> With stubborn and unalterable will,
> Even as a giant oak, which Heaven's fierce flame
> Hath scathèd in the wilderness, to stand
> A monument of fadeless ruin there;
> Yet peacefully and movelessly it braves
> The midnight conflict of the wintry storm,
> As in the sunlight's calm it spreads
> Its worn and withered arms on high
> To meet the quiet of a summer's noon."

In *Hellas*, Ahasuerus, having withdrawn from the world to an enchanted sea-cave, is reluctantly called forth by various magical spells to inform the tyrant, Mahmud, about the future. What in fact he tells him, however, is that both the future and the past "are idle shadows / Of thought's eternal flight" (783–4) and that he ought, as a result, to turn aside from them and focus his attention upon "the One, / The unborn and the undying" (768–9). He should, that is, withdraw from life altogether and commune with his own pre-existent reality rather than occupy himself with "this brief race whose crown is death" (856).

Over against this anagogical perspective, Shelley in one of the choral odes speaks of Christ as a Promethean hero whose cross still leads the generations on. Commenting on the ode in his notes on the drama (p. 478), he argues that the notions of Christianity in the popular mind are true in relation to the religions of Israel and Islam. Placed within a more universal perspective, these notions asume a very different character. Since, however, it is impossible for man in his present condition to disentangle "the Gordian knot of the origin of evil," the Christian myth, though "inexplicable and incredible," remains the most probable account. Thus, in the Prologue to *Hellas*,

Christ is presented before His Father's throne beseeching destiny to grant victory to the Greeks, while Satan, who is also present, argues that in the end the spoils of Christ's labours will be his. Shelley, it would appear, is exploring in his unfinished Prologue to *Hellas* the possibilities of using the Christian myth for the presentation of an ironic vision of the human predicament.

Christ, however, does not appear in the drama; his struggle with Satan, suggested in the unfinished Prologue, does not assume dramatic form. Instead, Shelley treats the subject lyrically, which he defines in his Preface (p. 446) as a series of "indistinct and visionary" pictures, suggesting, rather than delineating, some final victory for the Greeks. Thus the Chorus, which articulates the visionary hopes of the poet, emerges as the real hero of the lyrical drama.

The absence of any clearly delineated hero in *Hellas*, while partly explained by the fact that Shelley was improvising upon contemporary events the outcome of which was as yet unknown, is ultimately explained by Shelley's growing preoccupation with the One. In the second choral ode, the Chorus, describing Christ as a Promethean conqueror sent by the unknown God, declares that His mortal shape is like a dim vapour animated by the sun's light. The universe itself is merely the dust and light which gather around the chariot of the spirit in its unceasing flight back to its primal source. Ultimately, the vision of a reborn Greece is but a dream which will dissolve into nothingness when the dreamer awakes. For this reason, Shelley is loath to clothe the immortality of living spirit in the transience of matter, to delineate again the Promethean hero, this time in the figure of Christ. He has, as it were, awakened in *Adonais* from the dream of life, and the anagogical awareness of striking invisible nothings with his spirit's knife comes between him and his enthusiasm for the Greek revolt. In *Adonais*, he recognizes that what still is dear repels to make him wither because it forces his spirit back into a world which he now feels to be an illusion. And it is this sense of his imagination participating in illusion that best explains the failure of *Hellas* as a lyrical drama dedicated to Greek victory.

While composing *Hellas*, Shelley was also working sporadically at *Charles the First*, which he began in January of 1820. In a letter to Gisborne on January 26, 1822 (X, 355), he confesses that he finds it impossible to seize upon "the conception of the subject as a whole."

His intention was presumably to write a purely human drama, some-what in the manner of *The Cenci*, which would describe the collapse of monarchy, on the one hand, and the Cromwellian attempt to build an ideal commonwealth, on the other. The fragment ends with Crom-well and his followers about to set out for America, full of visions of a floating Eden in the Atlantic, unaware that the King has signed a warrant to detain them.

Shelley's inability to seize upon his conception of the drama would appear to reflect his gradual loss of faith in the millennium. Attendant upon this loss of faith, however, he dimly perceived the possibility, essentially Byronic in nature, of viewing his earlier visionary hopes in ironic terms. And this ironic perspective he achieves through Archy, the court jester, whose vision has been tempered by the vices of the age. Archy, modelled on Lear's fool, realizes that the King is doomed and that the future, if there is a future, lies with Cromwell. He cannot appear to take Cromwell's visionary hopes seriously, however. Thus he tells the King that what Cromwell hopes to create is "a commonwealth like Gonzalo's in the play, / Gynaecocoenic and pantisocratic" (362–3). The King, who knows nothing of Shelley's favourite play or his earlier notions of free love or his earlier enthusiasm for Newton's variation of panti-socracy, does not understand. Thus, Archy explains (364–6):

> New devil's politics.
> Hell is the pattern of all commonwealths:
> Lucifer was the first republican.

Shelley is here treating ironically the "new devil's politics" which were the basis of his Promethean vision. Irony, it would appear, pro-vided the only alternative to the lyric mode as he defines it in the Preface of *Hellas*. Had Shelley been able to develop this ironic mode in order to define his conception, it is possible that he might have been able, like Byron, to develop a latent satirical gift, already mani-fest in *Swellfoot the Tyrant* and *Peter Bell the Third*, into a coherent vision of life. In his treatment of Archy, Shelley, it would appear, was attempting to move from the lyric to the ironic mode without rejecting the visionary idealism that lay at the basis of the lyric. Through irony he could render that idealism even more indistinct and therefore less remote from the realities it sought to redeem.

The basis of Shelley's ironic vision which dominates the poetry of his last year lay in viewing both the familiar world and its imaginative re-creation in poetry from the perspective of the One. In *Adonais*, as Professor Wasserman argues, Shelley's vision "gains its energy from a system of ironies whose function is to compel a progressive revelation," the substance of which "is superior to author and audience."[2] Each succeeding configuration of images, as a result, throws into ironic relief those which precede it with the result that the process of gradual revelation becomes a process of images constructed only to be dissolved in order to arrive at the "deep truth" which is "imageless." In *The Triumph of Life*, this "system of ironies" achieves its apotheosis. The shaping spirit of imagination, treated ironically within the dialectical process in *Adonais*, is relegated from the outset to a world of illusion (*T. of L.*, 248–51):

> "Figures ever new
> Rise on the bubble, paint them as you may;
> We have but thrown, as those before us threw,
>
> "Our shadows on it as it passed away."

The substance of *The Triumph of Life*, as of *Adonais*, therefore, ultimately resides outside the poem in the realm of the One which must remain imageless. For this reason, Shelley locates himself at the outset in a world of thoughts "which must remain untold" (21) and remains throughout the vision (which he describes as the product of the fancy) a spectator rather than a participant. Unlike *Adonais*, therefore, the poem has no pattern of progressive revelation. Shelley, as it were, returns to the second movement of *Adonais* and traces the full cycle of those who remain faithful to Urania as contrasted with those, like Keats, who escape her deluding embrace.

Essential to this reading of the poem is an understanding of Shelley's chariot image. Professor Bloom in his analysis of the poem argues that the chariot is an image of life in the familiar and habitual sense and therefore radically opposed to the imagination, the function of which is to release man from life in the familiar sense. What, as a result, he sees in Shelley's use of the image, derived, he believes, from the fourfold tradition of Ezekiel, Dante, Milton and Blake, is the "terrifying irony of contrasts" with which Shelley treats this traditional

[2]Earl R. Wasserman, "Adonais" in *The Subtler Language* (Baltimore: The Johns Hopkins University Press, 1959), pp. 360, 361.

symbol of man's ascending spirit.[3] This interpretation assumes that Shelley in *The Triumph of Life* is reaffirming the views of the imagination which he presents in his *Defence of Poetry*, that he is still concerned with poets as the "unacknowledged legislators of the world." Shelley, however, is no longer concerned with poets as re-creators of the universe; he is concerned with the One which transcends the universe, reducing it by comparison to a world of shadow and dream. The poem, that is, must be read in the light of *Adonais* rather than in the light of *A Defence of Poetry*.

The "terrifying irony of contrasts" in *The Triumph of Life* does not reside in the distinction between the creative imagination and natural life; it resides in two distinct ways of viewing the imagination. Shelley's chariot remains an emblem of the creative imagination and the irony lies in the change of perspective. He is viewing the imagination in terms of its inability to penetrate the veil of life and arrive at the "intense inane" (*P.U.*, iii, iv, 204) where eternity abides. Those who place their ultimate faith in the creative faculty, as Shelley was tempted to do in *A Defence of Poetry*, must in the end "keep / With phantoms an unprofitable strife" (*Adonais*, 345–6). When viewed in this perspective, the imagination, at best a "fading coal" creating a feeble reflection of the poet's original conception, is like "cold hopes" which "swarm like worms within our living clay" (*Adonais*, 351).

Consistent with his interpretation of the chariot, Professor Bloom goes on to argue that Iris in *The Triumph of Life* is the light of the everyday world which tramples into dust Rousseau's "spark of imaginative vision."[4] Once again, however, he fails to grasp the irony involved in Shelley's view of the imagination. Rousseau's immortal spirit, imprisoned in flesh, seeks to ascend, chariot-like, towards "Heaven's light" which "forever shines" (*Adonais*, 461). Iris, goddess of the rainbow, is the refraction of that light, the "dome of many-coloured glass" which in *Adonais* "stains the white radiance of Eternity." She is, then, as Professor Baker (among others) argues, Rousseau's epi-psyche,[5] the created image of his own buried divinity which in itself

---

[3]Harold Bloom, *Shelley's Mythmaking* (New Haven: Yale University Press, 1959), p. 242.

[4]*Ibid.*, p. 257.

[5]Carlos Baker, *Shelley's Major Poetry: The Fabric of a Vision* (Princeton: Princeton University Press, 1948), pp. 264–5.

is imageless. As long as Rousseau fails to distinguish between the "white radiance" and its refracted form (Iris' "many-coloured scarf" and "crystal glass"), he lacks the "purer nutriment" (202) which would allow him to transcend Iris and achieve union with the One.

In Rousseau's account of Iris, Shelley vividly describes the ironic situation of the mind in creation. The mind, struggling, as Shelley says in the *Defence* (VII, 137), to redeem from decay "the visitations of the divinity in Man," is fighting a losing battle. The visitation works against the poet, fleeing the poet's attempt to redeem it by receding into oblivion. Thus, the poet is left with a feeble reflection of his original conception, haunted by the sense of his own failure. "I doubt whether I *shall* write more," Shelley wrote to his publishers on January 20, 1821 (X, 232). "I could be content either with the Hell or the Paradise of poetry; but the torments of its purgatory vex me, without exciting my power sufficiently to put an end to the vexation."

Professor Wilson, therefore, accurately observes that for Shelley "the created poem is the purgatory of the imagination."[6] The torments of Shelley's purgatory, however, do not necessarily purify the soul. The imaginative vision which Shelley explores in the second movement of *Adonais* can either sink back into the material annihilation of the first movement or be transcended as in the third. For this transcendence, however, a "purer nutriment," which allows the poet to recognize the true nature of Urania, is required. Rousseau, attached to Iris, lacks it. Thus, in *The Triumph of Life*, the first two movements of *Adonais* fuse to become a single cyclic vision of Nature, leaving Rousseau spiritually annihilated by matter. Like Keats, he is made one with Nature. But there the process stops; the "plastic stress" (381) of the one spirit is arrested in Rousseau. He cannot, as a result, burst out of Nature into the "Heaven's light." Unlike Keats, Rousseau "waited the full cycle," filling his "crescent sphere" (241–2) to suffer the fate that Keats would have suffered if Urania had had her way, that is, kept him chained to time, unable to depart.

What, then, Shelley explores in *The Triumph of Life* is the "full cycle" in which the poet fills his "crescent sphere." The cycle begins with Rousseau awakening from his Saturnian sleep to find Nature still bathed in the light of that idyllic world. This "light diviner than

[6]Milton Wilson, *Shelley's Later Poetry* (New York: Columbia University Press, 1959), p. 301.

the common sun" (338) is Iris who grants the poet an ecstatic vision of Nature. She is, then, the spirit of beauty in Nature, which in itself is but the "awful shadow of some unseen Power." As such, she functions through the imagination, visiting the world with "inconstant glance," belonging as she does to the world of mutability.

While in the *Hymn to Intellectual Beauty*, Shelley could rejoice in the fleeting presence of this shadow, believing that through its power the world might be freed from its "dark slavery," in *The Triumph of Life* he recognizes that his radical hopes for a renovated society are a delusion. Thus he emphasizes the negative aspects of Iris. The power of Iris resides in the imaginative vision of a recreated Nature. Because it is limited to Nature, it ties man to an idealized world of sense which, if not transcended, robs him of his spirit's pre-existent world (382–8):

> "And still her feet, no less than the sweet tune
> To which they moved, seemed as they moved to blot
> The thoughts of him who gazed on them; and soon

> "All that was, seemed as if it had been not;
> And all the gazer's mind was strewn beneath
> Her feet like embers; and she, thought by thought,

> "Trampled its sparks into the dust of death."

The sparks upon which Iris tramples are the embers of the "fire for which all thirst," the purpose of which, Shelley argues in *Adonais* (485–6), is to consume "the last clouds of cold mortality." And it is precisely for this reason that she tramples upon them. Iris, like Urania, belongs to time and mutability. As the refractor of Heaven's light, she clothes the insubstantial in earthly forms, reducing the "intense inane," from which Rousseau's soul descended, to multicoloured images. Iris' function, like that of Urania in *Adonais*, is to come between the poet and the object of his quest, which is reunion with the One.

Rousseau, then, is betrayed by his love of Iris even as Shelley in *Adonais* realized that he had been betrayed by his love of Urania in whose honour, he told Peacock, he had written *A Defence of Poetry*. And it is this sense of betrayal that graphically illustrates the opposition, within Shelley's vision, of what Professor Wilson describes as the radical and the Platonic.[7] Shelley's radical vision conducts to the millennium; his Platonic vision conducts to apocalypse. The former conceives of eternity as in love with the productions of time; the latter conceives of eternity as standing outside of time in opposition to it. Shelley could embrace Urania as his muse so long as he could conceive of the imagination as the consolidation of the temporal into a vision of the eternal, so long, that is, as he could accept the Godwinian notions of progress and perfectibility. At the same time, however, Shelley's passion for the Greeks led him to conceive of history as a recurrent cycle in which whatever is consolidated is inevitably disentangled. Thus, in his visionary works, his desire to reform the world is always crossed by a desire to transcend it. And it is the opposition of these two points of view that best explains the lack of a unified vision in most of his major works. Both *Adonais* and *The Triumph of Life* are exceptions. *Adonais* is unified by its dialectic; *The Triumph of Life* is unified because Shelley's desire to reform the world is no longer present to oppose the apocalyptic vision ultimately defined in *Adonais*.

In *The Triumph of Life*, Shelley rejects the radical Promethean strain in his poetry, thereby releasing, through negation, the transcendental. In this final work he identifies his vision of a renovated world with "the contagion of the world's slow stain" (*Adonais*, 356), that is, with a vision which is essentially cyclic, chained as it is to Nature. Poets as "unacknowledged legislators of the world" are rejected; only the "sacred few" who refused to submit to the contamination of Iris' refracted light remain. They alone were able to touch the world with "living flame" and fly back at once to their "native noon" (128–31). The rest, like Rousseau, are trapped in the cyclic round of Nature which in the end is what Iris turns out to be.

Rousseau's error is that he believes that the vision of Iris contains within itself the answer to the riddle of man's existence, that through her he will discover the "deep truth" which is "imageless." As Demogorgon points out to Asia, however, the "deep truth" can never be penetrated by gazing upon the revolving world. To commit oneself to Iris is to commit oneself to illusion; the "deep truth" can be discovered only when the spirit, withdrawing from "invulnerable noth-

[7]*Ibid.*, p. 253.

ings," darts "beyond all worlds" to "satiate the void circumference" (*Adonais*, 419–20).

Thus Rousseau is like Shelley in the second movement of *Adonais*: one who, having gazed upon "Nature's naked loveliness," is led astray in the "world's wilderness" (275–7), cursed by a vision the limitations of which rob him of his goal. Rousseau's purpose, then, is to warn Shelley of what lies ahead for him if he continues to pursue his "coy mistress" (188–9):

> "If thou canst, forbear
> To join the dance, which I had well forborne!"

And Shelley, by way of reply (243–8), reaffirms the decision arrived at in *Adonais*:

> "Let them pass,"
> I cried, "the world and its mysterious doom
>
> "Is not so much more glorious than it was,
> That I desire to worship those who drew
> New figures on its false and fragile glass
>
> "As the old faded."

In his *Defence of Poetry*,[8] Shelley focuses primarily upon the notion of time as a "mediator" and "redeemer" and is thus able to view poets as "mirrors of the gigantic shadows which futurity casts upon the present." Believing that this prophetic spirit was abroad in his own day, he considered his own contemporaries to be compelled as poets to minister to the "spirit of good," even though they abjured it as men. In *The Triumph of Life*, this view of time and the poet is rejected so that what Shelley witnesses in the vision of the chariot is "the spent vision of the times that were / And scarce have ceased to be" (233–4). The spell cast by his imagination in *Prometheus Unbound*, already in the process of dissolution in *Hellas*, is finally broken. Shelley has come to agree, not with Prometheus, but with Prometheus' tempters (*T. of L.*, 228–31):

> And much I grieved to think how power and will
> In opposition rule our mortal day,
>
> And why God made irreconcilable
> Good and the means of good.

[8]VII, 138, 140.

In agreeing with Prometheus' tempters, Shelley is admitting that the imagination cannot either destroy evil or convert it into good. Prometheus cannot prevent some future disentangling of doom. What presumably he can do is quicken the moral will to bring it under control. He can do this, however, only so long as men place their faith in imaginative vision and allow it to take up residence in the soul as a model of the virtuous life. With a loss of faith in the world of the imagination, however, the very foundation of the moral will is undermined. And this is precisely what the rejection of Urania in *Adonais* leads to. Contrasting *Prometheus Unbound* and *Adonais*, Professor Wilson makes this penetrating comment:

In *Prometheus Unbound* there was something to do; and I mean not only to perfect the will by casting out hate, self-contempt, and despair, by returning good for evil, and by maintaining an independent and resolute will in the face of persecution; but also (it is surely implied) by such political action as time, power, and opportunity permit. In *Adonais* there is nothing for the mourners to do but wait until death shatters the many-coloured dome. The ethical will has shrunk to insignificance. Keats did not slay the unpastured dragon, and the mourners are not being prepared for the role of St. George. Nor are they asked to prepare themselves for the burning fountain by slaying the old Adam (or perhaps the self-love of the *philosophes*) in themselves.... No such ethical imperative is given the mourners, the elect of a Platonic heaven.[9]

The absence of any ethical imperative (more needed by the critics than the mourners) is, however, perfectly consistent with Shelley's anagogical perspective. To view the cyclic round of Nature from the vantage point of the One is to view life immobilized, devoid of meaning. The cyclic vision is simultaneously a vision of life and death; to view Adonis rising is also to view him dying, that is, if you view him as *Adonais* does. And so it is with Iris, whose very nature is to wax and wane, to consecrate Nature with her own hues one moment and then withdraw the next, leaving it "vacant and desolate." Her nature is as much revealed in her presence as in her absence. Winter and spring are but different states of Nature's spirit. The world of imagination, Iris' cyclic spirit working in the poet, is present in the vision both of life and of death. To argue, as Shelley does in *A Defence of Poetry* (VII, 136) that poetry is "the record of the best and happiest moments of the happiest and best minds" ignores the fact that some of

[9]*Shelley's Later Poetry*, p. 299.

his best poems are filled with despair. The argument is very much like Coleridge's declaration in a poem about dejection that joy is the basis of poetic power. Rousseau in *The Triumph of Life*, like Shelley in his *Defence*, is seeking the impossible: to arrest Iris, whose very essence is mutability. Iris cannot be arrested; she can be transcended, which is to reach beyond the range of poetry, or she can be explored in all her phases, which *is* the range of poetry.

In *Adonais* the visionary becomes a mystic, which no poet can become and remain a poet. In *The Triumph of Life* the mystic in Shelley gives way for the last time to the visionary to present a vision of Iris in her darkest phase. And he creates this dark vision because, as mystic dedicated to the One, the world of Iris can only appear as a temptation devoutly to be shunned. The "Shape all light" (352) which Rousseau encountered "in the April prime" (308) becomes first "that light's severe excess" (424) and finally the "cold bright car" (434) which Shelley, having explored in his poetry the other phases, first perceives as the grisly vision begins to unfold.

The waning of Iris is the full cycle which Keats in *Adonais* escaped, much to Urania's sorrow. Urania perceives that if Keats had lived he might have armed himself with the mirrored shield of wisdom and the spear of scorn and thus have been in a position to drive the "unpastured dragon" (238) from his den. He might, that is, have become a Promethean poet, an advance already in evidence in Keats's development from *Endymion* to *Hyperion* and its revision. While, as the disciple of Urania, Shelley rejoiced in Keats's awakening from his Saturnian sleep in order to take upon himself, as his own Prometheus had done, the plight of suffering humanity, he saw that in the end he would be defeated by the limitations of the imagination and emerge as yet another victim of the "world's slow stain." He would have followed the path of Rousseau in *The Triumph of Life*, thereby losing his place among the "sacred few" whose spirits, remaining pure and undefiled, flowed back to the burning fountain from which they came. Rousseau, unlike Keats, took on the corruption which his spirit ought to have disdained to wear by joining the throng which hurled itself in the path of the chariot. While Keats is the broken lily, its "petals nipped before they blew" (52), Rousseau is the "shut lily stricken by the wand / Of dewy morning's vital alchemy" (401–2) and therefore, like Shelley, "the withering flower" on which "the killing sun smiles

brightly" (286–7). Keats died on "the promise of the fruit" (53).
Rousseau fulfilled the promise only to discover, like Eve, its evil
nature. The "promise of the fruit," as Shelley describes it in the last
movement of *Adonais*, is "envy and calumny and hate and pain, /
And that unrest which men miscall delight" (353–4). It is "the
shadow of our night" (352) which the imagination cannot "outsoar."
This daemonic, as opposed to apocalyptic, perception of the imagination is summed up in the grotesque image of Urania embracing the
corpse of Keats, forcing for a moment "Life's pale light" to flash
"through those limbs, so long her dear delight" (220–1). The imagination embracing life in order to recreate it is, when anagogically
perceived, merely embracing death.

This anagogical focus reveals the irony of Iris' role in *The Triumph
of Life*. By trampling upon the smouldering embers of the fire from
the burning fountain, she makes the "shadow of our night" appear
as day. The intensity of her light (which Shelley associates with the
sun's light: Iris stands "amid the sun" as the sun "amid the blaze /
Of his own glory") puts out "even the least / Of heaven's living eyes"
(391–2) until, says Shelley, they are reillumined by "the breath /
Of darkness." This "breath" is presumably the "breath" whose might
descends upon Shelley at the conclusion of *Adonais* to carry his
spirit "darkly, fearfully" beyond the "massy earth and spherèd skies"
(491–2). As such, it reveals a spectacle of death, on the one hand,
and opens towards the "intense inane," on the other. For Rousseau,
committed to Iris, it is the daemonic vision that emerges. Professor
Bloom argues that Shelley chose Rousseau because "he is *the* poet,
above all others, of the natural man; the unique archetype of the celebrant of the body of this death, which is the human body of this life
as the poem views it."[10] Rousseau, however, is not, as Professor Bloom
argues, this unique archetype because he lacked the "spark of imaginative vision." He is the archetype (though certainly not "unique")
because he failed to transcend his imaginative vision. Rousseau became the "celebrant of the body of this death" because his imagination
could not of itself make him anything else.

In *The Triumph of Life*, the imagination is not conquered by life
because Shelley is viewing the imagination as a part of life. The
poem, therefore, is similar to the vision of life which Arnold presents

[10]*Shelley's Mythmaking*, p. 252.

in *Empedocles on Etna*: a vision "in which the suffering finds no vent in action; in which a continuous state of mental distress is prolonged, unrelieved by incident, hope, or resistance; in which there is everything to be endured, nothing to be done."[11] There is no "triumph" because there is no defined conflict. The vision, like the last movement of *Adonais*, is suicidal. It is the product of the poet who has rejected poetry. It is, in other words, Shelley's recantation.

All of this becomes clear enough in Shelley's account of the chariot. Here Shelley returns to his Dionysian vision which had provided him with the archetypal image of the creative faculty and explores not its apocalyptic, but its daemonic, aspects. In the *Ion*, Plato compares the divine madness of the poet to the Bacchantes who, when possessed of the god, draw honey and milk from the rivers only to discover, when they return to their senses, that it is nothing but simple water. Shelley, following Plato, argues in his *Defence* (VII, 137) that the poet is an alchemist who "turns to potable gold the poisonous waters which flow from death through life." In the Preface to *Alastor* (p. 15) he speaks of the necessity of the poet's being "duped" by an "illustrious superstition," and within the poem, having, like Rousseau in *The Triumph of Life*, lost his Iris, the poet yearns for "Medea's wondrous alchemy" (672). This identification of the poet with the magician is again brought out in *Prometheus Unbound* when Demogorgon at the end of the drama (IV, 468) identifies the poet's vision with fleeting "spells". Shelley, then, in *The Triumph of Life*, is, like Prospero at the end of *The Tempest*, abjuring his "rough magic." And he does it (138–69) by presenting the account of the chariot as a daemonic parody of the Dionysian vision of the last act of *Prometheus Unbound*:

> The wild dance maddens in the van, and those
> Who lead it—fleet as shadows on the green,
>
> Outspeed the chariot, and without repose
> Mix with each other in tempestuous measure
> To savage music, wilder as it grows,
>
> They, tortured by their agonizing pleasure,
> Convulsed, and on the rapid whirlwinds spun
> Of that fierce Spirit, whose unholy leisure

---

[11]"Preface to Poems, 1853" in *The Poetical Works of Matthew Arnold*, ed. C. B. Tinker and H. F. Lowry (London, New York, Toronto: Oxford University Press, 1950), p. xviii.

Was soothed by mischief since the world begun,
Throw back their heads and loose their streaming hair;
And in their dance round her who dims the sun,

Maidens and youths fling their wild arms in air
As their feet twinkle; they recede, and now
Bending within each other's atmosphere,

Kindle invisibly—and as they glow,
Like moths by light attracted and repelled,
Oft to their bright destruction come and go,

Till like two clouds into one vale impelled,
That shake the mountains when their lightnings mingle
And die in rain—the fiery band which held

Their natures, snaps—while the shock still may tingle;
One falls and then another in the path
Senseless—nor is the desolation single,

Yet ere I can say *where*—the chariot hath
Past over them—nor other trace I find
But as of foam after the ocean's wrath

Is spent upon the desert shore;—behind,
Old men and women foully disarrayed,
Shake their gray hairs in the insulting wind,

And follow in the dance, with limbs decayed,
Seeking to reach the light which leaves them still
Farther behind and deeper in the shade.

The passage has been quoted at length because of the light it casts upon the significance of the daemonic vision in *The Triumph of Life*. The "fierce Spirit" which drives the company on in its whirlwind measures is the "fierce splendour" (359) that falls from Iris and assumes, as she recedes, the form of the chariot. The dancers "tortured by their agonizing pleasure" are the purgatory of the imagination, the "unrest which men [including Shelley in his *Defence*] miscall delight" (*Adonais*, 354). The image of the maidens and youths (Maenads and Satyrs) who "bend within each other's atmosphere" to "kindle invisibly" recalls in *Prometheus Unbound* the chariot-moon revolving around the chariot-earth, like a Maenad around the cup of Agave, to kindle new life within her womb. The image of them as moths attracted and repelled by the light that leads them to their "bright destruction" echoes the "one annihilation"

(587) of the lovers in the *Epipsychidion*. Both of these poems, however, present the apocalyptic vision of "Love's rare universe" (589) imaged as the psyche's union with its epipsyche, which dissolves in the presence of Demogorgon in *Prometheus Unbound* and, as Shelley's curious Advertisement suggests, conducts to death in the *Epipsychidion*. The description of the chariot passing over the dancers leaving no further trace than that of foam after the ocean has spent its force echoes the image of Iris receding from the brain of Rousseau like a wave removing the trace of deer from the sand. Behind the chariot follow the old men and women who "shake their gray hairs in the insulting wind" and are therefore associated with those in *Adonais* (358) whose heads have "grown gray in vain." With the extinction of their "spirit's self," Shelley observes in *Adonais*, they merely "load an unlamented urn" with "sparkless ashes" (360). And this is precisely what Shelley is doing in his ironic elegy.

In his account of the chariot in *The Triumph of Life*, Shelley reinforces the sense of "invulnerable nothings" (*Adonais*, 348) to which the deluded crew has sacrificed itself by emphasizing the blindness of the four-faced charioteer who "could not pierce the sphere / Of all that is, has been or will be done" (103–4). The poet's vision, in other words, cannot penetrate beyond the veil of time. Hence, the poet sits within the chariot (88–90)

> as one whom years deform,
>
> Beneath a dusky hood and double cape,
> Crouching within the shadow of a tomb.

This account of the "Shape" within the chariot finds its parallel in Shelley's description of himself in *Adonais*. Realizing that "tears and gall" are all that remain, he turns from "the world's bitter wind" to "seek shelter in the shadow of the tomb" (457–8). The image of Shelley, yearning for death yet fearing it (lingering, turning back, shrinking), is strongly echoed (and reinforced) in the Shape in *The Triumph of Life*, carried along by the chariot while remaining completely withdrawn.

One may therefore conclude that the "thoughts which must remain untold," which evoke the vision in *The Triumph of Life*, are, in part, the suicidal thoughts which Shelley expresses in the last movement of *Adonais* (469–71):

Why linger, why turn back, why shrink, my Heart?
Thy hopes are gone before: from all things here
They have departed; thou shouldst now depart!

These thoughts are inspired by the Platonic Eros whose function is to guide the soul away from the world's contagion back to the One. The vision of Eros is a vision of death in which the soul is released from the stain of the "dome of many-coloured glass" and restored to its original divinity in the "white radiance of Eternity." This vision of Eros as the apocalyptic awakening to the One led Shelley to assume death's role in *The Triumph of Life* and trample into fragments the "prismatic and many-sided mirror" of Iris in which he had earlier sought, as the disciple of Urania, to collect "the brightest rays of human nature."[12]

Shelley was led by Eros to annihilate the world of his imaginative vision, to reject his earlier Promethean role as "the saviour and strength of suffering man" (*P.U.*, i, 817). Mankind is totally abandoned in *The Triumph of Life*, relegated as it is to the Platonic hell of the chariot of life (which includes the imagination). Shelley was therefore forced in the end to realize that the roles of Eros and the imagination are incompatible. The way of the imagination is the way of incarnation, as Shelley points out in his Preface to *The Cenci*; the way of Eros is the way of transcendence. In terms of Eros, the incarnation is but a dim vapour that veils the omnipotent spirit. By transforming Christ into an Orphic, Shelley ultimately robbed him of his redemptive role.

There is, then, a terrifying irony in Shelley's attempt, essential to an understanding of his apocalyptic vision, to transform Christ from the Hebrew Son of Jehovah into the Orphic emanation of the One. Shelley considered Christ, as the Son of Jehovah, to be the instrument of God's tyrannical revenge upon man. Christ becomes in this context "a hypocritical Daemon, who announces Himself as the God of compassion and peace, even whilst He stretches forth His blood-red hand with the sword of discord to waste the earth, having confessedly devised this scheme of desolation from eternity." Shelley goes on in his notes on *Queen Mab* (p. 820) to contrast this distorted view foisted on men by their enslavement to Jehovah with what he considers (though not in the poem) to be the true nature of Christ: one

[12]*A Defence of Poetry*, VII, 121.

of those "true heroes who have died in the glorious martyrdom of liberty, and have braved torture, contempt, and poverty in the cause of suffering humanity." This vision of Christ is, of course, that of the "Promethean conqueror" whose cross still "leads the generations on."[18] But this view of Christ also turns out to be a disguise, belonging as it does to the radical vision of the imagination rather than the Platonic vision of the One. As an Orphic, Christ is concerned not to redeem but to transcend. His martyrdom, like the martyrdom of Keats, serves no redemptive function; it simply releases Him from the stain of flesh which, as Rousseau points out, man's spirit ought to disdain to wear. Christ belongs to the "sacred few" because He did disdain it; his "living spirit," having touched the world, returned at once to the "burning fountain" (Adonais, 339). Christ, as Eros, teaches the way back, which is the way of death. His purpose is not to recreate the body of the world but to destroy it in order to release the spirit from its prison. The vision of The Triumph of Life is the Orphic vision of an annihilated world, created by the disciple of Eros, who is concerned only to remove the veils that hide the "intense inane."

Confronted by the spectacle of ruin in The Triumph of Life, which is, of course, the ruin of his Promethean vision, Shelley must have seen something of what he saw in Michelangelo's vision of the Last Judgment: the God of compassion and peace unveiling His true identity as His scheme of desolation unfolds. Did Shelley realize that the author of A Defence of Poetry emerges in one sense as a "hypocritical Daemon" in The Triumph of Life, that what he was after was not a recreated universe but an annihilated one? Did he realize that his imaginative vision was merely the mask and mantle to hide his real apocalyptic intention? What ultimately were the "thoughts which must remain untold," out of which the "strange trance" (28) in The Triumph of Life emerges? Did he after Adonais conclude, at least in part, that his own poetic vision, like Milton's vision in Paradise Lost, contained a refutation of the very system which it appeared to support? Was this realization embedded in the ironic mode which he was beginning to explore without quite allowing himself to seize upon the conception as a whole? When, in Adonais, Urania scanned "the stranger's mien" and murmured "Who art thou?" the poet did not answer. Instead, with "sudden hand," he "made bare his branded and ensanguined brow / Which was like Cain's or Christ's" (302–6).

[18]Hellas, 212, 224.

INDEX